Develop Evaluative Judgement in Higher Education

A key skill to be mastered by graduates today is the ability to assess the quality of their own work, and the work of others. This book demonstrates how the higher education system might move away from a culture of unhelpful grades and rigid marking schemes, to focus instead on forms of feedback and assessment that develop the critical skills of its students.

Tracing the historical and sociocultural development of evaluative judgement, and bringing together evidence and practice design from a range of disciplines, this book demystifies the concept of evaluative judgement and shows how it might be integrated and encouraged in a range of pedagogical contexts. Contributors develop various understandings of this often poorly understood concept and draw on their experience to showcase a toolbox of strategies including peer learning, self-regulated learning, self-assessment and the use of technologies.

A key text for those working with students in the higher education system, *Developing Evaluative Judgement in Higher Education* will give readers the knowledge and confidence required to promote these much-needed skills when working with individual students and groups.

Professor David Boud is Foundation Director of the Centre for Research in Assessment and Digital Learning (CRADLE), Deakin University, Australia.

Dr Rola Ajjawi is Senior Research Fellow at CRADLE.

Associate Professor Phillip Dawson is Associate Director of CRADLE.

Dr Joanna Tai is Research Fellow at CRADLE.

Developing Evaluative Judgement in Higher Education

Assessment for Knowing and Producing Quality Work

Edited by
David Boud, Rola Ajjawi,
Phillip Dawson and Joanna Tai

Routledge
Taylor & Francis Group
LONDON AND NEW YORK

First published 2018
by Routledge
2 Park Square, Milton Park, Abingdon, Oxon OX14 4RN

and by Routledge
711 Third Avenue, New York, NY 10017

Routledge is an imprint of the Taylor & Francis Group, an informa business

British Library Cataloguing-in-Publication Data
A catalogue record for this book is available from the British Library

Library of Congress Cataloging-in-Publication Data
Names: Boud, David, editor.
Title: Developing evaluative judgement in higher education / edited by David Boud, Rola Ajjawi, Phillip Dawson, Joanna Tai.
Description: Abingdon, Oxon ; New York, NY : Routledge, 2018. | Includes bibliographical references.
Identifiers: LCCN 2017057256 (print) | LCCN 2018009589 (ebook) | ISBN 9781138089341 (hbk) | ISBN 9781138089358 (pbk) | ISBN 9781315109251 (ebk)
Subjects: LCSH: College students – Rating of. | Students – Self-rating of. | Learning strategies. | Education, Higher – Evaluation.
Classification: LCC LB2368 (ebook) | LCC LB2368 .D47 2018 (print) | DDC 378 – dc23
LC record available at https://lccn.loc.gov/2017057256

ISBN: 978-1-138-08934-1 (hbk)
ISBN: 978-1-138-08935-8 (pbk)
ISBN: 978-1-315-10925-1 (ebk)

Typeset in Minion
by Florence Production Ltd, Stoodleigh, Devon, UK

MIX
Paper from responsible sources
FSC www.fsc.org FSC® C013056

Printed and bound in Great Britain by
TJ International Ltd, Padstow, Cornwall

Contents

Illustrations

Contributors

Rola Ajjawi is a Senior Research Fellow at the Centre for Research in Assessment and Digital Learning, Deakin University. She holds a Bachelor's Honours degree in physiotherapy and worked as a physiotherapist and clinical educator before moving into academia. She has since led a programme of research on workplace learning, with a particular interest in assessment and feedback.

Elizabeth Barrett is a Lecturer in the Division of Speech and Hearing Sciences, Faculty of Education, University of Hong Kong. Her main teaching area includes topics related to human development. Her research explores factors that influence cognition, such as childhood bilingualism, music and visual impairment.

Margaret Bearman is an Associate Professor (Research) at the Centre for Research in Assessment and Digital Learning, Deakin University. She has received formal recognition for her work as an educator, including awards from the Australian Office of Learning and Teaching and Simulation Australasia. Margaret's publication record reflects her interests in assessment and feedback, simulation and digital technologies, sociomateriality, and educational workforce development.

Sue Bennett is Professor and Head of the School of Education at the University of Wollongong. Sue's work investigates how students and teachers engage with technology in their everyday lives and in educational settings. A key strand of her research focuses on supporting teachers to improve their design practices and to integrate information and communication technologies effectively, and how students learn effectively when supported by technology.

David Boud is Professor and Foundation Director of the Centre for Research in Assessment and Digital Learning, Deakin University, Professor of Work and Learning at Middlesex University and Emeritus Professor at the University of Technology Sydney. He has been a pioneer in developing learning-centred approaches to assessment across the disciplines, particularly in student self-assessment, building assessment skills for long-term learning and new approaches to feedback. He is an Australian Learning and Teaching Senior Fellow.

Jaclyn Broadbent is Associate Head of School (Teaching and Learning) in Psychology and Research Fellow at the Centre for Research in Assessment and Digital Learning, Deakin University. Jaclyn's research focuses on development, evaluation, and translation of effective teaching strategies to ensure student success. Research interests include: the role of self-regulation in learning; the use of feedback and online technologies to ensure positive student outcomes in large cohorts; and determinants of student success, engagement, and retention. She has received an Australian Award for University Teachers.

Alison Bullock has a background in educational studies. She took up her current post as Professor and Director of the Cardiff Unit for Research and Evaluation in Medical and Dental Education, Cardiff University, after researching healthcare education at the University of Birmingham. The three strands of her work encompass medical education, dental education, and knowledge mobilisation. She is an experienced project lead and has published in a range of medical and dental education journals, as well as in health services research.

David Carless is a Professor in the Faculty of Education, University of Hong Kong, specialising in learning-oriented assessment and sustainable feedback. His signature publication is the book *Excellence in University Assessment: Learning from Award-winning Practice.*

Barney Dalgarno is Professor and Director of Learning Online at Charles Sturt University, leading strategic innovation for Australia's largest online learning provider. His research contributions have been in three areas: the relationship between learning technology and learning theory; learning in polysynchronous learning environments, including 3D virtual environments; and university teacher and student use of learning technologies.

Gloria Dall'Alba is Associate Professor in the School of Education at the University of Queensland. Her research focuses on learning and teaching in higher education and the workplace, with a particular interest in educating for the professions and the philosophy of higher education. In her work, she predominantly adopts a lifeworld approach in line with hermeneutic phenomenology, while also drawing on other research traditions.

Phillip Dawson is an Associate Professor and Associate Director of the Centre for Research in Assessment and Digital Learning at Deakin University. He holds degrees in education, artificial intelligence and cybersecurity. His research focuses on assessment and learning matters like rubrics and academic integrity, often with influences from computer science.

Cath Ellis is Associate Dean (Education) in the Faculty of Arts and Social Sciences at the University of New South Wales. She has a research interest in electronic assessment management and academic integrity.

Peter Goodyear is Professor of Education at the University of Sydney. He is an Australian Learning and Teaching Fellow and an Australian Research Council Laureate Fellow. He was founding co-director of Sydney's Centre for Research on Learning and Innovation. His research focuses on methods for the analysis and design of complex learning environments, professional education and the nature of professional knowledge. His latest books are *Epistemic Fluency and Professional Education* and *Place-based Spaces for Networked Learning.*

John Hattie is Professor and Deputy Dean of the Melbourne Graduate School of Education, Director of the Melbourne Educational Research Institute at the University of Melbourne, Chair of the Australian Institute of Teaching and School Leaders, and Co-Director of the Science of Learning Research Centre. His areas of interest are measurement models and their applications to educational problems, and models of teaching and learning.

Michael Henderson is an Associate Professor in the Faculty of Education at Monash University. He researches the complex relationship between education and technology, with particular interests in the use of new media in instructional design and their implications for teaching and learning. His focus ranges from early childhood through to higher education, and he is known for work in social media risks as well as multimodal feedback designs.

Christina Johnson is Director of Monash Doctors Education and a consultant in general and geriatric medicine at Monash Health in Melbourne. She is currently undertaking a PhD in medical education. Her research is focused on identifying essential ingredients in effective feedback, examining feedback episodes in the healthcare workplace, and developing the Feedback Quality Instrument.

Gordon Joughin has written extensively on assessment in higher education, with an emphasis on oral forms of assessment and the influence of assessment on learning. He is the editor of *Assessment, Learning and Judgement in Higher Education* and is currently an Honorary Professor in the Centre for Research in Assessment and Digital Learning at Deakin University. He is a former Director of the Teaching and Educational Development Institute at the University of Queensland.

Kennedy Kam Ho Chan is an Assistant Professor in the Division of Mathematics and Science Education, Faculty of Education, University of Hong Kong. His main areas of research include pedagogical content knowledge, teacher noticing, using videos to promote teacher learning, and formative assessment.

Gregor Kennedy is the Pro Vice-Chancellor (Teaching and Learning) at the University of Melbourne and Director of the Melbourne Centre for the Study of Higher Education. Gregor has spent two decades conducting and overseeing research and development in educational technology in higher education. His current research interests include: students' motivation and self-regulation;

understanding confusion and the provision of feedback to students engaged in digital tasks; and the use of learning analytics for improved learning design, teaching and student support.

Romy Lawson is currently Deputy Vice-Chancellor (Education) at Murdoch University. She was previously Director of Learning, Teaching and Curriculum at the University of Wollongong, where she led teams in areas including strategic curriculum development, technology-enhanced learning and learning development. Romy has also held key learning and teaching positions at James Cook University and University of Technology Sydney.

Margaret Lo is an Assistant Professor in the Division of English Language Education, Faculty of Education, University of Hong Kong. Her main areas of research are language teacher education, multiliteracies and social justice pedagogies.

Lori Lockyer is Professor and Dean of the Graduate Research School at the University of Technology Sydney, responsible for leading the strategic direction and policy development for research training across the University. She researches learning technology, learning design and teacher practice. Her research projects investigate how students' learning is influenced by their emotions and self-regulation in digital learning environments, and how teacher thinking influences the design of the learning experiences they create for their students.

Jason M. Lodge is Senior Lecturer in Higher Education at the University of Melbourne and an experienced educator in psychology and higher education. He is a psychological scientist by profession and is affiliated with the national Australian Research Council-funded Science of Learning Research Centre. Jason's areas of expertise are in cognitive science, educational psychology, higher education and educational technology. His research focuses on the cognitive and emotional factors that influence student learning and the student experience in higher education.

Lina Markauskaite is an Associate Professor in the Centre for Research on Learning and Innovation, University of Sydney. Her work spans three related areas: students' and teachers' ICT capabilities; professional learning for complex inter-professional knowledge work; and emerging ICT-enhanced interdisciplinary research methods. Her most recent book is *Epistemic Fluency and Professional Education.* She is currently co-authoring a book, *Education for Practice in Hybrid Spaces: Enhancing Professional Learning with Mobile Technology.*

Karen L. Mattick is Professor of Medical Education and Co-Lead for the Centre for Research in Professional Learning at the University of Exeter, with a strong track record in teaching and research. She is a Principal Fellow of the Higher Education Academy. Her research explores the experiences of medical students and junior doctors, especially during the transition to clinical practice and in relation to prescribing medications.

Elizabeth Molloy is Professor of Work Integrated Learning in the Department of Medical Education, Melbourne Medical School, University of Melbourne.

Elizabeth has researched feedback, assessment, and professional transitions in the health workplace. She teaches short courses and award courses designed to develop the educational skills of clinical educators.

Lynn V. Monrouxe has a cognitive linguistics and educational background. She is Professor and Director of the Chang Gung Medical Education Research Centre at the Chang Gung Memorial Hospital group in Taiwan. She has developed a strong research profile in healthcare professionalism, professional identities, cross-cultural issues and transitions into practice. Lynn is a deputy editor of *Medical Education.*

Robert Nelson is Associate Professor and Associate Director (Student Learning Experience) at Monash University. Trained in the history of art and architecture, he makes use of philological methods to connect the aesthetic and the moral across many cultural forms and in education. Robert has been art critic for Melbourne's *The Age*, and he is the author of seven books, the latest of which – *Creativity Crisis: Toward a Post-Constructivist Educational Future* (in press) – deconstructs the convention of learning outcomes. Robert is also a scene painter for Polixeni Papapetrou.

Ernesto Panadero is a Senior Researcher (Ramón y Cajal Programme) at the Faculty of Psychology, Universidad Autónoma de Madrid, and an Honorary Professor at Deakin University. His research interests are self-regulated learning and educational assessment. His publications have explored the effects of different assessment methods (e.g., self-assessment and rubrics) on the regulation of learning, along with reviewing a number of areas, including self-regulated learning, peer feedback and peer assessment interpersonal factors.

Michael Phillips is a Lecturer in the Faculty of Education at Monash University and co-leads the Learning with New Media Research Group. His research largely focuses on teachers' knowledge and how it is shaped across contexts. His book *Digital Technology, Schools and Teachers' Workplace Learning: Policy, Practice and Identity* explores the role of identity and its connection to education practices. Michael is also recognised for his research relating to multimodal assessment feedback.

Charlotte E. Rees is Director of the Monash Centre for Scholarship in Health Education, Director of Curriculum (Medicine) and Chair of Diversity and Inclusion at the Faculty of Medicine, Nursing and Health Sciences, Monash University. She was previously Professor of Education Research and Director of the Centre for Medical Education, University of Dundee, and Founding Director of the Scottish Medical Education Research Consortium. Charlotte was also a member of the UK 2014 sub-panel for education from 2011 to 2014.

Tracii Ryan is a Research Fellow in the Faculty of Education at Monash University, and is project manager for the OLT-funded Feedback for Learning project. Tracii researches digital tools for assessment and feedback purposes, as well as the motivations, outcomes, and individual differences associated with social media use.

Samantha Sevenhuysen is a Lecturer and Research Assistant in the Faculty of Medicine, Nursing and Allied Health at Monash University, and the manager of the Elective Surgery Program at Monash Health in Melbourne. Sam has a background in physiotherapy and is an experienced clinical educator and coordinator of large workplace education programs. Sam's research interests include peer-assisted learning and clinical placement models. Her work has focused on the translation of evidence to practice and the implementation of alternative education models in the clinical setting.

Joanna Tai is a Research Fellow at the Centre for Research in Assessment and Digital Learning at Deakin University. Her research interests include peer-assisted learning, developing capacity for evaluative judgement, student perspectives on learning and assessment, and research synthesis. She has published peer-reviewed papers on a range of health professions education topics, and presented at local and international conferences.

Darrall G. Thompson holds a PhD in Education and a Masters in Design, along with awards for the implementation of equity, diversity and social justice and the innovative use of technology in teaching and assessment. His research has contributed to the higher education literature on assessment and includes the design of assessment software for use in universities and high schools. He is currently Associate Head of the School of Design and a Learning Futures Fellow at the University of Technology Sydney.

Jessica To is a Post-Doctoral Fellow in the Division of English Language Education, Faculty of Education, University of Hong Kong. Her research interests lie in exemplar use, assessment feedback and other aspects of assessment for learning in higher education.

Acknowledgements

We would like to acknowledge the timely work of Dr Helen Walker, Paige Mahoney and Kevin Dullaghan in helping prepare the manuscript for publication.

Introduction: what is evaluative judgement?

Phillip Dawson, Rola Ajjawi, David Boud and Joanna Tai

Henry is a new graduate working in finance. He graduated with excellent grades, and he is delighted to be in his dream job. Henry attributes his success to his skills at negotiating university assessment processes: by the end of his studies he was able to interrogate a rubric and really give his markers what they wanted. But now Henry has been asked to lead a big new report, and his manager hasn't given him anything that looks remotely like a criteria sheet or marking guide. Henry's manager is starting to seem frustrated with Henry's requests for formative feedback on his work in progress.

Henry excelled at university assessment. However, university assessment processes have failed Henry in one important respect: they did not cultivate his understanding of what quality work looks like. Throughout his studies, Henry developed an unsustainable dependence on others to assess his work.

This book argues that university assessment can and should be reframed to enable students to thrive in a world without marks, grades, rubrics, explicit criteria and markers. The book advances the concept of evaluative judgement, which can be defined as the "capability to make decisions about the quality of work of self and others" (Tai et al. 2017, 5). In the above example, Henry has poor evaluative judgement, despite his great grades. Throughout this book, we and other researchers discuss the nature of evaluative judgement, why it is important, how it connects with other theories, and how it can be developed in our students.

Evaluative judgement is not a new concept in the literature; however, in practice it often tends to be ignored or taken for granted. Evaluative judgement is rarely an explicit outcome for students. However, at the risk of over-dramatising, evaluative judgement is in some cases actually a matter of life and death. A medical graduate who thinks they know how to perform a procedure, but does not know what an acceptable performance of that procedure looks like, is a dangerous person. Similar scenarios can be drawn from law, engineering, teaching, counselling and other professions. Evaluative judgement is simply too important to be left to chance.

How, then, can evaluative judgement be developed? Throughout this book, a range of pedagogies from different disciplines and contexts are presented to develop evaluative judgement. These include peer learning, feedback, dialogues about exemplars of quality work, and self-assessment.

If you've been concerned with students' understandings of quality for some time, you may be wondering: how is evaluative judgement different from self-assessment? Taking the definition of evaluative judgement posed earlier, an obvious difference is that evaluative judgement relates not just to one's own work, but also to the work of others. However, a more important distinction is that evaluative judgement is a capability – not an act or a pedagogy. Engaging in self-assessment activities may develop one's capability for evaluative judgement. This capability may be applied not only to one's own work, but also to the work of others. Self-assessment is therefore but one pedagogical approach in a toolbox for developing evaluative judgement.

Evaluative judgement is a much more challenging capability to develop than the ability to guess one's grades or compare oneself with others. Evaluative judgements are complex and incorporate many criteria. Evaluative judgement is also concerned with the quality of work in contexts where quality may be difficult to define, even for experts. The reasoning behind an evaluative judgement is as crucial as the judgement itself. Most importantly, evaluative judgement is a capability not applied to the self, but to work.

In this book, we advance evaluative judgement as a concept to be developed rather than a construct to be measured. Too much of the prior research into self- and peer-assessment has focused on the differences between scores given by novices and scores given by experts. Over several decades, meta-analyses have been published showing that students give different scores to teachers (e.g., Li et al. 2015; Falchikov and Goldfinch 2000; Falchikov and Boud 1989). However, in the absence of standardised tests and highly prescriptive analytic rubrics, even experts can give very different marks on the same pieces of work (Bloxham et al. 2016). Rather than being a book about better measuring or eliminating this variability, this book asks more fundamental questions about how evaluative judgement works and how it can be developed.

To get the most out of this book, we encourage you to read Chapter 1 next. This chapter traces the historical development of evaluative judgement over time. It also situates evaluative judgement within other key concepts in the literature, such as self-regulated learning and metacognition.

The remaining chapters can be read in any order. The first few chapters theorise evaluative judgement in terms of student capabilities. Dall'Alba situates evaluative judgement within epistemological (what students know and can do) and ontological (what students are learning to be) dimensions. Goodyear and Markauskaite theorise evaluative judgement as an epistemic capability, which students use in determining if they can act in particular situations that are changing dynamically.

The next section of the book applies disciplinary and theoretical perspectives to evaluative judgement. Ajjawi and Bearman take us through representational and sociocultural perspectives of standards, and suggest a view of evaluative judgement as "performing the standard". Nelson takes a creative and historical perspective and proposes different types of evaluative judgement, all of which require us to "make peace with lingering doubt". Joughin takes a cognitive perspective, incorporating work on decision-making. Lodge, Kennedy and Hattie draw on the science of learning and investigate the psychological processes within evaluative judgement.

A range of approaches to developing evaluative judgement are studied in the next section. Two chapters apply self-regulated learning (SRL): Panadero and Broadbent explore activities with potential to develop evaluative judgement alongside SRL, while Bennett, Lockyer, Kennedy and Dalgarno propose open-ended online tasks as a useful pedagogy for developing evaluative judgement, and provide a case study of this approach. The next two chapters focus on exemplars, from very different perspectives: Dawson draws on research in artificial intelligence and uses it to build an exemplar pedagogy based on how computers can learn about quality, while Carless, Chan, To, Lo and Barrett share their experiences and empirical work using scaffolding and dialogue with exemplars to develop evaluative judgement. The following three chapters consider evaluative judgement development at scale. Henderson, Phillips and Ryan explore how technology can enable some of the practices closely associated with evaluative judgement development in a massified setting, and propose a design for technology-enabled dialogic feedback. Ellis argues that for evaluative judgement to be developed en masse, we need to focus on technology that enables the workflows of massified education systems. Thompson and Lawson advance approaches founded in curriculum design, technology and stakeholder engagement.

The final section of the book focuses on evaluative judgement for learners' practice and work. Bearman explores agency and disciplinary identity, and provides implications for authentic assessment design. Tai and Sevenhuysen focus on professional learning contexts and analyse two cases of how peer learning can develop evaluative judgement. Johnson and Molloy also report on empirical research conducted in a workplace setting, focusing on the opportunities for verbal feedback dialogues to understand and calibrate evaluative judgement. Rees, Bullock, Mattick and Monrouxe study newly qualified professionals in the workplace, and what their narratives reveal and hide about their evaluative judgement.

The final chapter of the book acts as a call to action: what next must we do to advance evaluative judgement as a concept in practice?

Returning to Henry from the opening vignette, imagine a different reality where, instead of teachers giving him prescriptive rubrics, he was required to identify criteria himself. Instead of over-emphasising teacher-provided grades, Henry has learnt that his ability to judge the quality of work matters too. Rather than just teaching Henry how to do good work, Henry is now engaged in activities where he has to judge what constitutes "good work". This is a world where the approaches and conceptualisations in this book are used in practice. In such a reality, Henry would better possess "the capability to make decisions about the quality of work of self and others". Henry would have improved his evaluative judgement.

References

Bloxham, S., B. den-Outer, J. Hudson, and M. Price. 2016. "Let's stop the pretence of consistent marking: exploring the multiple limitations of assessment criteria." *Assessment & Evaluation in Higher Education* 41 (3): 466–481. doi:10.1080/02602938.2015.1024607.

Falchikov, N., and D. Boud. 1989. "Student self-assessment in higher education: a meta-analysis." *Review of Educational Research* 59 (4): 395–430. doi:10.3102/00346543059004395.

Falchikov, N., and J. Goldfinch. 2000. "Student peer assessment in higher education: a meta-analysis comparing peer and teacher marks." *Review of Educational Research* 70 (3): 287–322. doi:10.3102/00346543070003287.

Li, H., Y. Xiong, X. Zang, M. L. Kornhaber, Y. Lyu, K. Sun Chung, and H. K. Suen. 2015. "Peer assessment in the digital age: a meta-analysis comparing peer and teacher ratings." *Assessment & Evaluation in Higher Education*: 41 (2): 245–264. doi:10.1080/02602938.2014.999746.

Tai, J., R. Ajjawi, D. Boud, P. Dawson, and E. Panadero. 2017. "Developing evaluative judgement: enabling students to make decisions about the quality of work." *Higher Education*. doi:10.1007/s10734–017–0220–3.

SECTION 1

Conceptualising evaluative judgement

CHAPTER 1

Conceptualising evaluative judgement for sustainable assessment in higher education

Rola Ajjawi, Joanna Tai, Phillip Dawson and David Boud

How can we usefully think about developing evaluative judgement? This chapter introduces a framework for evaluative judgement that underpins discussion in subsequent chapters. We start by identifying what we mean by evaluative judgement and examining why it is a necessary idea for organising courses and designing assessments. We suggest that the development of students' evaluative judgement is an important and underexplored aspect of assessment which enables us to consider the longer-term influence of assessment activities on learning. We then describe the historical evolution of the term "evaluative judgement", and its related antecedents in the assessment literature. In one sense, evaluative judgement may not be a new concept, in that many graduates would have developed this capability. However, we argue that considering it explicitly and systematically, and using it as an integrative and organising framework for designing assessment in higher education, contributes an important and novel perspective. We conclude by examining how common assessment practices – such as rubrics, exemplars, self-assessment, peer assessment and feedback – can be better tailored towards developing students' evaluative judgement.

We have defined evaluative judgement as "the capability to make decisions about the quality of work of self and others" (Tai et al. 2017, 5). What this definition focuses on is the need for learners to understand what constitutes quality and how to make judgements about their own work and those with whom they operate. It is a vital element of being able to work and learn in any context – in study, employment, and more broadly in society. Evaluative judgement is required to judge one's own work, and to determine if a colleague's work is good enough.

Why evaluative judgement and why now?

The ability to engage effectively in lifelong learning is a crucial twenty-first-century capability. Graduates are facing an uncertain future, with the rapidly changing nature of work and workplaces, multiple career shifts, and evolving roles and responsibilities (Oliver 2015). The future for graduates is less clear, and more than ever the role of education is to provide capability to learn and adapt. However, the current pace of change is unprecedented and exceeds the pace at which higher education is changing. Recent reports of workforce trends, such as the Committee for Economic Development of Australia's report (den Hollander 2015), indicated that jobs of the future are changing more rapidly and unpredictably than they have in the past, due to technological changes and disruption. Oliver (2015, 63) argues that students and graduates need to be able to "discern, acquire, adapt and continually enhance the skills, understandings and personal attributes that make them more likely to find and create meaningful paid and unpaid work that benefits themselves, the workforce, the community and the economy". This is where evaluative judgement can play an important role.

In the increasingly massified context of higher education, assessment and feedback practices have been described as "resistant to change" (Ferrell 2012) and are frequently critiqued for being unidirectional and content-focused, and for positioning students as passive recipients (Boud and Molloy 2013; Ajjawi and Boud 2017; Nicol 2010). Traditional assessment structures in higher education privilege the primacy of teachers, as experts, making judgements about the quality of students' work. This creates dependence on the teacher in the absence of other opportunities for students to make judgements, such as in self-assessment or peer assessment (Sadler 2010). Such learnt dependency is counterproductive for the working world into which students will graduate.

The reason for developing evaluative judgement is about more than helping students to get a job (be employable) or be job ready (employability); it is about ensuring that graduates are safe and effective in whatever roles they take on. The notion of evaluative judgement acknowledges the complexity of contextual standards and performance, and seeks to support the development of learning trajectories and mastery. The ability to produce appropriate judgements also underpins the ability to engage in feedback conversations and thus learn effectively from the multiple opportunities that present themselves in courses, workplaces and beyond. Enhancing students' ability to accurately self-evaluate, and evaluate others, should be implemented in a way that transfers into their working lives beyond university. Within the workplace, graduates need evaluative judgement to be able to tell if their work meets standards and, more importantly, when they need to ask for assistance from others or undertake further learning.

While Sadler's (1989) pioneering paper forecast the importance of developing students' evaluative judgement, only with recent advances in the conceptions and practices of assessment and feedback has it been considered in more detail (Carless 2015; Nicol et al. 2014; Tai et al. 2016; Cowan 2010). Arguments have also been made about the potential for new digital pedagogies such as interactive feedback dialogue, MOOCs and flipped classroom approaches to develop related constructs such as self-determination or self-regulation (Gašević et al. 2014; Abeysekera and Dawson 2015; Barton et al. 2016); however, there is no systematic body of evidence about effective learning designs or appropriate learning analytics that help develop evaluative judgement.

Features of evaluative judgement

Several aspects of our view of evaluative judgement should be noted. First, in order to make decisions about the quality of any work one must have an understanding of quality; that is, what enables one to distinguish good from not-so-good work. Second, necessary for understanding quality is reference to a standard (where the standard can be implicit or explicit). Standards may be written in formal documents; however, they may also exist in exemplars of good work, and understandings in the minds of expert practitioners which may be difficult to articulate. These standards of quality are contextually bound within disciplinary notions of knowledge and/or professional practice.

In order for good evaluative judgement to be developed, there should be a desire, opportunity or habit developed in learners for making these judgements, as a way of *being* that is contextual, social and cultural. That is, one should take into account the circumstances and expectations of the context in which work is conducted, as well as where it will be used. In making (and articulating/justifying) these judgements, students can further refine or advance their understandings of quality and their capabilities to make judgements, linking to learning beyond the task. In educational settings, learners' evaluative judgements need to be developed so that they can apply their capability for judgement to an increasingly wider scope of work and in a greater range of contexts. Surprisingly, little work has been undertaken on how evaluative judgement comes to be developed, and how theories of learning support this concept. There is a paucity of evidence to support educational and assessment design that promotes the development of students' evaluative judgement.

Evaluative judgement is not to be confused with self-assessment. Students may use and develop their evaluative judgement capability through engagement in tasks that involve various forms of self-assessment. However, unlike self-assessment, which is a localised *activity*, evaluative judgement is a *capability* that extends beyond the individual and any immediate piece of work. Evaluative judgement is a fundamental attribute needed by those who are competent to operate unsupervised and manage their own learning and work.

While it may be easy to agree that developing students' evaluative judgement might be worthwhile, there are other ideas used in considering learning which touch upon what we have discussed. So, do we then need a new term? Evaluative judgement is clearly related to and sits alongside concepts such as decision-making, metacognition, self-assessment, self-regulated learning and connoisseurship. Indeed, there are overlaps, and there are chapters in this book that address each of these terms in their own right (see e.g. Chapters 6, 7, 8, 9 and 5, respectively). However, none of these ideas entirely captures the reciprocal transfer of current understandings of quality and potential for future improvement in any given work that occurs between the assessments of others and assessments of self (or vice versa), though all of these concepts may aid in understanding what "evaluative judgement capability" is, and how we can develop it. For example, self-regulation of learning includes the notion of self-assessment (monitoring and improving performance), yet it doesn't incorporate an explicit making and articulation of judgement in relation to peers' work. Metacognition inhabits a cognitive psychology space, oriented towards self, which doesn't take into account disciplinary notions of being and becoming. Connoisseurship, often associated with evaluative judgement in the arts, doesn't have the reach/appeal that it might across higher education, and does not necessarily mean that the connoisseur is a producer of work as well as an evaluator. In advancing evaluative judgement as a concept, we seek not to subsume or supersede these concepts, but to integrate elements from each that relate to decisions about quality into a core capability for all university graduates. Each of these concepts comes from a particular disciplinary origin, and we have found that they do not sit as easily in the discourse of academics from other disciplines as the notion of evaluative judgement.

The historical development of evaluative judgement

A key step in introducing evaluative judgement to discussion of learning and assessment in higher education can be found in the work of Sadler (1989), who argued for the role of formative assessment in developing students' "evaluative knowledge" and "evaluative expertise". These were posited as capabilities that students must progressively develop to become independent of their teachers. Sadler argued that for students to improve, they need to develop the capacity to monitor the quality of their own work. This capacity is underpinned by an appreciation of what high-quality work is (i.e., an understanding of standards, criteria and quality), which is necessary for students to appreciate feedback about their performance. Students then need to develop "the evaluative skill necessary for them to compare with some objectivity the quality of what they are producing in relation to the higher standard, and that they develop a store of tactics or moves which can be drawn upon to modify their own work" (p.119). Academics could promote this through engaging students in "direct" and "authentic" evaluative experiences, in order to develop a concept of quality and the "facility" to make complex, multi-criterion judgements (Sadler 1989). For assessment to be transformative, students need to know what high-quality work looks like and how their work compares with that standard, and have the ability to improve their work.

The desire to move students beyond the protected environment of courses and teaching (a necessary condition of work following graduation) is encapsulated in Boud's (2000, 152) concept of sustainable assessment: "assessment that meets the needs of the present without compromising the ability of students to meet their own future learning needs". The focus of sustainable assessment is on helping students become more effective learners, through engagement in carefully designed assessment activities that meet the current requirements and build their capacity to judge their work beyond the immediate assessment context. This work was progressed through consideration of how assessment might be designed for future learning. Boud (2007) proposed five steps for promoting what he termed students' informed judgement (closely akin to evaluative judgement) from the perspective of the learner, which consisted of: (1) identifying oneself as an active learner; (2) identifying one's level of knowledge and the gaps in this; (3) practising testing and judging; (4) developing these skills over time; and (5) embodying reflexivity and commitment.

In his later writing, Sadler (2010) suggested that in order for students to make the relevant complex appraisals in relation to an assessment task, they need to grasp and apply three related concepts: the assessment genre, quality and criteria. He argued that the development of these capabilities should be one of the purposes of assessment in higher education. Sadler's notions of developing students' appraisal were picked up by Nicol (2010), who critiqued the predominantly monologic way feedback is delivered in the higher education sector and instead proposed that feedback should serve the function of progressively enabling students to better monitor, evaluate and regulate their own learning, independently of the teacher. Tutors' tacit knowledge around assessment was the result of multiple evaluative judgements and seeing different ways of addressing the task (Nicol and Macfarlane-Dick 2006). Therefore, tutors developed an internal calibration for quality and comparability through these activities of reading, critiquing and evaluating pieces of work. Similarly, students should be given the opportunity to take part in the processes of making academic judgements to help them develop "appropriate evaluative expertise themselves" (appropriating Sadler's 1989 term), and so make more sense of, and take greater control of, their own learning (Nicol 2010). Such structured opportunities could help students to develop the ability to evaluate the quality, completeness and/or accuracy of their work, and also to develop the confidence to communicate their judgements. We turn to this pedagogical imperative next.

Strategies for developing evaluative judgement

As mentioned, evaluative judgements can be developed through explicit and scaffolded educational designs that require students to (1) evaluate their own and others' work and (2) to make interpretive judgements of their evaluations against criteria gathered from external sources, including tutors, peers and others (e.g., patients, students or clients when doing work-integrated learning). Evaluative judgements require an internal calibration of quality that is influenced by external information, and can be applied both reflexively and to others (Tai et al. 2016). The curriculum may serve the function of inducting and socialising learners into a discipline; however, learners also need opportunities to take part in the processes of making judgements, which cannot occur if they are always judged unilaterally by others (Boud and Soler 2016).

Pedagogic strategies that may be suitably adapted and optimised to enable students to exercise their evaluative judgement include rubrics, exemplars, self-assessment, peer assessment and feedback. A core principle to keep in mind, borrowed from Sadler (2009, 822), is that: "bringing students into a knowledge of standards requires considerably more than sending them one-way messages through rubrics, written feedback or other forms of telling". Rust et al. (2003)

showed that articulation of assessment criteria and standards is not sufficient to develop a shared understanding between staff and students. We instead need to engage students in activities such as co-construction of rubrics, standards and assessment criteria; encourage discussion, critique and debate of standards and quality; involve students in critiquing exemplars; as well as promoting self- and peer-evaluation of work. These activities place the student in a more active role than is typically seen in assessment practices. Broadly speaking, these activities and the underlying assumptions about learning that we make in the following sections take a social constructivist view of learning, where students actively and situatedly construct their knowledge (Talja et al. 2005).

Rubrics

Rubrics come in many formats, but commonly they contain concrete descriptors of standards associated with constituent criteria (Dawson 2015). They are often used to make learning outcomes and standards explicit and therefore to guide learning. Some researchers hail the value of rubrics in making learning "transparent" for students (Panadero and Jonsson 2013), and in some circumstances they have been shown to improve students' work (Lipnevich et al. 2014). At face value, rubrics contribute to evaluative judgement through the above-mentioned functions, becoming a substrate from which quality judgements and comparisons are developed. However, a more nuanced consideration of rubrics is required, as students have been shown to lack understanding of these inherent meanings, and can find criteria and feedback comments based on criteria difficult to interpret and operationalise (Higgins et al. 2001). Assessment criteria and guidelines are an attempt to represent standards to students, but they do not fully communicate the complex tacit knowledge embedded in practice (Hager 2000; Eraut 2004). Attempting to fully represent practice in such statements may result in atomisation of criteria, which would be counterproductive or even impossible (Sadler 2009). Rubrics may also encourage instrumentalism where demonstrated compliance with criteria replaces learning (Torrance 2007).

If rubrics are to be used to develop students' evaluative judgement they should be highly context-specific, and designed and used in ways that reflect the nuanced understandings of quality that experts use when making judgements about a particular type of task while acknowledging the complexity of the practices they represent. If expert evaluative judgement usually consists of detecting the presence or absence of particular pieces of information, then analytic rubrics may be very appropriate representations of evaluative judgement capability – however, if experts take a more holistic or intuitive approach to making evaluative judgements, holistic rubrics may be more appropriate. While evaluative judgement could be seen as the ability to apply an analytic rubric to a piece of work – both one's own and others' – a less reductionist, more holistic understanding of quality could be developed through discussion on the matter, and repeated interactions with artefacts, items or exemplars of work. Much like a moderation or calibration process, it requires multiple inputs and is a continual renegotiation of standards as the world changes and practices develop. As proposed by Panadero and Jonsson (2013), rubrics could be used as a scaffold – beginning as more explicit and analytic in earlier years of study or phases of a course, and becoming more complex and holistic, or even absent, as students progress in their learning within a field. Care should be taken to help students make links between unit and course learning outcomes, standards and criteria, as well as profession-sanctioned standards and criteria, should they exist.

Exemplars

Exemplars offer instantiations of quality for a particular task or activity. Research into exemplar use has seen a renaissance of late, oriented towards strategies for increasing active participation by students in the evaluative process. Dialogue is an active ingredient driving much of the exemplar research. For example, Orsmond et al. (2002) identified that student discussion regarding a range of exemplars in the absence of grades aided in understanding notions of quality. To and Carless (2016) advocated a dialogic approach involving student–peer participation as well as teacher guidance. However, teachers may need to reserve their own judgements to allow students to co-construct understandings of quality (Carless and Chan 2016), as students have been shown to value teacher explanation more than their own interactions with exemplars (Hendry and Jukic 2014). The use of exemplars in developing evaluative judgement is likely to require a delicate balance, where students are scaffolded to notice various examples of quality, without explicit "telling" from the teacher.

Self-assessment

Self-assessment involves students appraising their own work. Earlier studies focused on student-generated marks as their end point, comparing student marks with those generated by teachers – also referred to as "grade guessing" (Boud and Falchikov 1989). For the development of evaluative judgement, the emphasis of self-assessment must be on eliciting and using criteria and standards as an embedded aspect of learning and teaching strategies (Thompson 2016), not simply as a means of generating grades. We advocate that students should be engaged in selecting, generating and appraising criteria and standards, and making qualitative evaluative judgements in relation to these. While the universal provision of standards and criteria may exemplify transparency and accountability in course provision, it can also act as an inhibitor to students developing their own ability to ascertain what yardsticks they should apply to their work. Students can be encouraged to provide a judgement (what) of the level they have achieved for each criterion, alongside justification (why) for their choices. Despite the seeming focus on self-assessment for particular tasks, consistent invitations for students to self-assess across a programme of study can inculcate habits of explicit evaluation of their own work; and through the process (including feedback dialogue), they learn to refine their understandings of quality and calibrate their judgements in relation to the disciplinary community in which they operate (Boud et al. 2013, 2015).

Peer assessment

Similar to the literature on self-assessment, studies of peer assessment have overemphasised the accuracy of marks generated and the potential for peer assessments to contribute to grades (Falchikov and Goldfinch 2000). This emphasis has only intensified in the age of technology-mediated peer assessment (Li et al. 2016). Traditionally, the primary benefit of peer assessment was perceived to exist for the students receiving feedback from their peers. However, this perception is shifting, with students providing feedback now seen to be the main beneficiaries (Nicol et al. 2014) due to their more critical engagement with the criteria and others' work. This benefit is optimised when students have the opportunity to modify their own work after being engaged in peer review (To and Carless 2016). By engaging more closely with criteria and standards, and having to compare these with peers' work, students have reported a better understanding of quality work (McConlogue 2012; Tai et al. 2016). The assessee may also stand to benefit from a deeper engagement in the task, showing higher metacognitive awareness, better scores on a concept map and greater motivation towards the peer assessment activity (Kim 2009). For instance, assessees may be asked whether or not they agreed with the assessor's opinion for each criterion (e.g., "Do you agree with your peer's opinion? Why or why not?").

Feedback

Feedback has been the focus of renewed interest in higher education (e.g., Boud and Molloy 2013), particularly models of feedback that place students in a more active role in generating and responding to information from others. Such models go some way to demonstrating how feedback may assist the development of evaluative judgement. Despite the reams of literature on feedback, however, monologic feedback practices generally persist (Shute 2008; Nicol 2010). Such practices typically position the student as the passive receiver of a teacher's expert input, ignoring the complex credibility judgements that students make about the task, content and feedback source – and, importantly, also ignoring the effect of feedback on the learner. Time is often named as the limiting factor here; however, many more productive feedback practices require less time, more usefully deployed, on the part of teachers. Where students' evaluative judgements (what and why) are in accord with those of the other (e.g., teacher), then, in principle, less time needs to be spent providing feedback comments as many routine comments can be avoided. Feedback matters most where there is discrepancy between students' evaluative judgements of quality work and standards as set or used within a discipline. Feedback comments should therefore be deployed to help students calibrate their own judgements, rather than to simply provide information about the task (Boud et al. 2015). Feedback dialogue, participation and guidance towards the future goals of linked tasks and judgement-making are also required. In order for students to engage meaningfully with feedback comments, they need an understanding of the standards and criteria that govern the work.

Conclusion

In this chapter, we have argued for evaluative judgement as an integrative concept that underpins existing pedagogical practices. Evaluative judgement is essential to being a competent practitioner, performing better-quality work, and learning beyond the end of a course. It entails understandings of quality, and the ability to make and learn from judgements on one's own and others' work. Existing teaching strategies can be refined to explicitly promote learners' evaluative judgements and shared understandings of standards – through engaging learners in disciplinary or professional discussions, and providing opportunities for learners to make evaluative judgements of work and to articulate and defend these judgements. The concept of evaluative judgement supports the argument that assessment should be *for* learning and sustainable. Future research considerations may include examining how we can track the development of learners' evaluative judgement, in order to better understand the effects of assessment activities on our students.

References

Abeysekera, L., and P. Dawson. 2015. "Motivation and cognitive load in the flipped classroom: definition, rationale and a call for research." *Higher Education Research & Development* 34 (1): 1–14. doi:10.1080/07294360.2014.934336.

Ajjawi, R., and D. Boud. 2017. "Researching feedback dialogue: an interactional analysis approach." *Assessment & Evaluation in Higher Education* 42 (2): 252–265. doi:10.1080/02602938.2015.1102863.

Barton, K. L., S. J. Schofield, S. McAleer, and R. Ajjawi. 2016. "Translating evidence-based guidelines to improve feedback practices: the interACT case study." *BMC Medical Education* 16 (1): 1–12. doi:10.1186/s12909–016–0562-z.

Boud, D. 2000. "Sustainable assessment: rethinking assessment for the learning society." *Studies in Continuing Education* 22 (2): 151–167. doi:10.1080/713695728.

Boud, D. 2007. "Reframing assessment as if learning was important." In *Rethinking Assessment in Higher Education: Learning for the Longer Term*, edited by D. Boud and N. Falchikov. London: Routledge.

Boud, D., and N. Falchikov. 1989. "Quantitative studies of student self-assessment in higher education: a critical analysis of findings." *Higher Education* 18: 529–549.

Boud, D., R. Lawson, and D. G. Thompson. 2013. "Does student engagement in self-assessment calibrate their judgement over time?" *Assessment & Evaluation in Higher Education* 38 (8): 941–956. doi:10.1080/02602938.2013.769198.

Boud, D., R. Lawson, and D. G. Thompson. 2015. "The calibration of student judgement through self-assessment: disruptive effects of assessment patterns." *Higher Education Research & Development* 34 (1): 45–59. doi:10.1080/07294360.2014.934328.

Boud, D., and E. K. Molloy. 2013. "Rethinking models of feedback for learning: the challenge of design." *Assessment & Evaluation in Higher Education* 38 (6): 698–712. doi:10.1080/02602938.2012.691462.

Boud, D., and R. Soler. 2016. "Sustainable assessment revisited." *Assessment & Evaluation in Higher Education* 41 (3): 400–413. doi:10.1080/02602938.2015.1018133.

Carless, D. 2015. "Exploring learning-oriented assessment processes." *Higher Education* 69 (6): 963–976. doi:10.1007/s10734–014–9816-z.

Carless, D., and K. K. H. Chan. 2016. "Managing dialogic use of exemplars." *Assessment & Evaluation in Higher Education* 42 (6): 930–941. doi:10.1080/02602938.2016.1211246.

Cowan, J. 2010. "Developing the ability for making evaluative judgements." *Teaching in Higher Education* 15 (3): 323–334. doi:10.1080/13562510903560036.

Dawson, P. 2015. "Assessment rubrics: towards clearer and more replicable design, research and practice." *Assessment & Evaluation in Higher Education* 42 (3): 347–360. doi:10.1080/02602938.2015.1111294.

den Hollander, J. 2015. "A brave new world of higher education." In *Australia's Future Workforce?*, edited by CEDA: Committee for Economic Development of Australia, 225–233. Melbourne: CEDA.

Eraut, M. 2004. "Informal learning in the workplace." *Studies in Continuing Education* 26 (2): 247–273.

Falchikov, N., and J. Goldfinch. 2000. "Student peer assessment in higher education: a meta-analysis comparing peer and teacher marks." *Review of Educational Research* 70 (3): 287–322. doi:10.3102/00346543070003287.

Ferrell, G. 2012. *A View of the Assessment and Feedback Landscape: Baseline Analysis of Policy and Practice from the JISC Assessment & Feedback programme.* UK: JISC.

Gaševic, D., V. Kovanovic, S. Joksimovic, and G. Siemens. 2014. "Where is research on massive open online courses headed? A data analysis of the MOOC research initiative." *The International Review of Research in Open and Distributed Learning* 15 (5): 134–176. doi:10.19173/irrodl.v15i5.1954.

Hager, P. 2000. "Know-how and workplace practical judgement." *Journal of Philosophy of Education* 34 (2): 281–296. doi:10.1111/1467–9752.00173.

Hendry, G. D., and K. Jukic. 2014. "Learning about the quality of work that teachers expect: students' perceptions of exemplar marking versus teacher explanation." *Journal of University Teaching & Learning Practice* 11 (2): 1–10.

Higgins, R., P. Hartley, and A. Skelton. 2001. "Getting the message across: the problem of communicating assessment feedback." *Teaching in Higher Education* 6 (2): 269–274. doi:10.1080/13562510120045230.

Kim, M. 2009. "The impact of an elaborated assessee's role in peer assessment." *Assessment & Evaluation in Higher Education* 34 (1): 105–114. doi:10.1080/02602930801955960.

Li, H., Y. Xiong, X. Zang, M. L. Kornhaber, Y. Lyu, K. S. Chung, and H. K. Suen. 2016. "Peer assessment in the digital age: a meta-analysis comparing peer and teacher ratings." *Assessment & Evaluation in Higher Education* 41 (2): 245–264. doi:10.1080/02602938.2014.999746.

Lipnevich, A. A., L. N. McCallen, K. P. Miles, and J. K. Smith. 2014. "Mind the gap! Students' use of exemplars and detailed rubrics as formative assessment." *Instructional Science* 42 (4): 539–559. doi:10.1007/s11251–013–9299–9.

McConlogue, T. 2012. "But is it fair? Developing students' understanding of grading complex written work through peer assessment." *Assessment & Evaluation in Higher Education* 37 (1): 113–123. doi:10.1080/02602938.2010.515010.

Nicol, D. 2010. "From monologue to dialogue: improving written feedback processes in mass higher education." *Assessment & Evaluation in Higher Education* 35 (5): 501–517.

Nicol, D., and D. Macfarlane-Dick. 2006. "Formative assessment and self-regulated learning: a model and seven principles of good feedback practice." *Studies in Higher Education* 31 (2): 199–218. doi:10.1080/03075070600572090.

Nicol, D., A. Thomson, and C. Breslin. 2014. "Rethinking feedback practices in higher education: a peer review perspective." *Assessment & Evaluation in Higher Education* 39 (1): 102–122. doi:10.1080/02602938.2013.795518.

Oliver, B. 2015. "Redefining graduate employability and work-integrated learning: proposals for effective higher education in disrupted economies." *Journal of Teaching and Learning for Graduate Employability* 6 (1): 56–65. doi:10.21153/jtlge2015vol6no1art573.

Orsmond, P., S. Merry, and K. Reiling. 2002. "The use of exemplars and formative feedback when using student derived marking criteria in peer and self-assessment." *Assessment & Evaluation in Higher Education* 27 (4): 309–323. doi:10.1080/0260293022000001337.

Panadero, E., and A. Jonsson. 2013. "The use of scoring rubrics for formative assessment purposes revisited: a review." *Educational Research Review* 9: 129–144. doi:10.1016/j.edurev.2013.01.002.

Rust, C., M. Price, and B. O'Donovan. 2003. "Improving students' learning by developing their understanding of assessment criteria and processes." *Assessment & Evaluation in Higher Education* 28 (2): 147–164. doi:10.1080/02602930301671.

Sadler, D. R. 1989. "Formative assessment and the design of instructional systems." *Instructional Science* 18 (2): 119–144.

Sadler, D. R. 2009. "Indeterminacy in the use of preset criteria for assessment and grading." *Assessment & Evaluation in Higher Education* 34 (2): 159–179. doi:10.1080/02602930801956059.

Sadler, D. R. 2010. "Beyond feedback: developing student capability in complex appraisal." *Assessment and Evaluation in Higher Education* 35 (5): 535–550. doi:10.1080/02602930903541015.

Shute, V. J. 2008. "Focus on formative feedback." *Review of Educational Research* 78 (1): 153–189. doi:10.3102/0034654307313795.

Tai, J., R. Ajjawi, D. Boud, P. Dawson, and E. Panadero. 2017. "Developing evaluative judgement: enabling students to make decisions about the quality of work." *Higher Education.* doi:10.1007/s10734–017–0220–3.

Tai, J., B. J. Canny, T. P. Haines, and E. K. Molloy. 2016. "The role of peer-assisted learning in building evaluative judgement: opportunities in clinical medical education." *Advances in Health Sciences Education* 21 (3): 659–676. doi:10.1007/s10459–015–9659–0.

Talja, S., K. Tuominen, and R. Savolainen. 2005. " 'Isms' in information science: constructivism, collectivism and constructionism." *Journal of Documentation* 61 (1): 79–101. doi:10.1108/00220410510578023.

Thompson, D. G. 2016. "Marks should not be the focus of assessment – but how can change be achieved?" *Journal of Learning Analytics* 3 (2): 193–212.

To, J., and D. Carless. 2016. "Making productive use of exemplars: peer discussion and teacher guidance for positive transfer of strategies." *Journal of Further and Higher Education* 40 (6): 746–764. doi:10.1080/0309877X.2015.1014317.

Torrance, H. 2007. "Assessment *as* learning? How the use of explicit learning objectives, assessment criteria and feedback in post-secondary education and training can come to dominate learning." *Assessment in Education: Principles, Policy & Practice* 14 (3): 281–294. doi:10.1080/09695940701591867.

CHAPTER 2

Evaluative judgement for learning to be in a digital world

Gloria Dall'Alba

If the broad benefits of higher education are to be achieved, it is necessary to cultivate what students know and can do – an epistemological dimension – as well as how they are learning to be – an ontological dimension (Dall'Alba 2005, 2009). Evaluative judgement is crucial not only for enhancing how students perform course-related tasks, but also how they are learning to be, both in the present and for the world beyond higher education. This chapter explores issues relating to the development of evaluative judgement in supporting both epistemological and ontological dimensions of learning from higher education in our digitally enabled world.

While the notion of evaluative judgement is receiving attention in literature on assessment for learning (Ajjawi et al., Chapter 1), it also has broader applicability and relevance for learning in higher education more generally. Judgement about the quality of students' performance on assessable work can be distinguished from judging their preparedness for practice within a particular profession. For instance, judging students' capability to create a captivating sculpture, develop a convincing philosophical argument or reach a well-informed medical diagnosis is not equivalent to judging their preparedness as a sculptor, philosopher or medical practitioner. While these judgements can be distinguished from one another, the performances on which they are based are nonetheless interrelated and overlapping. Developing a capability for evaluative judgement is crucial, then, not only for enabling students to enhance their performance on course-related assessments or tasks, but also for how they are learning to be for the world beyond higher education (see also Boud and Soler 2016; Nguyen and Walker 2016). Below, I outline how I use the term evaluative judgement. The chapter then explores the importance of evaluative judgement for learning to be in the present, and the world beyond higher education, before pointing to some ways in which evaluative judgement can be enhanced in an increasingly digital world.

Following Ajjawi et al. (Chapter 1), evaluative judgement is taken to mean "the capability to make decisions about the quality of work of self and others". This decision-making typically occurs in relation to standards that may be implicit or explicit. While judging quality may be self-evaluative or based on appraisals by others, the two forms are not entirely independent. This is because appraising quality is not an isolated event, but is contextualised within an extended process of developing skilfulness in a field of expertise (Sadler 1989; see also Bearman, Chapter 15). Evaluative judgement develops through learning what constitutes quality in a performance or work produced within the practice or field in question. The "performance or work produced" is broadly conceived here, and so may or may not be intended for formal assessment purposes; for instance, it may consist of an argument a student poses during a regular online discussion, blog post, seminar or laboratory class. Making evaluative judgement becomes meaningful with reference to the practice or field of expertise within which it is embedded. So although the term evaluative judgement may imply coming to a (final) judgement, enhancing the *process of learning to form judgements about quality* in the present and for life beyond formal education is also of particular interest in educational settings.

Embodying evaluative judgement

In promoting evaluative judgement, Royce Sadler (1989, 2010) emphasises providing students with experience of appraising the quality of a range of performances or work produced. The aim of this experiential activity is to "induct students into sufficient explicit and tacit knowledge of the kind that would enable them to recognise or judge quality when they see it and also explain their judgements" (Sadler 2010, 542). This emphasis on experiential activity calls attention to what and how students are learning in the present, as a means of preparing for making evaluative judgements into the future. Sadler (1989) also distinguishes appraising quality from producing the performance or work oneself, such as in the case of art criticism. The remainder of this chapter relates primarily to evaluative judgement for enhancing performance or work produced, as this is an expectation commonly held of students in higher education. The points made are also applicable to appraising quality as a performance or end in itself, although this is not the focus of this chapter. In the following section, I outline features of developing evaluative judgement that hinge upon the embeddedness of this judgement within the practice to which it relates. These features include: learning to embody the practice in question; integrating epistemological with ontological dimensions of learning; embodying the use of tools and instruments; and the multiplicity of practice in a personal-social process of learning to form evaluative judgements.

Embodied experience of practice worlds

While experiential activity is valuable when learning to appraise quality, the experiential basis of evaluative judgement is integral to its very development. More particularly, not only is evaluative judgement contextualised within a developing capacity to engage in a practice or field, but it is reliant upon this emergent capacity. In other words, promoting evaluative judgement for enhancing performance relies upon learning to enact the practice in question. As Maurice

Merleau-Ponty ([1945] 1962) points out, the understanding we develop is based upon our embodied experience of being embedded within, and directed towards, the world we inhabit. This includes our engagement in practice worlds, such as the world of medicine, economics or social work. As we learn bodily perceptions, sensations and movement that enable us to engage in a particular practice world, these settle into habits over time, providing resources for participating in practice in increasingly sophisticated ways.

Embodied experience is made possible through our entwinement with others and things as we engage in, and across, practice worlds (see Dall'Alba 2009 for elaboration). Due to our entwinement with others and things, evaluative judgement can be informed by our interactions with others and also by the manner in which things in the world "speak back" (see also Goodyear and Markauskaite, Chapter 3), such as when we destroy equipment through misuse or employ resources in sustainable ways. Evaluative judgement takes on meaning and significance within the context of embodied experience in sociomaterial worlds. For example, physics students' efforts to make decisions about quality in their simulations of how galaxies form are meaningful in the context of human beings' endeavours to interrogate and understand our place in the larger universe.

Coming to an informed judgement about quality – or developing a "feel" for what constitutes quality in a field – is, therefore, reliant on embodied experience of the practice in question (including when the practice is art criticism). For Merleau-Ponty, "bodily actions or habits make thinking possible in the first place. And so the body and its habitual actions constitute forms of knowledge in themselves about how to be particular kinds of human beings in particular social settings" (Scully 2012, 144). This means that when we enact what we know, we embody ways of being in the world. As Martin Heidegger argues, our modes of knowing, such as occupational therapy, accountancy and history, are ways of being human, directed to our world ([1927] 1962, 33).

Integrating epistemological with ontological dimensions of learning

Developing capacity among students to engage in a practice world thus involves cultivating what they know and can do (an epistemological dimension), as well as how they are learning to be (an ontological dimension) in this practice world (Dall'Alba 2005, 2009). For instance, as engineering students learn to distinguish engineering concepts, employ computer software and laboratory equipment, and report on experiments or projects they conduct, they also learn to be engineers. When students gain knowledge and skills, this knowledge and skills may be integrated to varying extents into their ways of engineering, nursing or teaching.

Developing a capability for informed evaluative judgement is central to enhancing both epistemological and ontological dimensions of learning in higher education, so that what students know and can do becomes integrated into their ways of being. Enabling students to enhance their own and others' practice requires that students be engaged in appraising the quality of what they know and can do, within a process of learning to be the professionals in question, both in the present and into the future. Forming evaluative judgements about their own and others' practice can become habituated through interrogating and enhancing their practice, both individually and collectively. Students can be encouraged to embody this predisposition to enhance practice through evaluative judgement, so it becomes integral to enacting practice. In contrast, placing emphasis on either gaining knowledge and skills in the present or their application in the future can undermine the forging of strong relationships between what is learnt in the present for the future.

Embodying the use of tools and instruments

Learning to embody practice includes employing the tools and instruments that form part of that practice. Merleau-Ponty points out that we extend the body through incorporating tools and instruments, such as in a blind person's use of a cane: "The blind man's stick has ceased to be an object for him, and is no longer perceived for itself; its point has become an area of sensitivity, extending the scope and active radius of touch, and providing a parallel to sight" ([1945] 1962, 143). In a similar way, our digitally enabled world extends the potential reach of our experiential activity and embodied learning, through entwining our here and now with others and things removed in space and time. For example, archaeology students can digitally explore distant sites and artefacts, while also consulting others whom they may never meet in person. Science students can operate laboratory equipment located elsewhere, monitoring the effects "over there" of their actions carried out here. Appraising their own and others' use of tools and instruments is highly relevant for enhancing students' performance or work produced, including when activities are digitally enabled.

Multiplicity in personal-social evaluative judgement

As noted above, learning to form evaluative judgements is contextualised within developing capacity to engage in a practice world. This means evaluative judgement is not an exclusively individual matter as it develops intersubjectively, with reference to what constitutes quality among those engaged in the practice in question (see also Sadler 2010). Learning to form evaluative judgements is, then, a personal-social process, occurring in relation to ways of being in particular practice worlds. As practice changes over time and across settings, judgements about quality also shift. For instance, evaluating the quality of work produced by computer science students today varies from what such students achieved two decades ago, as well as what is possible in many "developing" nations (see Nguyen and Walker 2016 for cross-cultural comparisons of assessment practices). Thus, informed evaluative judgement is not achieved once and for all, but alters as practice changes (see also Goodyear and Markauskaite, Chapter 3).

Even within a single practice setting, practice is enacted in diverse ways (Dall'Alba 2009; Mol 2002), as evidenced in differing levels of skilfulness that may not be tied to length of experience and also in varying ways of embodying practice at a similar skill level (Dall'Alba and Sandberg 2006). For instance, some recent teaching graduates might enable student learning to a greater extent than some experienced teachers, while teachers who demonstrate a similar level of skilfulness may teach in differing ways. This multiplicity of practice highlights the personal-social in learning to form evaluative judgements, in that socially agreed practices are taken up and enacted in personalised ways. Such multiplicity provides fertile ground for developing practice in diverse directions, but it also contributes to tension in forming evaluative judgements, as it is not usually self-evident which (or whose) judgement serves as a "golden standard". Moreover, the very notions of evaluating and judging imply weighing up and coming to some decision. However, the need for evaluative judgement indicates there remains "lingering doubt" (Nelson, Chapter 5).

Enhancing evaluative judgement in a digitally enabled world

As learning to form evaluative judgements is contextualised within developing capacity to engage in a practice world, enhancing this judgement relies upon enabling students to extend and deepen their understanding of what this practice world entails. Given the prevalence of newer digital technologies in wealthy nations, and their continuing emergence elsewhere, it is timely to consider how they can be harnessed for developing evaluative judgement in the context of extending capacity to engage in varied practice worlds.

Employing technologies for pedagogical purposes

Beyond hype about newer digital technologies, in an informed manner we can ponder the possibilities they afford in preparing students for the complexities of life beyond higher education. By thoughtfully incorporating digital technologies into educational programmes, we can provide students with experience in using these technologies for professional purposes, in ways with which they might not be familiar, as indicated below. This has potential benefits in preparing students for practice in an increasingly digital world, while recognising that the pace at which new technologies are emerging suggests proficient use of specific digital technologies is unlikely to be a sufficient learning outcome in itself.

Moreover, while the functionality of technologies must be given careful consideration in educational settings, this alone is not sufficient. Rather, how technologies are employed for pedagogical purposes impacts the contributions they make to supporting students in developing evaluative judgement towards becoming professionals. It is therefore imperative that the usage of these technologies is continually and critically interrogated against the pedagogical purposes for which they are employed.

Evaluating development towards professional aspirations

In educating students in evaluative judgement, what is foregrounded and how this is done has importance for the learning that follows. Curriculum design and pedagogy therefore have a key role in providing an experiential basis for students to develop evaluative judgement in, and of, practice. Purposeful opportunities for forming evaluative judgement are required throughout the curriculum if this capability is to be developed in a sustainable manner. It would be important, too, that students come to understand what evaluative judgement entails in particular practice, and also its purpose in preparing them for the complexities of this practice following higher education.

Fostering such understanding requires assisting students to enhance their evaluative judgement of what they themselves (or others) know and can do, in a manner that becomes integrated into how they are learning to be professionals in a digitally enabled world. For instance, architecture students learn to access a range of building designs in varied locations to inform their design ideas for a particular building or building complex in a specific site, while they may also use design software in working on emergent design ideas. In encouraging students to make evaluative judgements about their own and others' work, the focus could be on decisions about the quality of the knowledge and skills they bring to bear in their designs and related work. Alternatively, making decisions about the quality of this knowledge and skills can be embedded within a process that supports students in articulating, and forming judgements about, the architect(s) they aspire to be.

In promoting evaluative judgement among students, learning tasks could periodically require them to evaluate their development towards the professionals they aspire to be, while steering them away from highly general or idealised aspirations. Evaluating development towards their aspirations will be of value to students when grounded in interrogating their emergent capacities, as well as their own assumptions about the practice or profession to which they aspire. Both peers and teachers can make valuable contributions to ensuring criticality in this process of becoming professionals. Enabling students to embody a predisposition for interrogating and enhancing practice through evaluative judgement can support them in integrating knowledge and skills into ways of being professionals, both in the present and into the future.

Promoting an informed stand in the learning journey

Within purposeful curriculum design, teachers – as relative experts in the field – can model how to engage in evaluative judgements of practice and of becoming professionals, including through the emphases we demonstrate. This can powerfully influence students as they attempt to gain footholds in negotiating the complexities of the practice world in which they seek to become a part.

A challenge for teachers in modelling practice, including evaluative judgement, is to avoid simply turning our students into imitations of ourselves. Digital technologies can assist in addressing this challenge by organising, and making visible, the learning journey students can expect within single units of study or educational programmes, as well as their achievements towards becoming the professionals they aspire to be. This organising and making visible provides a structure for individualising achievements to date, while pointing students towards the learning to come. Although such a structure opens opportunities for students in conceptualising and enacting practice, this structuring nonetheless simultaneously limits the multiple options that may be open for students.

An additional means of re-directing attention from imitation is encouraging students to take an informed stand on what they are learning and how it is becoming integrated into the professional (and person) they are learning to be. With its focus on decisions about quality, enhancing evaluative judgement can contribute to the informed stand students take on the learning and development of themselves and others. It provides a means of both facilitating and highlighting the integration of what students know and can do with how they are learning to be. However, it is necessary that this integration is an explicit focus in curriculum, pedagogy and student learning if it is to be enabled through educational programmes in a manner that extends, rather than limits, students' becoming (Dall'Alba 2009).

Encouraging creativity and diversity in becoming professionals

In addition to modelling by teachers, a commonly used strategy in providing guidance for students as they engage in coursework or in decision-making about quality is to provide examples of work produced or past performances (Sadler 2010). Digital environments can be employed to provide examples that students can access from many locations and revisit as needed. Although examples can inform students' work, they also risk curtailing creativity. Making available a range of diverse examples, including varied formats, can help to reduce this risk while also increasing students' exposure to possible ways of engaging in practice. As the range of digital formats expands, they can contribute to the options available, while also preparing students for practice worlds that are increasingly digitally enabled. A diverse range of examples and formats also serves to demonstrate that there is not only one appropriate way of approaching or completing a task (McWilliam 2009) – thus reflecting the multiplicity of practice. This multiplicity can form a point of discussion in itself, as a means of preparing students for becoming professionals who can accommodate the complexities of practice.

A further strategy for encouraging creativity and diversity is to enable options within a broadly delimited task, so that not all students complete exactly the same task. This strategy may also provide some associated benefits for promoting academic integrity. In English literature, for instance, students may be required to make evaluative judgements about literary work they produce or perform, while being given a choice about the topic, setting, geographical location depicted or format to be employed, including digital options. These evaluative judgements can be contextualised within learning to be creative writers, poets, playwrights and so on, whether or not this is the students' intention in learning about these forms of being and becoming. Similarly, teacher education students could make decisions about the quality of lesson plans that they produce towards preparing school students for our digitally enabled world. For example, they could evaluate how they employ digital learning technologies for differing school settings (such as inner urban and rural), class levels (beginning and advanced) and/or topics to be taught, within the context of their preparedness to be teachers in multiple settings.

An additional benefit of promoting creativity and diversity is that students have varying strengths and can perform distinctly differently on disparate tasks. For instance, some students present well in oral or visual form, while others perform better in written or auditory formats. As the range of available digital forms expands, they can be utilised in allowing students' differing strengths to emerge and be developed through coursework, including assessable work.

Reducing bias in evaluative judgement

In the various ways identified above, newer digital technologies can be harnessed for enhancing evaluative judgement, as students interrogate the quality of their own and others' learning towards the professionals they aspire to be in our digitally enabled world. There is a risk, however, that evaluative judgement can be clouded when students know who has performed or produced the work – also a risk in judgements by teachers (Malouff and Thorsteinsson 2016). Those considered to be high achievers may be expected to produce high-quality work and be evaluated accordingly, with lower expectations of those perceived as less strong achievers.

A strategy that teachers use to reduce biased judgements is moderating anonymously against agreed criteria and standards, with opportunities for later re-assessment of the workability and validity of the criteria and standards. Students can be given similar opportunities in learning to form evaluative judgement, with digital technologies facilitating both the anonymisation process and the collective revision of criteria and standards by teams of students. Anonymising student work is not always a feasible option, however. For example, anonymity may not be possible when students make judgements about quality based on observing performance by their peers, or when they have witnessed the process of producing work they are to evaluate, such as in architecture studios or engineering laboratories. In these instances, comparing and discussing judgements about quality for the same performance or work can still contribute to learning. Moreover, calling attention to the challenges of forming defensible evaluative judgements can itself become part of the learning process – including ethical aspects of making fair and balanced judgements of quality, as professional practice demands. Gordon Joughin elaborates further on biases in his chapter (Joughin, Chapter 9).

Concluding comments

Developing evaluative judgement has meaning and significance for improving how students perform course-related tasks, and also how they learn to engage in the practice worlds they aspire to enter. Given learning to form evaluative judgement is contextualised within developing capacity to engage in practice worlds, it can support students in learning from higher education how to progress towards fuller participation in our digitally enabled world. As complexities of practice mean that lingering doubt remains an inevitable feature of evaluative judgement, this doubt provides a means of promoting necessary tolerance of uncertainty and multiplicity in informed, skilful professional practice. Recognising such uncertainty and multiplicity can provide impetus for deepening understandings about practice, as well as about what is entailed in being professionals within particular practice worlds. Enhancing evaluative judgement has importance, then, in supporting both epistemological and ontological dimensions of learning to be in the present and for the world beyond higher education.

The rapid pace of contemporary life, in which digital technologies play a part, can give us pause to consider the ways and extent to which the use of digital technologies provides space and opportunities for students; that is, the chance to "let them learn" deeply (Heidegger 1968, 15), including making decisions about the quality of their own and others' work. Harnessing emergent digital technologies for embodying evaluative judgement in becoming professionals remains a challenge into the future.

References

Boud, D., and R. Soler. 2016. "Sustainable assessment revisited." *Assessment & Evaluation in Higher Education* 41 (3): 400–413. doi:10.1080/02602938.2015.1018133.

Dall'Alba, G. 2005. "Improving teaching: enhancing ways of being university teachers." *Higher Education Research and Development* 24 (4): 361–372. doi:10.1080/07294360500284771.

Dall'Alba, G. 2009. *Learning to be Professionals.* Dordrecht, The Netherlands: Springer.

Dall'Alba, G., and J. Sandberg. 2006. "Unveiling professional development: a critical review of stage models." *Review of Educational Research* 76: 383–412.

Heidegger, M. (1927) 1962. *Being and Time.* Translated by J. Macquarrie and E. Robinson. New York: SCM Press.

Heidegger, M. 1968. *What is Called Thinking?* Translated by T.F.D. Wieck and J.G. Gray. New York: Harper Row.

Malouff, J. M., and E. B. Thorsteinsson. 2016. "Bias in grading: a meta-analysis of experimental research findings." *Australian Journal of Education* 60 (3): 245–256. doi:10.1177/0004944116664618.

McWilliam, E. 2009. "Teaching for creativity: from sage to guide to meddler." *Asia Pacific Journal of Education* 29 (3): 281–293. doi:10.1080/02188790903092787.

Merleau-Ponty, M. (1945) 1962. *Phenomenology of Perception.* Translated by C. Smith. London: Routledge & Kegan Paul.

Mol, A. 2002. *The Body Multiple: Ontology in Medical Practice.* Durham, NC: Duke University Press.

Nguyen, T. T. H., and M. Walker 2016. "Sustainable assessment for lifelong learning." *Assessment & Evaluation in Higher Education* 41 (1): 97–111. doi:10.1080/02602938.2014.985632.

Sadler, D. R. 1989. "Formative assessment and the design of instructional systems." *Instructional Science* 18 (2): 119–144. doi:10.1007/BF00117714.

Sadler, D. R. 2010. "Beyond feedback: developing student capability in complex appraisal." *Assessment & Evaluation in Higher Education* 35 (5): 535–550. doi:10.1080/02602930903541015.

Scully, J. L. 2012. "Disability and the thinking body." In *Embodied Selves*, edited by S. Gonzalez Arnal, G. Jagger, and K. Lennon, 139–159. Basingstoke, UK: Palgrave Macmillan.

CHAPTER 3

Epistemic resourcefulness and the development of evaluative judgement

Peter Goodyear and Lina Markauskaite

In this chapter, we examine some ideas about the development of evaluative judgement in the context of preparation for the professions. Universities have long been important sites for education that is directed towards membership of a specific profession; it is a significant area of activity for many contemporary universities. There is, of course, considerable diversity among programmes of education for the professions, reflecting both diversity among the professions and diversity in educational approaches. It can be dangerous to generalise across the whole of university-level professional education. Nevertheless, it may enrich conceptions of evaluative judgement if we consider it from a range of positions in that broad space. Not least, it can test some assumptions about the development of evaluative judgement that may go unquestioned in the classic disciplines of academia, but prove problematic in other areas of knowledge work.

Our chapter is primarily a contribution to the task of theorising evaluative judgement. While we believe that this has practical educational payoffs, which we outline in the final section of the chapter, we are also motivated by a curiosity about the kinds of work and capabilities that are involved in evaluative judgement – both within and for professional action. In a nutshell, we argue in this chapter that evaluative judgement can be seen as an *epistemic* capability, useful in assessing one's ability to engage in knowledgeable action in specific, dynamically changing situations. We draw on some of our recent empirical and theoretical research to show how a broad range of examples of professional knowledge work can be categorised within a taxonomy of *epistemic games*. The ability to recognise and participate in these games is a manifestation of *epistemic fluency* and we can think of the corresponding personal capabilities in terms of *epistemic resourcefulness*. We illustrate this approach to conceptualising evaluative judgement, and its development, with a discussion of one particularly relevant kind of professional epistemic game: the evaluation game. From this base, we develop an argument about the need for evaluative judgement to be considered from a generative perspective. In rapidly changing and uncertain times, professionals cannot get by with methods and standards for assessing worth or quality that are carved in stone. Epistemic resourcefulness enables people to formulate novel, principled approaches to the making of evaluative judgements.

In considering the needs of future professionals – including the capacities they will require in order to make defensible judgements about the quality of their own work, and the work of others around them – we identify four significant trends that are (re)shaping professional practice. The first of these is the growing social expectation that professional practice will entail the *generation of evidence* to justify courses of action. (This is associated with, but not wholly caused by, the imposition on professions of an audit culture – see, e.g., Beck and Young 2005; Guile 2011.) A second, related trend is the need to work appropriately with *second-hand knowledge*: knowledge generated by others (Bromme et al. 2010). The third trend involves the growing importance of *relational expertise* – which is essential for inter-professional working as well as for working across professional–lay boundaries (Edwards 2010). The fourth trend is also connected to this: the *opening out of professional service delivery*, associated with service clients being actively engaged in co-producing services (Cipolla and Manzini 2009; Manzini 2015).

These trends are placing additional stress upon curriculum and assessment design in programmes of professional preparation in higher education. One synoptic way of thinking about this is in terms of a tension between the need for ever-greater quantities of firm, rigorous, codified knowledge on the one hand, and the need to nurture adaptability and flexibility on the other. Some commentators on higher education suggest that this tension can be resolved by moving away from knowledge itself (e.g., Barnett and Griffin 1997; Barnett 2009). As researchers, our choice is to head in the opposite direction: to look more closely at professional knowledge and knowing. Taking this path leads to a recognition of the fundamental importance of epistemic fluency and epistemic resourcefulness (Markauskaite and Goodyear 2017). In taking knowledge more seriously, we believe we can also make a useful contribution to clarifying some ideas whose haziness restricts our collective ability, as educators, to design better opportunities for our students. For example, in the years that have elapsed since Royce Sadler's seminal work on tacit evaluative knowledge (Sadler 1989), researchers analysing expertise have identified some important distinctions between different types of tacit and explicit knowledge, and between different types of expertise (e.g., Collins 2007, 2010). Different kinds of personal knowledge are developed in different ways – opening up some possibilities for supplementing experiential learning with more structured educational designs.

Epistemic fluency and epistemic games

We have been carrying out a programme of empirical research into the form of, and rationale for, a wide range of assessment tasks taken from university-level programmes that are preparing students for one of the professions. We have drawn examples from 20 courses in pharmacy, teacher education, nursing, social work and school counselling. Our collection centres on assessment tasks situated on the boundaries of academic and professional worlds – notably, tasks that relate to periods in which students are having practical "workplace" experiences, such as through a practicum. In addition to collecting documents containing task specifications, we observed students working on tasks, interviewed them, and interviewed their teachers.

One of our primary goals has been to identify qualitative variations in the kinds of knowledge work being done by students in response to each of these assessment tasks, as well as to discover teachers' intentions with respect to how the tasks connected with two valued elements of professional practice: current and future-oriented.

In professional practice, there is an understandable focus on working knowledge, practical knowledge or *actionable knowledge*: knowledge that is particularly useful for getting things done in complex practical activities (Yinger and Hendricks-Lee 1993; Bereiter 2013; Markauskaite and Goodyear 2014, 2017). New knowledge, including new actionable knowledge, is created in various ways. One family of knowledge-creating methods is enquiry. When people engage in enquiry – whether scientific, moral, political, legal or other – characteristic moves occur again and again (Perkins 1997). Patterns of enquiry, including patterns of enquiry that we observe in professional work, have characteristic forms, moves, goals and rules: in combination, these constitute characteristic *epistemic games* (Perkins 1997; Collins and Ferguson 1993). "Game" is used deliberately, with three sets of allusions – to Wittgenstein's "language games" (and the interweaving of language and action); to the distinct combination of rules, moves, strategies etc. whose mastery is implicated in fluent playing of a game; and to the fact that most games are played with and against other people.

A strength of the construct of epistemic games is that it helps resolve some issues of specificity and generality of knowledge. Evaluative judgement occurs concretely in context – it mobilises a mixture of generic and specific criteria and connects them with specific qualities of the work at hand. It needs to be understood as an instance of situated knowledgeable action. Nevertheless, general knowledge and capabilities are also involved. Epistemic games encapsulate the rules and strategies with which legitimate, situated, evaluative moves are made.

(Professional) epistemic fluency can be thought of as the capability to recognise and participate in a number of (professional) epistemic games. Among other things, it entails the ability to:

- Integrate different kinds of knowledge;
- Co-ordinate different ways of knowing; and
- Configure and reconfigure one's epistemic environment (which includes the material, digital and social resources that "come to hand" during situated acts of knowledge construction).

We supplemented our analysis of the epistemic activity involved in the various assessment tasks that our teaching colleagues provided with a review of relevant literature and related studies. Through this, we identified a range of distinct ways of working with knowledge, each of which can be labelled a professional epistemic game. The resultant taxonomy of epistemic games includes both formal and functional epistemic games (Greeno 2012; Markauskaite et al. 2014). Formal epistemic games are patterns of enquiry that are used in (normative) systems of formal professional reasoning and judgement. Functional epistemic games are patterns of enquiry that contribute to the ways in which professionals generate (situated) knowledge to inform their actions.

Epistemic games are identified and distinguished from one another by reference to four distinct aspects: (a) their goals; (b) their outcomes; (c) their characteristic moves, rules and principles of procedure; and (d) the kinds of expertise entangled with them. So, for example, we can usefully distinguish between meta-professional, trans-professional and translational public discourse games. Meta-professional games focus on sharpening professional perception by re-describing actions and products within a shared professional community framing. Some of these games involve articulation of otherwise invisible features of a professional phenomenon in a specialist language (e.g., making tacit knowledge explicit). Others involve evaluation and judgement. All such meta-professional games are played *within* a profession. Trans-professional and translational public discourse games create links between cognate professional knowledges and between professional and lay/client knowledges respectively. In each case, they enhance possibilities for joint knowledgeable action, which sometimes entails weaving together different kinds of epistemic games.

Evaluation games

An important class of meta-professional epistemic games are *evaluation games.* Evaluation games

> . . . follow recognised, explicit rules for evaluating certain professional things, resources, actions and other professional objects, from a particular shared perspective.
>
> (Markauskaite and Goodyear 2017, 421)

Depicting and judging important properties of a pharmaceutical product, evaluating a teaching resource, observing and peer-assessing a lesson taught by a pre-service teacher and other games that use agreed evaluation schemes and criteria belong to this group of epistemic games. Some evaluation games are played independently (e.g., during conventional formative or summative evaluation), but many evaluation games are also played as part of larger learning and professional tasks (e.g., evaluating the appropriateness of a teaching resource for a designed lesson, or the appropriateness of a medication for a particular patient).

Evaluation games involve the consistent application of a relevant epistemological framework, and professional evaluation discourse can be characterised by such rules as explicitness of criteria and consistency (cf. Sadler 1989, 134–136). In our studies, evaluation games were used by (university) teachers to develop *capacities for skilled professional perception*, such as – among student teachers – an ability to notice important features of a lesson plan from a social justice perspective.

Identifying the ways evaluation games are played in a profession, and in preparation for that profession, can help inform curriculum and assessment design. In other words, students can be helped to learn how to make good evaluative judgements by understanding the rules (etc.) of the evaluation games characteristic of their field/profession. But simply having an abstract account of the evaluation game is not enough. Students also need opportunities to obtain personal experience of playing evaluation games, in order to learn how to co-ordinate generic forms of knowledge with their actions and their situated experiences – a knowledge-creating capacity that we refer to as "epistemic resourcefulness" (Markauskaite and Goodyear 2017, 523–552). Allan Collins (Collins and Kapur 2014) provides a useful tennis analogy. One cannot become a good (fluent, effective) tennis player simply by knowing the rules, reading about or watching the game. One needs to play it with other people – and one can sometimes learn faster by playing with people who are better at the game. The notion that a capacity for evaluative judgement cannot be attained without appropriate personal experience is already reflected in writing on the topic (e.g., Ajjawi et al., Chapter 1). A second claim we can make for connections between epistemic resourcefulness and evaluative judgement is through highlighting the intrinsically multimodal and dynamic nature of actionable knowledge. David Turnbull (2000) speaks of an "assemblage" of knowledge practices as:

> . . . the amalgam of places, bodies, voices, skills, practices, technical devices, theories, social strategies and collective work that together constitute technoscientific knowledge/ practices.
>
> (Turnbull 2000, 43–44)

So we can say that the epistemic is not merely mental, social or technological – it is an interdependent, multimodal, dynamic and complex system. And when we think of an "epistemic environment", we are thinking of something social and material, in which a rich meshwork of tools and other artefacts, infrastructure, people, inscriptions and speech *afford* epistemic activity. For example, what counts as a high-quality lesson plan or a well-taught lesson cannot be grasped simply by looking at general criteria that are applied when making such judgements (Table 3.1). What counts as "appropriate assessment strategies", or a sufficient "range of communication strategies", must be judged in relation to the content that is taught, available classroom facilities, student misunderstandings encountered during teaching sessions, and even the teacher's personal embodied qualities (e.g., a natural pitch of the voice) and experiences (i.e., what is "appropriate" for a novice is not necessarily appropriate for an experienced teacher, and vice versa). This *grounded* interpretation of epistemic resourcefulness helps explain why direct experience is necessary in the development of evaluative judgement. It also suggests that fluency in evaluative judgement may benefit from an ability to reconfigure one's environment to make important qualities of the *evaluand* more visible.

Table 3.1 An extract from the assessment criteria used by university academics and peers for evaluating pre-service teachers' lesson plans and peer teaching

LESSON PLAN EVALUATION			*TEACHER-STUDENT INTERACTION*
Outcomes	*Y*	*N*	*Comments*
Planned and implemented a range of strategies to motivate and gain students' attention and interest			
Provided clear instructions and directions			
Effectively implemented planned procedures taken in account collective and individual student needs			
Demonstrated effective management of student interaction and participation in learning tasks			
Attempted to implement a variety of management strategies that are responsive to the needs of students and school and DET requirements/policies			
Created and maintained learning environments that are interesting, challenging, orderly, safe, purposeful and supportive of students			
Clearly and effectively used oral and written English language to communicate with students and other members of the school community			
Used voice, gestures, eye contact and movement to enhance teaching effectiveness			
Developed a range of communication strategies such as questioning, exposition and leading discussions, to facilitate student inquiry and understanding			

Continued

Table 3.1 Continued

LESSON PLAN EVALUATION			*PLANNING AND PREPARATION*
Outcomes	*Y*	*N*	*Comments*
Identified clear and appropriate purposes for the lesson			
Planned teaching experiences that demonstrate an understanding of how students develop and learn			
Showed evidence of thorough knowledge of the visual arts in the context of the prescribed syllabus			
Selected knowledge and resources appropriate to syllabus requirements and the needs, interests and abilities of the individuals and groups			
Planned a variety of lesson structures, teaching strategies and resources across the lesson sequence			
Planned a range of appropriate assessment strategies to provide feedback to students and about their progress			
Demonstrated an awareness of, and planned appropriately for individual differences and the varying needs of students			

Designing enquiry and innovation in evaluation

A further connection we want to make to ideas about the development of evaluative judgement is to say that the ubiquity of innovation in skilled professional work means that there cannot always be established standards against which to judge the quality of one's work, or that of one's peers. Rather, evaluative judgement in changing times must also call upon a capacity to *dynamically establish appropriate criteria*, against which novel accomplishments can be judged.

This brings us into a more complicated and demanding space of epistemic activity. One way to describe this is to say that the would-be evaluator needs to move up a level: from *enacting* enquiry to *designing* enquiry, with evaluation in mind. An example of such a situation is when the student/professional finds themselves involved in a "wicked" problem (Rittel and Webber 1984; Farrell and

Hooker 2013). The complexity of a wicked problem emerges from a lack of a consensus about the nature of the problem, how it should be tackled, and what constitutes a solution. People may not agree about what a useful, trustworthy evaluation would look like. Shared understandings of the problem and of candidate solutions have to be developed together. Even more demanding are situations in which wicked *systemic* problems prevail (Markauskaite and Goodyear 2017, 553–594). Such problems are not uncommon in professional practice. Wicked systemic problems occur when development of an understanding of the problem, and enactment of candidate solutions, are distributed across multiple actors and across time. Wicked systemic problems change over time, sometimes in response to the (problem-solving) actions taken; therefore, a complete strategy cannot be worked out in advance. Joint action and shared enquiry (deep collective learning) are both needed – often in a loosely yoked way. Implementing a complex teaching and learning innovation within a school in order to improve students' learning outcomes, or designing a new health intervention in order to tackle persistent health issues, are examples of such problems. Shared enquiry is needed so that collective sense can be made of the problematic situation in which the professionals are engaged, as well as of candidate actions that some/all of the professionals might need to take.

Bringing this back to evaluative judgement, the issues just described require capable professionals to be able to do much more than assess the quality of their work against accepted standards. New standards have to be created and justified. Neither is it as simple as applying accepted standards for gathering evaluative data in unfamiliar circumstances; one cannot dodge the issue by shifting the focus of evaluation from established professional knowledge (what is known) to established methods of creating new knowledge (enquiry techniques). Important though this capability may be, it is not (yet) enough to allow professionals to judge whether they are dealing well with wicked systemic problems. That needs additional capabilities: to *weave* evaluation games with trans-professional and public discourse games. The need for such weaving is well illustrated in emerging approaches to *developmental evaluation* that underpin judgements in complex professional work and dynamic contexts (Patton 2011).

Looking at evaluative judgement through the lens of preparation for professional practice can be useful in other ways – for example, because it reveals and questions what can be quite deep, implicit assumptions about the nature of students' academic work. If one takes the academic essay as a canonical form of university student work, then (a) it seems entirely logical that experienced academics should be arbiters of quality – that students need to acquire a sense of quality in academic work by attending carefully to feedback from those who have spent years being socialised into a discipline; and (b) one naturally thinks of good student work as being faithful to the state of knowledge and ways of knowing prevailing in the academic discipline concerned.

In contrast, in many of the tasks we observed students carrying out, the purpose of writing texts was more performative than representational. The purpose of the text that they were producing was to guide their future action in the world, rather than to represent some existing, agreed set of knowledge claims about the world. Producing a lesson plan is a simple example. A good lesson plan is principled, for sure, but its fundamental purpose is to scaffold future action.

Once this distinction between representational and performative functions of the artefacts students are producing is acknowledged, we can expand the concept of evaluative judgement. Staying with the example of the lesson plan, its evaluation is not a matter of academic connoisseurship; evaluation in this kind of case has to take into account how the lesson went. Feedback from the world of action is an important ingredient in making an appropriately comprehensive evaluative judgement.

Generalising this a little, we might say that there is an under-acknowledged capacity that students should find useful in a large subset of circumstances in which evaluative judgement is required. We can think of this as a kind of reconfiguration of the epistemic environment such that data (feedback) from the world become more accessible, timely and usable. One cannot always rely on extrinsic feedback from academic or professional experts; one needs to be able to generate intrinsic feedback from the situation in which one is working. In many areas of practice, when we make a mistake, the world "bites us back". It can be very unforgiving. Knowing how to arrange things in the world so that early intrinsic feedback can be sensed – before irrecoverable mistakes are made – is a useful epistemic capability.

Practical implications for curriculum and assessment design

The stronger our collective theorisation of evaluative judgement, the better placed we are to help educators improve curriculum, pedagogy and assessment design.

We know from recent, extensive reviews by Winstone et al. (2017) that university students say they do not get enough training in how to make productive use of feedback, but also that they worry about the time needed by interventions that are aimed to provide just such experiences. We also know that end-of-course feedback rarely has a positive effect on subsequent courses – that is, fragmentation of programmes makes it harder to help students make better use of feedback. Positive results have been achieved in a number of ways – notably through engaging students in peer review, in co-creating rubrics and, more generally, in getting them to use and discuss assessment criteria (Winstone et al. 2017).

One implication of our research is that giving students opportunities to engage in a mix of evaluation games, appropriate to their field or discipline, could provide a tighter structure for curriculum design than is currently available to those who want to help students develop evaluative judgement.

In part, this is because epistemic games offer a useful level of abstraction when programme teams are working together to codify and represent how knowledge work is actually done in their disciplines and/or professional fields. Turning more specifically to professional education programmes, it is often the case that these are staffed by a mixture of people who identify as primarily academic, primarily professional, or as a hybrid of the two. Such professional education staff can have very different experiences of socialisation into a field/discipline, and may well draw on very different qualities when exercising connoisseurship. Our insights suggest that if these staff combine their perspectives to create representations of how epistemic work gets done in their areas of practice – such as by identifying sets of epistemic games – then they will be better placed to design developmental paths for their students' growing evaluative judgement, and for students' ability to integrate different perspectives in forming such judgements.

References

Barnett, R. 2009. "Knowing and becoming in the higher education curriculum." *Studies in Higher Education* 34 (4): 429–440.

Barnett, R., and A. Griffin. 1997. *The End of Knowledge in Higher Education.* London: Cassell.

Beck, J., and M. F. D. Young, 2005. "The assault on the professions and the restructuring of academic and professional identities: a Bernsteinian analysis." *British Journal of Sociology of Education* 26 (2): 183–197.

Bereiter, C. 2013. "Principled practical knowledge: not a bridge but a ladder." *Journal of the Learning Sciences* 23 (1): 4–17.

Bromme, R., D. Kienhues, and T. Porsch. 2010. "Who knows what and who can we believe? Epistemological beliefs are beliefs about knowledge (mostly) to be attained from others." In *Personal Epistemology in the Classroom,* edited by L. D. Bendixen and F. C. Haerle, 163–193. Cambridge, UK: Cambridge University Press.

Cipolla, C., and E. Manzini. 2009. "Relational services." *Knowledge, Technology & Policy* 22 (1): 45–50.

Collins, A., and W. Ferguson. 1993. "Epistemic forms and epistemic games." *Educational Psychologist* 28 (1): 25–42.

Collins, A., and M. Kapur. 2014. "Cognitive apprenticeship." In *The Cambridge Handbook of the Learning Sciences,* edited by R. Keith Sawyer, 109–127. Cambridge, UK: Cambridge University Press.

Collins, H. 2007. *Rethinking Expertise.* Chicago, IL: The University of Chicago Press.

Collins, H. 2010. *Tacit and Explicit Knowledge.* Chicago, IL: The University of Chicago Press.

Edwards, A. 2010. *Being an Expert Professional Practitioner: The Relational Turn in Expertise.* Dordrecht, The Netherlands: Springer.

Farrell, R., and C. Hooker. 2013. "Design, science and wicked problems." *Design Studies* 34 (6): 681–705.

Greeno, J. G. 2012. "Concepts in activities and discourses." *Mind, Culture, and Activity,* 19 (3): 310–313.

Guile, D. 2011. "Interprofessional activity in the space of reasons: thinking, communicating and acting." *Vocations and Learning* 4 (2): 93–111.

Manzini, E. 2015. *Design, When Everybody Designs: An Introduction to Design for Social Innovation.* Cambridge, MA: MIT Press.

Markauskaite, L., and P. Goodyear. 2014. "Professional work and knowledge." In *International Handbook of Research in Professional and Practice-based Learning,* edited by S. Billett, C. Harteis, and H. Gruber, 79–106. Dordrecht, The Netherlands: Springer.

Markauskaite, L., and P. Goodyear. 2017. *Epistemic Fluency and Professional Education: Innovation, Knowledgeable Action and Actionable Knowledge.* Dordrecht, The Netherlands: Springer.

Markauskaite, L., P. Goodyear, and A. Bachfischer. 2014. "Epistemic games for knowledgeable action in professional learning." In *Proceedings of the International Conference of the Learning Sciences (ICLS) 2014. Learning and Becoming in Practice*, edited by J. Polman et al., 1289–1292. Boulder, CO: International Society of the Learning Sciences.

Patton, M. Q. 2011. *Developmental Evaluation: Applying Complexity Concepts to Enhance Innovation and Use.* New York: Guilford Press.

Perkins, D. N. 1997. "Epistemic games." *International Journal of Educational Research* 27 (1): 49–61.

Rittel, H., and M. Webber. 1984. "Planning problems are wicked problems." In *Developments in Design Methodology*, edited by N. Cross, 135–144. New York: Wiley.

Sadler, D. R. 1989. "Formative assessment and the design of instructional systems." *Instructional Science* 18 (2): 119–144.

Turnbull, D. 2000. *Masons, Tricksters and Cartographers: Comparative Studies in the Sociology of Scientific and Indigenous Knowledge.* Amsterdam, The Netherlands: Harwood.

Winstone, N. E., R. A. Nash, M. Parker, and J. Rowntree. 2017. "Supporting learners' agentic engagement with feedback: a systematic review and a taxonomy of recipience processes." *Educational Psychologist* 52 (1): 17–37.

Yinger, R., and M. Hendricks-Lee. 1993. "Working knowledge in teaching." In *Research on Teacher Thinking: Understanding Professional Development*, edited by C. Day, J. Calderhead, and P. Denicolo, 100–123. London: Falmer.

SECTION 2

Alternative theoretical perspectives on evaluative judgement

CHAPTER 4

Problematising standards: representation or performance?

Rola Ajjawi and Margaret Bearman

Increasing public accountability, due to the commodification of higher education, has seen a rise in standards-based assessment (Boud 2017). Central to standards-based assessment is the notion that all students should meet the explicated standards. This has led to the common practice of providing learning outcomes as expressions of what students should be able to do as a result of completing their studies. Ideally, standards-based assessment is underpinned by constructive alignment, whereby course learning outcomes are aligned with unit learning outcomes, which are also aligned with assessments and within-unit learning activities (Biggs and Tang 2007). Rubrics are frequently used to capture the criteria by which students can meet the learning outcomes at various levels of quality (Dawson 2015). Academics then make judgements about what students know or can do in relation to these criteria and standards (Torrance 2007).

Students may be unconcerned with standards except when specifically oriented towards them through rubrics or similar assessment documents. In these instances, students make evaluative judgements about their work in relation to implicit and/or explicit standards. Judging how "good" work is requires an understanding of what constitutes "good". From a student perspective, this is the key role of standards. Ideally, this interaction with standards takes place when students assess their own and others' work in relation to the given criteria, on multiple occasions, with feedback to help calibrate these judgements.

The broad discourse of standards-based assessment skirts around the complexities that underpin learning outcomes, rubrics and other similar texts. In this chapter, we seek to problematise notions of standards within the assessment discourse and particularly in relation to evaluative judgement. Standards in higher education are already the subject of some debate. We review these debates and then introduce an alternative, sociomaterial account. Our core argument is that a standard is not a static representation of either an absolute truth or a subjective interpretation of a culturally generated artefact, but a dynamic and emergent "performance". We then consider the implication of this view for assessment in general and evaluative judgement in particular.

Standards in the assessment literature

Bowker and Star (1999) state that standards are any set of agreed-upon rules for the production of textual or material objects. This broad definition includes all rubrics, guidelines, aims and objectives that contribute to the production of assessment. In short, assessment standards describe what teachers think learners should achieve in a uniform manner. There are reasons of equity underpinning this: the expected standard for one learner's work should be the same as for another at the same level. Further, standards help give all students an equal footing regarding expectations, thereby overcoming aspects of cultural capital learnt at home from professional parents or through their social networks.

Standards assist students to navigate the learning landscape. Research shows that when teachers make standards explicit, learning improves (Andrade and Valtcheva 2009; Panadero and Jonsson 2013). Standards are generally adjusted according to the level of the student, so that standards for the first year can be quite different for later years, which can be different again from workplace or professional standards. Standards also communicate to employers and the public a minimum level of achievement and expectation. Much of the assessment literature promotes transparency of standards as benefiting teachers and learners alike and, regardless, they are here to stay – at least for the foreseeable future (Boud 2017).

The literature on academic standards has been summarised as containing two perspectives (Bloxham and Boyd 2012). Some take a techno-rational or representational view, where standards are untainted by values, culture or power. Others hold a sociocultural perspective wherein standards are context-dependent, socially situated and interpretive (continuously created by academic communities). We will review each of these.

A representational view of educational standards holds that the standard is a stable artefact that describes particular realities of practice, often expressed as prescribed lists of competencies or learning outcomes (Mulcahy 1999). These representations aim at capturing the knowledge, values and competencies of a profession or discipline. This representational epistemology holds that knowledge is an accurate representation of something that is separate from the knower (Mulcahy 2014). This may become a problem where the representation is conflated with how the world *really* is.

Sociocultural perspectives, on the other hand, take context and its social and cultural relations into account. Standards do not exist in a vacuum but are deliberately constructed, typically through consensus. Thus, standards reside in the practices of academic and professional communities, underpinned by tacit and explicit knowledge (O'Donovan et al. 2004). Once prescribed, they are often set and sustained over time (although not indefinitely, as they are refined and revised). They are then viewed as comparable across time and space, but are often manifested for different assessment tasks, courses and disciplines (Sadler 2009).

Fenwick and Edwards (2013) argue that educational practices tend to be primarily representational (or techno-rational), focused on the development of individuals and their cognitive acquisition of knowledge and skills. From a sociocultural perspective, the representational view of standards in higher education is limited. This dominant model of transparency and sharing of standards relies on explicit criteria and level descriptors, which have been shown to be inadequate because many aspects of quality cannot be communicated through explicit criteria (Hudson et al. 2017). We concur with this view and explore some of its implications later. However, a sociocultural view itself may also have limitations, as it foregrounds the expert construction of standards. There is an implicit assumption that standards represent the explicit and tacit expertise of their creators – albeit expertise that is shifting, subjective and practice-based. This ignores the role of the standard-as-written. We suggest the standard-as-written cannot "accurately" capture a sociocultural practice any more than the consensus can capture an external and objective list of what constitutes quality.

We introduce an alternative perspective to the debate, taking a sociomaterial framing of standards. This offers richness to the existing debates of standards in the assessment literature and provides a more generative conceptualisation. When it comes to evaluative judgement, Sadler (1989, 121) points out that an indispensable condition for improvement in student learning is that "the *student* comes to hold a concept of quality roughly similar to that held by the teacher". What makes a sociomaterial view different from a sociocultural one is that the ultimate aim shouldn't be seeking alignment with the teacher's view, but a more dynamic perspective of standards.

A sociomaterial framing of standards

Sociomateriality contends that the material and the human work together to enact social practices. Thus, "teaching is not simply about the relationships between humans but is about the networks of humans and things through which teaching and learning are translated and enacted . . ." (Fenwick and Edwards 2013, 54). There is less of an emphasis on individual or social motivations and a greater focus on what *happens*. This view offers a conceptual foundation upon which to understand the complexities associated with developing and using standards as part of assessment. Studies of standards in healthcare (Timmermans and Berg 2003; Timmermans and Epstein 2010) and education (Mulcahy 2011; Tummons 2014b, a) inform this discussion.

From a sociomaterial perspective, standards are *reified*. That is, they are ideas made into concrete artefacts such as rubrics or competency frameworks. In this way, the text itself holds a particular view of quality, which is separate from its progenitors. This takes the standard out of the internal cognitive processes of the individual and even beyond the "way things are done around here" of the social. It places standards artefacts in powerful positions: they can mobilise (and constrain) human action.

Standards artefacts do not carry a single, agreed meaning. The act of reading itself necessitates interpretation and negotiation of meaning, based on the lenses or frames of reference the reader brings to the text and the relevant social, cultural and historical milieu. This act of meaning-making is further complicated by distance, with artefacts spanning institutional, organisational or geographic boundaries (Tummons 2014b). For example, consider a unit rubric that spans multiple tutorial classes, delivered online and face-to-face, at multiple campuses of a university. The same rubric is enacted differently due to local interpretations in different contexts. In this way, standards do double work; they are enacted locally through judgements of competence (e.g., when an assessor judges a trainee's performance against a standard), but they also work globally through ordering practice at a distance, with the promise of consistency and comparability (Fenwick 2010).

Performing educational standards

From a sociomaterial perspective, a standard is always both a stable, constant artefact and an unstable, inconstant interpretation. The disjuncture between the artefact and the interpretation is bridged by conceptualising a standard as an activity in which people might participate. In other words, assessment standards, such as checklists and rubrics, are *performative* (Mulcahy 1999). To put it another way, what are the standards actually *doing*? To achieve anything they must be read, circulated, quoted, acted on or otherwise manipulated. Standards are constituted and enacted by people and materials in complex social arrangements (Mulcahy 2012). The underpinning notion that reality is constructed through enactment is sometimes called a "performative ontology" (Fenwick and Edwards 2013).

A performative ontology challenges held assumptions about the stability of standards across space, time, people and materials. Each enactment of a standard results in a new performance as individuals engage with it, making their own meanings and constructing their own usage. How then, if it is always a new performance, is there a standard? Microadjustments (referred to as 'tinkering') are sufficient to permit a performance of the standard to be necessarily adjusted, as required by the context and purpose, but not adjusted so far that it is no longer recognisable as the standard (Mol 2009).

Tinkering permits the standard to be used across time and space: "made and unmade at the same time" (Mulcahy 1999). Mulcahy (1999) found that teachers tinkered with standards in an attempt to manage the representational ambiguity between the enacted and the formal standard. Teachers in her study enacted translations of the standards to settle the problem of difference at the local level. In synthesising the varied literature on how people organise and reorganise their practices when their local circumstances do not match the prescribed categories or standards, Bowker and Star (1999, 294) comment: "using any kind of representation is a complex accomplishment, a balance of improvisation and accommodation to constraint". These balances are seen in the well-documented subjectivities of assessors who vary in their interpretation of standards and use of marking criteria (Bloxham et al. 2016). However, this is not the same as having no marking criteria; simultaneously, standards attempt to order practice at a distance with the promise of consistency and comparability (Fenwick 2010). Moreover, standards are often nested within other standards.

To give a concrete illustration of a sociomaterial construction of standards playing out across time and space, consider the Australian Medical Council competency framework for newly graduated doctors. These competencies are nested within other standards that inform each year of study of a university curriculum, within which sit yet more standards for each unit of study. The same competency framework standards document applies across all medical schools in Australia; yet it is "performed" sufficiently differently by each medical school to fit with each medical school's vision and aspirations for its graduates, while still being sufficiently similar across each of the schools to be recognisable by the accrediting body. There is then the dance between these professional standards, those stipulated for higher education by national quality assurance agencies, and those required within a specific hospital where a medical student is undertaking a placement. Consider a final-year medical student on rotation, trying to complete a clinical assessment "competently", where the formal criteria for "competence" draw from standards nested within and across the university, professional bodies, regulatory bodies and the workplace. The student's enactments of the standard are informed by a long chain of performances that occur at multiple levels by multiple people, organisations and communities (Bearman and Ajjawi 2017).

This example articulates the complexity of the role of standards within a single piece of assessment. If we take a representative/techno-rational view, we risk becoming glib about standards and uniformity. From an assessment perspective, we need to be mindful of how criteria are used, rather than simply accepting them as given. We propose a more nuanced approach to standards in assessment, with the recognition that how they are used is not necessarily closely aligned to the intentions that underlie the tool.

Implications for assessment and evaluative judgement

From a student perspective, each act of evaluative judgement is a performance of the standard. With every engagement in a task or a learning activity, through watching others and appraising their work using criteria and other standards, learners start to construct their notions of quality for different response genres. Through performing these standards, students can come to understand and embody notions of quality, assisted by formal and informal feedback mechanisms and interpretations of exemplars and other cues. This process can take place across different contexts and with increasing complexity, helped if the learner is attuned to the overlap of criteria across tasks. Research suggests that student co-creation of rubrics may support the development of evaluative judgement (Fraile et al. 2017). Students' notions of quality may be refined with each iteration of a learning task and associated engagement with standards.

A performative view alerts us to dangers: some evaluative judgements may focus purely on the standardised deficits, so that it becomes a question of self-assessment against the standard but not a question of quality – "how can I get over the line?" rather than "how good is this?" That is, the learner is trying to subjectively gauge how good they or others are at a particular task. We are not the first to argue against the dominance of "grade guessing" types of design – whether of one's own work or that of others – or against the unhelpfulness of giving a "mean mark" in peer assessment activities, which "will not help students develop judgements about the value of their own and others' work" (McConlogue 2012, 120). McConlogue goes on to argue that we need to challenge students' assumptions that marking can be objective, or that criteria and grades may be true representations of what a student can actually do. Indeed, the aggregation of marks, across multiple competencies and standards, to achieve a solitary number that enables students' classification is antithetical to the development of students' evaluative judgement. By thinking about performing the standards, we shift this focus towards building complex professional discourses, recognising that judgements occur at local and global levels that provide some boundaries from which a practice can be realised. Education that seeks to develop evaluative judgement fits a discourse of aiming to develop equity, subject expertise and a high degree of autonomy to exercise professional judgement.

There are occasions when the standards of the assessment – the professional competencies or the criteria in the rubric – do not seem to support learning. We can see these instrumental effects of performing inappropriate standards in documented, unintended consequences of assessment. For example, medical students learning the surface communication when performing checklists in a clinical skills examination (Hanna and Fins 2006; Wear and Varley 2008). This has the pernicious effect of discouraging reflective practice, instead promoting a tick-box mentality whereby learners disengage from assessment tools that do not match their everyday practice (Elmholdt et al. 2016). Rather than enacting formal standards, students may throw back to implicit and idiosyncratic standards, learnt ad-hoc with individual supervisors and not in keeping with the community of practice, leading to a narrowing of what constitutes quality and loss of opportunities to further refine understandings of quality. It is ironic that the act of rejecting the formal standard as not meaningful is itself an enactment of evaluative judgement.

From a learning perspective, we need to become curious about the ways in which our students perform standards across units and in different contexts – including how (and why) they inform students' interpretations and understandings of quality, and how these relate to the messy complexities of practice. Loose standards may provide greater adaptability than rigidly defined ones (Timmermans and Epstein 2010). By developing students' evaluative judgement we empower them to enact standards in a sufficiently uniform way for the task at hand, but also help them to articulate the uncertainty and situatedness inherent in their enactment. They can become adept at questioning and interrogating the gaps between the formal/global interpretations and localised enactments and judgements. This then becomes a generative exercise, without betraying the standard. We do this through supporting students, in dialogue and practice, to make sense of quality across tasks and, importantly, across institutions as they transition to the workplace, re-examining the vulnerability of standards as they are locally constituted, enacted, tinkered with and "unmade".

Ongoing dialogue about the role of standards may assist here. In our medical student example, discussing these enactments at each level (with a view to the course-level outcomes) introduces students to the communities of practice that construct these standards and how local interpretations might differ; this ultimately might help students with the complexities of tacit knowledge and practice. Students may also usefully explore how, in professional practice, the experts who develop the standards are typically removed from the actual practitioners who enact them (Reich et al. 2015). Students can come to grips with the responsibility for what is included or excluded in standards, and how these artefacts constitute practice and ultimately affect their own notions of quality.

These complex engagements with standards are best built over time. Assessment design can present standards multiple times for multiple performances, link standards across tasks, and focus on the educational processes that promote shared understanding of quality and recognise the layers of complexity in the standards. Such a view enables judicious tinkering within the performance of the standards that remains true to the response genre of the task. Educators, in their modelling of practice, can highlight how they are enacting standards (including the multiple layers of standards) and adjusting them in relation to the intended purpose, thereby actively constituting quality. As Sadler (2009, 822) argues, "bringing students into a knowledge of standards requires considerably more than sending them one-way messages through rubrics, written feedback or other forms of telling". Processes built around standards require a moving back and forth between the enactment and its manifestation in text.

This alternative way of thinking of standards may also change institutional practices. Universities as a whole could engage with the view that the application of assessment criteria (at course and individual unit levels) is a complex judgement and there is rarely an incontestable interpretation of their meaning. Bringing students into a particular community of practice could include student involvement with standards across courses, units and tasks. This may be easier to facilitate with assessment which is integrated across an entire programme:

> A focus on programme outcomes and standards rather than incremental outcomes provides students with a more holistic view and where there is a greater sense of the holistic programme students are likely to achieve higher standards than on more fragmented programmes.
>
> (Havnes 2007 cited in Price et al. 2017)

If students are given the opportunity to engage with standards then they might not make assumptions about criteria being objective, but instead come to recognise the nature of holistic judgements.

Future research

Research that focuses on the standards artefacts themselves, rather than the educational processes that render the standards valuable, is limited. Rather, research is needed into the interplay of multi-layered standards and how they are performed, translated and tinkered with in the context of assessment and learning in higher education. A performative research agenda, compared to representationalism and socioculturalism, shifts the focus from questions of correspondence between descriptions and reality (e.g., do they mirror nature or culture? does this accord with my teachers' concept of quality?) to matters of practices/doings/actions (Barad 2003, 802). Research in this performative genre would trace a standards artefact such as curriculum documents and assessment instruments through educational practices. Such research would "follow the materials" and see how texts and the activities of assessment actually interweave. For example, researchers might follow how rubrics: come into being; are enacted by students in different contexts; are used by markers; or are referred to in discussions between first and second markers. Thus, researchers can trace the negotiations and performances through which educational standards are derived and sustained, highlighting rifts between prescribed and enacted standards (Fenwick 2010).

Conclusions

Standards-based assessment is a key concern in higher education. In this chapter, we have reviewed representational and sociocultural perspectives of standards within higher education, before presenting a sociomaterial view. In this performative ontology, the focus shifts to the educational processes of enacting an evaluative judgement. We suggest that thinking about evaluative judgement as "performing the standard" will help develop students' nuanced understandings and enactments of multiple layers of quality.

References

Andrade, H., and A. Valtcheva. 2009. "Promoting learning and achievement through self-assessment." *Theory Into Practice* 48 (1): 12–19. doi:10.1080/00405840802577544.

Barad, K. 2003. "Posthumanist performativity: toward an understanding of how matter comes to matter." *Signs: Journal of Women in Culture and Society* 28 (3): 801–831.

Bearman, M., and R. Ajjawi. 2017. "Actor-network theory and the OSCE: formulating a new research agenda for a post-psychometric era." *Advances in Health Sciences Education.* doi:10.1007/s10459–017–9797–7.

Biggs, J., and C. Tang. 2007. *Teaching for Quality Learning at University*, 3rd edn. Buckingham, UK: Society for Research in Higher Education and the Open University Press.

Bloxham, S., and P. Boyd. 2012. "Accountability in grading student work: securing academic standards in a twenty-first century accountability context." *British Educational Research Journal* 38 (4): 615–634.

Bloxham, S., B. den-Outer, J. Hudson, and M. Price. 2016. "Let's stop the pretence of consistent marking: exploring the multiple limitations of assessment criteria." *Assessment & Evaluation in Higher Education* 41 (3): 466–481. doi:10.1080/02602938.2015.1024607.

Boud, D. 2017. "Standards-based assessment for an era of increasing transparency." In *Scaling up Assessment for Learning in Higher Education*, edited by David Carless, Susan

M. Bridges, Cecilia Ka Yuk Chan and Rick Glofcheski, 19–31. Singapore: Springer Singapore.

Bowker, G. C., and S. L. Star. 1999. *Sorting Things Out: Classification and its Consequences.* Cambridge, MA: MIT Press.

Dawson, P. 2015. "Assessment rubrics: towards clearer and more replicable design, research and practice." *Assessment & Evaluation in Higher Education* 42 (3): 347–360. doi:10.1080/02602938.2015.1111294.

Elmholdt, K., C. Elmholdt, L. Tanggaard, and L. H. Mersh. 2016. "Learning good leadership: a matter of assessment?" *Human Resource Development International* 19 (5): 406–428. doi:10.1080/13678868.2016.1206362.

Fenwick, T. 2010. "(un)Doing standards in education with actor-network theory." *Journal of Education Policy* 25 (2): 117–133. doi:10.1080/02680930903314277.

Fenwick, T. J., and R. Edwards. 2013. "Performative ontologies: sociomaterial approaches to researching adult education and lifelong learning." *European Journal for Research on the Education and Learning of Adults* 4 (1): 49–63.

Fraile, J., E. Panadero, and R. Pardo. 2017. "Co-creating rubrics: the effects on self-regulated learning, self-efficacy and performance of establishing assessment criteria with students." *Studies in Educational Evaluation* 53: 69–76. doi.org/10.1016/j.stueduc.2017.03.003

Hanna, M., and J. Fins. 2006. "Power and communication: why simulation training ought to be complemented by experiential and humanist learning." *Academic Medicine* 81 (3): 265–270.

Hudson, J., S. Bloxham, B. den Outer, and M. Price. 2017. "Conceptual acrobatics: talking about assessment standards in the transparency era." *Studies in Higher Education* 42 (7): 1309–1323. doi:10.1080/03075079.2015.1092130.

McConlogue, T. 2012. "But is it fair? Developing students' understanding of grading complex written work through peer assessment." *Assessment & Evaluation in Higher Education* 37 (1): 113–123. doi:10.1080/02602938.2010.515010.

Mol, A. 2009. "Living with diabetes: care beyond choice and control." *The Lancet* 373 (9677): 1756–1757. doi:10.1016/S0140–6736(09)60971–5.

Mulcahy, D. 1999. "(Actor-net) working bodies and representations: tales from a training field." *Science, Technology and Human Values* 24 (1): 80–104.

Mulcahy, D. 2011. "Assembling the 'accomplished' teacher: the performativity and politics of professional teaching standards." *Educational Philosophy and Theory* 43 (sup1): 94–113. doi:10.1111/j.1469–5812.2009.00617.x.

Mulcahy, D. 2012. "Thinking teacher professional learning performatively: a socio-material account." *Journal of Education and Work* 25 (1): 121–139. doi:10.1080/13639080.2012.644910.

Mulcahy, D. 2014. "Re-thinking teacher professional learning: a more than representational account." In *Reconceptualising Professional Learning: Sociomaterial Knowledges, Practices and Responsibilities*, edited by T. Fenwick and M. Nerland, 52–66. Abingdon, UK: Routledge.

O'Donovan, B., M. Price, and C. Rust. 2004. "Know what I mean? Enhancing student understanding of assessment standards and criteria." *Teaching in Higher Education* 9 (3): 325–335. doi:10.1080/1356251042000216642.

Panadero, E., and A. Jonsson. 2013. "The use of scoring rubrics for formative assessment purposes revisited: a review." *Educational Research Review* 9: 129–144. doi:10.1016/j.edurev.2013.01.002.

Price, M., B. O'Donovan, C. Rust, and J. Carroll. 2017. Assessment Standards: A Manifesto for Change. www.heacademy.ac.uk/knowledge-hub/assessment-standards-manifesto-change.

Reich, A., D. Rooney, and D. Boud. 2015. "Dilemmas in continuing professional learning: learning inscribed in frameworks or elicited from practice?" *Studies in Continuing Education* 37 (2): 131–141. doi:10.1080/0158037X.2015.1022717.

Sadler, D. R. 1989. "Formative assessment and the design of instructional systems." *Instructional Science* 18 (2): 119–144.

Sadler, D. R. 2009. "Grade integrity and the representation of academic achievement." *Studies in Higher Education* 34 (7): 807–826. doi:10.1080/03075070802706553.

Timmermans, S., and M. Berg. 2003. *The Gold Standard: The Challenge of Evidence-based Medicine and Standardization in Health Care.* Philadelphia, PA: Temple University Press.

Timmermans, S., and S. Epstein. 2010. "A world of standards but not a standard world: toward a sociology of standards and standardization." *Annual Review of Sociology* 36 (1): 69–89. doi:10.1146/annurev.soc.012809.102629.

Torrance, H. 2007. "Assessment as learning? How the use of explicit learning objectives, assessment criteria and feedback in post-secondary education and training can come to dominate learning." *Assessment in Education: Principles, Policy & Practice* 14 (3): 281–294. doi:10.1080/09695940701591867.

Tummons, J. 2014a. "Professional standards in teacher education: tracing discourses of professionalism through the analysis of textbooks." *Research in Post-Compulsory Education* 19 (4): 417–432. doi:10.1080/13596748.2014.955634.

Tummons, J. 2014b. "The textual representation of professionalism: problematising professional standards for teachers in the UK lifelong learning sector." *Research in Post-Compulsory Education* 19 (1): 33–44. doi:10.1080/13596748.2014.872918.

Wear, D., and J. D. Varley. 2008. "Rituals of verification: the role of simulation in developing and evaluating empathic communication." *Patient Education and Counseling* 71 (2): 153–156. doi:10.1016/j.pec.2008.01.005.

CHAPTER **5**

Barriers to the cultivation of evaluative judgement: a critical and historical perspective

Robert Nelson

Evaluative judgement is implicitly a part of any syllabus. Sometimes, students make judgements of other students' work; sometimes they are called upon to discriminate among sources, contrary arguments, interpretation, even scientific opinion; sometimes they participate in debates and make judgements of a moral nature.

The more interesting and debatable the issue, the harder it is to assess. When we discriminate among plain dichotomies, where one story is right and the other wrong, we are not exercising evaluative judgement to an impressive degree. Meanwhile, the issue gains fascination and intrigue when there is *enduring doubt*, a subjective dimension where the values of the evaluator enter, requiring analysis and deconstruction. A further layer might be discerned where evaluative judgements occur in a creative proactive way, apparently inseparable from processes of construction, composition, writing or painting.

This chapter concentrates on the more subjective end of the spectrum, using a method that is both phenomenological and historical. I will first propose a cation of evaluative judgement, giving examples of three broad categories. To triangulate these speculations, I will draw upon the history of ideas to reveal how the development of language encourages a richer understanding of evaluative judgement. Finally, I turn to the suspected problem in fostering evaluative judgement in learning and teaching, where educational design flattens and disappoints the great historical nexus between evaluative judgement and creativity. Alas, the canonical themes of syllabus design have a withering effect on students gaining legitimate confidence in evaluative judgement.

A short taxonomy of evaluative judgement

It is helpful to distinguish between three types of evaluative judgement. Hard evaluative judgement arises when we discriminate on the basis of truth. Soft evaluative judgement arises when we discriminate on the basis of importance. Dynamic evaluative judgement arises when we discriminate on the basis of opportunity.

Hard evaluative judgement

All kinds of evaluative judgement have one motif in common: they involve a preference over which there is lingering doubt. If there is no lingering doubt, there is no need for an evaluative judgement, only empirical method. Nevertheless, there are forms of evaluative judgement that are much more objectively couched than others, more akin to analysis and other elements of empirical method. An example of analytical evaluative judgement is diagnosis. The training of students authentically follows the experience of doctors themselves when they are confronted with symptoms and seek to know their cause in order to propose a treatment. It is hugely important and depends upon a large amount of knowledge, excellent skills of observation and an ability to abandon premature theories that cross the clinician's mind. Imaginative ideas arise that could explain the symptoms; but they may not perfectly match the circumstance, in which case the fond but spurious explanations have to be discarded. The analyst must lay aside all convenience and continue to evaluate the circumstance, critically eschewing appealing but possibly wrong-headed explanations.

Soft evaluative judgement

Students and their lecturers also make judgements about values and quality, where the issue is not so much about right and wrong but how important things are. Many assertions can be deemed correct, dispelling doubt to some extent, but a prior judgement positions the issue as immaterial. If a painting is not seen as aesthetically worthy, it will not be discussed at all. All matters of inclusion in architectural or literary history, gender studies or film involve such judgements. The designer of the syllabus has already packaged a suite of judgements about what deserves study and what may be neglected; and the student learns a similar pattern, implicitly valorising what is studied (unless objects are held up to critical contempt) and dismissing the items neglected (unless they are seen as analogous to those that are included).

There are dangers in making such evaluative judgements, but they are called for in professions and even research. Editors, curators, producers of science programmes, librarians, website designers, festival managers: all make such judgements as part of their job. But personal confidence notwithstanding, the judgements are always vexed. There are bewildering variables, among which are legion past judgements and the conventions upon which they are based: ideas of acceptability, taste, decorum and popularity. The idea of value or worth, around which such judgements are constantly being made, is somewhat canonical in structure; and, alas, the agreement with past judgement or alignment with contemporary feeling is no guarantee of probity.

One of the most telling examples is the public reception of the baroque composer Telemann, a dazzlingly talented man who was greatly esteemed during his lifetime (1681–1767). Not long after his death, Telemann's fortunes went into decline and his music remained the object of scorn and derision for two centuries. In a book of chilling discoveries, the writer Eckart Klessmann (2005) documents how musical historians would regularly denounce Telemann's polygraphy, damning his music as shallow, artificial, routinely scribbled for occasions, having no musical integrity and never proceeding from a deeper understanding of human feeling or gravity. Today, Telemann's fortunes have been liberally redeemed and many of his chamber compositions count among the masterpieces of western music. How could it be, Klessmann asks, that the judgement of this self-evidently brilliant composer could have fallen so deeply in public regard that he became for so long a byword for musical superficiality? Klessmann argues that musical critics tend to rehearse the judgement that others have made, without independent or innocent encounters with the music.

The danger with evaluative judgement over cultural importance is that students simply learn the prejudice of their teachers and peers.

Dynamic evaluative judgement

Another vein of evaluative judgement may be distinguished, which involves writing, organising ideas in a creative or persuasive way, and all aesthetics, as with art or composition in music. Whenever we make something original, we face scores of decisions about the direction and emphasis of the work. There are normally too many decisions to name them all; but every decision requires further decisions, all based to some extent on an evaluative judgement of the efficacy of the previous decisions. In this creative context, one could define evaluative judgement as the editorial and censoring faculty that applies itself to imaginative processes.

It is seen in its purest form in the creative arts. If I have a melody that I want to elaborate in an instrumental form, everything that I write is meant to clinch the potential of the melodic motif; but equally, everything that I commit to the score has the capacity to wreck the flow, obscure the logic, create muddy sound, hijack the melody, cancel the musicality, or make pompous trifles of it, to the point that I am ready to discard what seemed so promising.

Dynamic evaluative judgement, which might strike you as the most esoteric, is in fact the most commonly practised; for instance, as with a lawyer preparing a statement. How to begin? With the client's background? With legal principle? With an admission? The whole of our communicative interactions is littered with evaluative judgement about the sensitivities and sympathies of our interlocutors. It is the case in social work where we need to establish in our own minds how receptive a person is to the prudent counsel that we might proffer. These tactics, if you will, are not about content but are instead judgements as to how to manage content – especially how to communicate it.

Historical judgement between prudence and perspicacity

Throughout the Renaissance, the zealous turns in the infinite prospect of studio practice were known as judgement. It was one of the most popular words in the artistic lexicon. In his *Lives of the Painters*, the sixteenth-century artist and biographer Giorgio Vasari uses the cluster of words (*giudicio*, *giudizio* or verbal *giudicare*) almost 250 times. Sometimes, the term indicates an awareness and skill deep inside the artistic process, and at all times it aligns implicitly with canonical classical taste; so, in recommending anything, one also recommends judgement. But the word subtly moves from the absolute to the instinctual. For example, a sculptor needs not only the perfection of organisational judgement but something absolute and instantaneous (*assoluta e subita*), to the point of understanding the inherence of a figure within the marble, such as Michelangelo fathomed divinely (*Lives*, proemio). In the absence of this happiness of judgement (*felicità di giudizio*), sculptors easily fall into errors that have no remedy and which remain witnesses in perpetuity to the faults of the chisel (*errori dello scarpello*) – which are irredeemable (*incorrigibili*) – or the scant judgement of the artist. Painters, meanwhile, can amend their lack of judgement and treat their errors (*medicarli*) with the same brush that commits them. But against that, painters need greater judgement (*maggior giudicio*) in composing multiple-figure compositions.

Though never defined in these creative epochs, judgement is nevertheless spread across all three categories and is not confined to just one of them.

The field of mobile criteria

The sixteenth-century philosopher Montaigne emphasises throughout his large collection of essays how chance operates through life, providing circumstances with unpredictable opportunities and risks. The same chaotic influences that might disrupt expectations in warfare are equally noticeable in creative endeavour. In speaking or writing, he explains, the circumstances dictate more than he can write, whence he discovers things that he would not find if he probed and engaged his wits by himself: "I don't find myself where I look [*je ne me trouve pas où je me cherche*] and I find myself more by encounters than by the investigation of my judgement" (*Essais* 1.10). In fact, judgement at a certain phase in formulating ideas has a corrosive effect, stymieing the nascent connexions that the imagination throws up. "If I took the razor to everything that occurs to me, I would be entirely despoiled" (*je me desferoy tout*). Two essays later, Montaigne directly invokes warfare, noting that discourse is somewhat inept in sorting out or fixing all the movements that occur; because what judgement could you make of the high and low sight of something so sudden (1.12)? In various conditions where we exercise "natural faculties", judgement only works by groping at things (*ne marche qu'à tastons*), staggering, tottering and flagging. In creative endeavours, where so many variables concatenate as a consequence of every action, the process cannot be designed or predicted. We react instinctively to each action according to our personality as much as to judgement.

To use Montaigne's word, it is proper to judgement to falter. Above all, when one judges between things that are legitimately in doubt – exciting things where the prospects are unknown in either direction – we cannot easily lay the doubt aside and sally forth with a conceit of perfect judgement. Rather, the creative skill is almost to keep the doubt alive. Around obscurities and among uncertain and false promises, it is unrealistic to establish any solid judgement (*Essais* 1.26). Going against the canon of perfection of judgement, the genial French philosopher proposes instead a spread of judgements (*diversité de jugemens*) among which one chooses, if one can; else one remains in doubt (*sinon il en demeurera en doubte*). Only fools, he concludes, are certain and resolute (1.26), quoting the beautiful line from Dante that "doubting pleases me no less than knowledge" ("*che, non men che saver, dubbiar m'aggrata*", *Inferno* 11.91).

So among all the challenges of evaluative judgement is the decision not to evaluate, to defer judgement, to imagine that things could go one way or another. The artist is, in many ways, not that resolute soul determined upon a canon but a changing, open mind until the final gesture, gathering chance and serendipity and forging the vision as much by mistakes as by resolve. In creative work of any kind, evaluative judgement is structured like a feedback loop: it informs, provisionally, a process of review that only occurs by doing, by making, by trying. It is not structurally fixed upon finality, but shifting opportunity.

Already in the Renaissance, then, there is not only a vivid celebration of evaluative judgement but a critique of it. What one generation esteems as perfect judgement, another will dismiss as anachronistic; and even our own judgement contradicts itself. How many things served us yesterday as articles of faith which today are fairy tales for us (Montaigne, *Essais* 1.27)? Montaigne insists that judgement operates in a field of not knowing things adequately: "the recognition of ignorance is one of the most beautiful and certain witnesses of judgement that I can find" (2.10).

Relationships between creativity and judgement

Throughout the Baroque, the term judgement was used as an absolute. One could lack judgement, but the term "bad judgement" – assuming a dichotomy between good and bad judgement, and hence acknowledging the relativity of judgement – is not to be found. It makes a difference to predicate judgement with an adjective. If there is good judgement, there is bad judgement; but if we just say "lacking judgement", it assumes that judgement is always good. The discovery that judgement is not absolute belongs to the modern age and does not appear in the pre-industrial period.

However, with whatever lexical attachment to the absolute, pre-industrial judgement is never really absolute in practice. How can it be if it is applied in a creative context? The final insight to emerge from the connexion of judgement with wit is that the evaluating person must be independent. The judgement of centuries is no guarantee of good judgement; judgement is not about numbers. As John Dryden says: "Nor is the people's judgment always true: / The most may err as grossly as the few" (Dryden [1681] 1966, 781–782). You can imagine any poet thinking in that way, especially in relation to wit. You create something witty and no one gets it. The absence of approval does not mean that it is not witty. This resolution on the part of the wit, to ignore the contempt of the many, is one of the hardest things to teach; first, because we do not like to cultivate conceit, and second, the many may, in the end, prove to be correct. The judgement of the wit can also err. But in the end, the autonomy of the wit must prevail, else there is no scope for undefended judgement nor a life for those who would profess it.

How to teach evaluative judgement

Evaluative judgement was never easy to teach. But there are structural reasons to suspect that it might be becoming harder to teach. Of the three forms already described, it was always easier to teach hard or analytical evaluative judgement than soft or dynamic judgement. With any analytical processes such as diagnosis, we can ply students with methods that are helpful and not too difficult to follow and learn. There are tree-like structures, gated flow charts with boxes linked by the interrogative particle 'if', which direct the inquiry on the basis of information to be gathered or that already lies to hand. This systematic map of decisions has few counterparts with artistic or synthetic processes, where we are called upon to judge not so much the truth or validity of claims against observations or logic but rather the intuition that something matters more than something else or that an opportunity avails – that, for instance, it might be a good idea to use blue as opposed to magenta or green, or to start the paragraph with a question or an image or a detail or a generalisation. No one can tell you, because it depends organically on what you are going to paint next or to say next. They are all potentially legitimate or misguided acts in a farrago of contingencies; and even if you could hypothetically isolate discrete stages (such as "apply blue here"), in reality, those myriad decisions and individual acts may be impossible to disentangle from one another. For the prudence of this decision or that, any of the options could be justified by a sufficiently persuasive sentence to follow; but what makes the sequence persuasive is always subjective. One reader will immediately respond favourably to the evocative character of an image and see the logic, whereupon the remainder is experienced rhapsodically, poetically reinforcing the intended point. Another reader, however, will find it obscure, requiring greater clarification and focus – the very evidential factuality that the other reader would find tedious.

Teaching evaluative judgement in any form of writing has always laboured under such problems of subjectivity. There would never have been a time when universal standards of imaginative essay-writing were agreed upon. It goes with the territory that the field is hard to regulate; the processes are difficult to define and judgement is somewhat unstable, conflicted, at times embarrassing. Each person's judgement is open to question and it is easy for a disaffected student to imagine that there is no real system, no real educational guidance, but only an arbitrary privilege among those who judge at the expense of the assessed. One may be rewarded by the coincidence of taste between evaluator and evaluated, or one could be punished as a result of their mutual alienation. The student who begins the essay with an outlandish paradox will excite the lecturer who takes similar liberties in momentarily confounding the reader. But another lecturer will despise the attempt at headlines and dismiss the effort as unacademic, journalistic, dilettantish. The evocation of some cultural circumstance will be well received by a reader with similar experiences; but the same evocation may be felt to be indulgent or belletrist by someone who does not share such experiences. Across the spectrum of teachers and students, the basis of evaluation could be considered capricious.

These vagaries might have gone on for decades, unchanged since the 1970s. The system was always capricious but it did not dull the capacity of the student to form evaluative judgements of the most sophisticated kind. It was, if you like, annoyingly educational: setting up students well for a career in editorial fields, industry or the public service, where attending to the desired rhetoric and casting content with a happy spin are life skills of an invaluable kind.

In due course, however, this crazy whimful economy of taste and guess was to come under unsympathetic review. The impetus was educational theory itself, with the enlightened writings of John Biggs (Biggs and Tang 2011), for example, insisting that learning is harmed when students are confused and disempowered, when items of content and disparate skill sets are strewn around them in no necessary relation to assessment or learning outcomes. With the doctrine of constructive alignment, students have the best possible chances to construct their knowledge actively, thanks to clear learning outcomes being stated, chased reliably by learning activities, presentations and discussions, and echoed scrupulously in the assessment. These elements are in alignment not just as content but also as ways of thinking, each mustering the same kind of lower- or higher-order cognitive effort.

The nicest expression of this cleansing of academic chaos is the alignment between assessment task and learning outcomes. Each assessment task must align with learning outcomes and be assessed according to criteria in similar agreement. To fulfil this laudable logic, it became common not just to publish the criteria for assessment but to also develop a marking rubric according to which each essay (or any other assessable genre) could be graded as satisfying the expectations to a greater or lesser extent. The rubric spells out the degree to which the desired content or technique is missing. Students are thus directed as exactly as possible. It is a responsible method and it now seems wayward and derelict to leave alignment to chance. We also mandate that the verbs used in learning outcomes be measurable, so that they reliably lead to logical discrimination and accurate marking.

Impediments to the pedagogy of evaluative judgement

What happens to our two forms of synthetic evaluative judgement (soft and dynamic) in this benign straightjacket? If I am following the rubric, I map out my writing strategically. I do not bother about decisions that involve colour, such as: should I start my essay with an image or a scene-setting quote or a gnomic paradox or any of the other dramatic resources available to a writer in any discipline? Rather, I will construct the essay as economically as possible in tight fulfilment of the rubric. I will begin with words such as: "in this essay I will analyse", because the rubric contains the word "structure" and I will want to signpost the structure from the beginning, lest I be accused of failing adequately to plan, announce the direction and conduct the reader along a logical development of ideas. Checklist in hand from the published rubric, I will then systematically go through all the points to which marks are accorded and thus attempt to wriggle into a high grade.

In all of this scoping and strategic manipulation of my knowledge in the grid of assessment criteria, I will only have exercised evaluative judgement confined to the mechanism of a checklist. It is thinking of a lower order, which in baroque language was called "ordinary" rather than imaginative. You do not decide anything on the basis of a creative intuition, holding out a hypothesis-in-miniature with every proposed wording – which you then test by writing it and thinking of its implications in further writing – but rather you look for a match amid the available options that best fits the criteria, cultivating minimal intellectual autonomy. Instead of evaluative judgement as a creative organic process, you employ evaluative judgement reactively, anxiously managing the content according to its assessment measures. Marking rubrics are the educational equivalent of colouring-in in art, where the process of learning is drained of creative evaluative judgement; consequently the attention of the student and the assessor turns to the minutiae of boring but measurable details, such as how well the bibliographic conventions are observed – which is like measuring how evenly the pressure has been applied in the colouring-in book and how neatly the outlines contain the hatching.

It is the reason, I believe, for the inordinate amount of attention given to referencing and bibliographic conventions in essays throughout humanities and social sciences. The element in learning that matters least ends up acting as the discriminator in assessments; because students are plied with resources and templates for handling the content; and all students who know how to read the marking rubric have a fair idea how to reach a similar standard as one another. Some, however, will foul themselves up on the conventions and their relative compliance thus affords a neater bell curve for the assessor. Our problem, I suggest, is that we have constructive alignment, with learning outcomes and rubrics to help confine the students to prescriptions.

Conclusion

This chapter has distinguished three types of evaluative judgement: (i) hard evaluative judgement, when we discriminate on the basis of truth; (ii) soft evaluative judgement, when we discriminate on the basis of importance; and (iii) dynamic evaluative judgement, when we discriminate on the basis of opportunity. Each requires us to make peace with lingering doubt; and only the first category is capable of proof in hindsight, as in a diagnosis being correct or a prescribed treatment helping to heal a patient. The categories of soft and dynamic evaluative judgement – both flooded with cultural contingencies – are seldom proven in hindsight, because another turn may have yielded an unknown and perhaps better result. These two categories are (a) identifiable historically across many centuries and languages, and (b) by no means confined to the creative arts.

In fostering the second and third kinds of evaluative judgement, learning and teaching are hampered by the structures of constructive alignment, which do not encourage the organic processes of conjecture and imagination that serve the more proactive dimensions of evaluative judgement. To optimise the discriminatory agility of students, a culture of learning outside the grid of learning outcomes is indicated.

References

Biggs, J., and C. Tang. 2011. *Teaching for Quality Learning at University.* Maidenhead, UK: Open University Press. Citation refers to 4th edn.

Dryden, J. (1681) 1966. *Absalom and Achitophel.* London: Oxford University Press.

Klessmann, E. 2005. *Ein Talent der flachsten Art: Georg Philipp Telemann im Urteil der Nachwelt.* Stuttgart, Germany: Franz Steiner Verlag.

CHAPTER **6**

Limits to evaluative judgement

Gordon Joughin

> The human understanding when it has once adopted an opinion draws all things else to support and agree with it. And though there be a greater number and weight of instances to be found on the other side, yet these it either neglects and despises, or else by some distinction sets aside and rejects, in order that by this great and pernicious predetermination the authority of its former conclusion may remain inviolate.
>
> (Francis Bacon, *Novum Organum*, 1620, cited by Baron 2008, 199)

> The act of self-assessment is an intrinsically difficult task...
>
> (Dunning, Heath, and Suls 2004, 69)

Dual processing systems of human judgement

In the literature on student evaluative judgement, it is often taken for granted that such judgement involves students reviewing their work in light of predetermined standards, communicated through such means as exemplars or statements of criteria and standards, with the latter often taking the form of rubrics. This process is seen as an analytical one whereby the student compares his or her work to the standard, evaluates that work against it, notes disparities and, hopefully, determines to address any disparities through more study and/or improved work. Such a view is most clearly articulated in the oft-cited work of Sadler (1989), and underpins much of the discussion of evaluative judgement in other chapters of this book. It is not the purpose of this chapter to argue against this understanding, but rather to draw attention to a strand of research and theory which suggests that other, parallel, processes may be at work in the process of evaluative judgement.

Research on judgement and decision-making in the social sciences over the past 60 years suggests that the understanding of judgement as a conscious, deliberative process may be only a partial representation of the process of judgement. "Dual process" or "dual system" theories of thought acknowledge a conscious, deliberate, effortful, analytical and "rational" approach to judgement while also positing an automatic, effortless, unconscious and "intuitive" process. The "intuitive" process has been designated System 1 and the "analytic" process

Table 6.1 System 1 and System 2 processes of judgement

System 1	*System 2*
Automatic	Controlled
Fast	Slow
Intuitive	Reflective
Heuristic	Analytic
Implicit cognition	Explicit learning
Effortless	Effortful
Holistic	Analytic
Rapid, parallel	Slow, serial
Skilled action	Rule application

System 2 (Stanovich and West 2000). Table 6.1 presents a selection of paired words from three summaries of the dual process approach (Evans and Frankish 2009; Kahneman and Frederick 2001; Stanovich and West 2000) to illustrate each system and contrast them with one another.

The automatic, "intuitive" judgements and decisions of System 1 have an important place in the routine decisions of daily life. They are also found in the thinking of experts with extensive experience in a particular field, who are able to recognise patterns in complex situations instantly and make immediate sound judgements on the basis of this "pattern recognition" (Simon 1955). Certain heuristics, or cognitive shortcuts, can facilitate such rapid, accurate judgements in situations requiring immediate action. On the other hand, for non-experts or those in novel situations, accurate judgement requires the activation of System 2 with careful, systematic, analytical thinking.

The evaluation of students' work could potentially utilise either system. Expert examiners will often make immediate judgements of student work without engaging in any conscious analytical process (Brooks 2012; Suto and Gatorex 2008). Their expertise arises from exposure to dozens, if not hundreds, of examples of student work, and is therefore far removed from the approach usually considered appropriate for students engaged in judging their own work at an undergraduate or postgraduate level. Dual process theory therefore draws our attention to the threat to evaluative judgement if students engage System 1 when the more deliberative System 2 is required, resulting in judgements that are "biased" – that is, which deviate from the more appropriate judgements that would be reached through a more thoughtful, effortful and analytical process.

Even when students approach evaluative judgement in a systematic, analytical way, might the biases associated with System 1 nevertheless intrude on, and distort, the deliberative process? Are Dunning et al. (2004, 69) right when, in summarising research in health, education and the workplace, they assert that "[t]he act of self-assessment is intrinsically difficult" and that "[s]everal psychological processes conspire to produce flawed self-assessments"? And might students, having formed an initial impression of their work, ensure that their initial judgement remains inviolate in the face of countering evidence? These are the questions addressed in the remainder of this chapter.

Heuristics and biases

The role of System 1 in leading to distorted judgement has been extensively examined in the "heuristics and biases" tradition (for summaries of this research, including references to an extensive range of heuristics and biases, see Gilovich et al. 2002; Kahneman et al. 2001; Keren and Wu 2015; Koehler and Harvey 2004; Newell 2013). This research has identified a range of heuristics – defined as unconscious mental shortcuts that lead to quick decisions – which, by eschewing a detailed analytical approach, have the potential to distort judgement. This work has only rarely been considered in the higher education literature, where Brooks' exploration of dual process theory in the context of teacher marking provides a useful introduction to issues that apply equally to student judgement (Brooks 2012). In this section, four specific heuristics – attribute substitution, anchoring and adjustment, overconfidence, and the endowment effect – are outlined, along with their potential interaction with student judgement, to illustrate the role that heuristics and biases could play in extending our understanding of evaluative judgement. While none of these heuristics have figured in evaluative judgement theorising or research to date, each would seem to have the potential to significantly distort students' judgement of their own work. Other heuristics, such as the affect heuristic (Slovic et al. 2002) or framing (Tversky and Kahneman 1981), could serve this illustrative purpose equally well.

Attribute substitution

Attribute substitution posits that "judgment is mediated by a heuristic when an individual assesses a specified *target attribute* of a judgment object by substituting another property of that object – the *heuristic attribute* – which comes more readily to mind" (Kahneman and Frederick 2001, 53). A less technical explanation is that "when confronted with a difficult question people often answer an easier one instead" (Kahneman and Frederick 2001, 53). Kahneman and Frederick cite as an example a college student survey where students were first asked about their general happiness and then how many dates they had been on in the past month. Presented in this order, the correlation between the questions was negligible; but when the order was reversed, and students had in mind the number of dates when they answered the happiness question, the correlation rose to 0.66. It appeared that many students, rather than answering the happiness question directly, substituted dating for happiness – dating came more easily to mind (Kahneman and Frederick 2001, 53).

An appropriate act of evaluative judgement can only occur if a student (a) understands the target attribute – that is, the specified criteria and standards – and (b) applies these in making a judgement. Consequently, if a student does not fully understand given criteria and standards, they may simply apply criteria and standards, of their own unconscious devising, that they *do* understand. A common example of this heuristic occurs when a student, finding specified criteria difficult to understand or apply to their work, unconsciously substitutes the amount of effort they have put into an assignment when considering its worth. Even if the student understands the criteria and standards, they still may not apply them if the circumstances are not propitious; for example, if they do not have enough time or if the benefits of a careful self-judgement are not apparent. Kahneman and Frederick postulate that attribute substitution will occur if

> (1) the target attribute is relatively inaccessible; (2) a semantically and associatively related [attribute] is highly accessible; and (3) the substitution of the heuristic attribute in the judgment is not rejected by the critical operations of System 2.
>
> (Kahneman and Frederick 2001, 54)

These first and second points have already been considered. The third point signals the vital role that might be played by a systematic, analytical process of judgement in countering the distortion in judgement which attribute substitution might cause.

Anchoring and adjustment

The *anchoring and adjustment* heuristic refers to the tendency of people, when presented with an initial value, to use this value as an "anchor" point from which they adjust their subsequent decisions or judgements. Such adjustments are typically insufficient in comparison to what their judgement would have been in the absence of that anchor point (Tversky and Kahneman 1974). Tversky and Kahneman give the example of students who, when presented with a random number between 0 and 100 and then asked for the percentage of African countries in the United Nations, report percentages significantly influenced by the random number – that is, the higher their random number, the higher their percentage estimate. Anchoring effects have been described as "among the most robust and ubiquitous psychological phenomena in judgement and decision making" (Mussweiler et al. 2004, 196; see also Furnham and Boo 2011).

From the perspective of the teacher/examiner, this heuristic has been demonstrated in studies of second marking, where second markers know the first grade awarded to a piece of work rather than marking blind. While this biasing effect is well established (Brooks 2012), Garry et al. (2005) explicitly link this phenomenon to the anchoring and adjustment heuristic in their work identifying the biasing effect in teachers' marking of politics essays.

How might this heuristic impact on students' judgement of their own work? It is commonly asserted that all judgement is comparative, and indeed this understanding is the basis of Laming's text on human judgement (Laming 2004) and Abercrombie's classic work, *The Anatomy of Judgment*, wherein she asserts that "[o]nly by seeing how we resemble and differ from other people do we understand ourselves" (Abercrombie [1960] 1989, 58). Similarly, Brooks notes in her work on assessment as judgement that "[j]udgment does not take place in a vacuum, it requires some form of comparator", often in the form of criteria, norms, or one's own previous work (Brooks 2012, 68). To these comparators we must add exemplars, which are typically presented to students as examples of work of different levels of quality, often with a grade to indicate the level. (See the work of Carless et al., Chapter 11 for an important variation on the use of exemplars.)

The question raised in considering students' evaluative judgement is whether such commonly used comparators may act as anchors, with students making insufficient adjustments in relation to their own work. For example, could a student, in light of an exemplar of outstanding work, recognise their work to be not at that level but still rate it more highly than they might have done in the absence of the anchoring exemplar? In light of the Dunning–Kruger effect discussed in the next section, might students of different levels of ability, self-efficacy or confidence experience the anchoring and adjustment heuristic in different ways? This heuristic, with its potential to interact with some of the most common practices in self-assessment, opens an important field for research into student evaluative judgement.

Overconfidence

Overconfidence refers to an exaggerated valuing of our self-assessments, often accompanied by an unwarranted degree of certainty attached to such judgements. Students' overrating of their work is a clear example of this heuristic. Overconfidence has figured prominently in the literature on judgement and decision-making, as it is seen as ubiquitous and can have serious consequences in any context where important decisions are being made or judgement is exercised (see Berner and Graber 2008; Hammond et al. 2013; Kahneman 2011). Kahneman's popular text on biases (Kahneman 2011) devotes five chapters to overconfidence, while others have described overconfidence as one of the most common traps in decision-making, and one that must be guarded against (Hammond et al. 2013; Kahneman et al. 2013).

While heuristics and biases have received little attention in the higher education literature (Joughin et al. 2016), overconfidence is an exception, with the work of Kruger and Dunning complementing and extending previous work in this tradition (Dunning 2011; Dunning et al. 2004; Dunning et al. 2003; Ehrlinger et al. 2008; Krueger and Mueller 2002; Kruger and Dunning 1999; Schlösser et al. 2013. See also reference to this work in Lodge et al., Chapter 7). The process and findings of this research can be summarised as follows. In an initial series of studies, participants were given tests on humour, logical reasoning and English grammar, and were asked to estimate: their ability in these areas; their estimated test results; and how these results would compare with those of other participants. Those students who were deemed less competent (since their performance placed them in the bottom quartile) consistently overrated their performance relative to their actual results and relative to those of the other participants; they were less able to gauge the performance of others; and they failed to gain insight into their own performance by seeing the performance of their peers. On the other hand, running somewhat counter to the overconfidence heuristic, students in the top quartile tended to underrate their own performance but became better calibrated by viewing other students' (lower) performance and could consequently more accurately rate their own performance in relation to that of their peers.

Kruger and Dunning speculated that overrating by the less able students may have been due to two factors: namely, that the skills involved in evaluating one's work are the same as those involved in producing the work, and a belief that simply having done one's best was likely to produce a reasonable grade. They posited that, conversely, higher-performing students tend to erroneously believe that other students have performed similarly well to themselves and consequently underestimate their standing in relation to their peers.

Finally, Kruger and Dunning found that, by providing training in logical reasoning, less competent students became as good at grading their own performance in this area as students in the top quartile who had not yet received this training, thus reinforcing their belief that the skills of self-assessment are closely aligned with content knowledge.

The endowment effect

The *endowment effect* (Kahneman et al. 1991; Thaler 1980, 2015) refers to the overvaluing of objects for which we hold a sense of ownership. Kahneman gives the example of the worker who doesn't care which of two offices she is allocated until she is allocated one of them – the day after which, she refuses to swap (Kahneman 2011, 299)! The endowment effect suggests that students who are influenced by this heuristic, at the expense of more thoughtful analysis of their work, may tend to overrate that work. This proposition has not yet been researched in the context of education, but surely warrants serious investigation. The somewhat related "IKEA effect" concerns the overvaluing of items that we not only own but have at least partly created (Norton et al. 2012). Here a sense of ownership may be in play, but so too might be a sense of the time spent on the task and the positive feelings associated with its successful completion: all results of a process that encourages "co-creation" of an object. While research into the IKEA effect is limited, and it has not yet been applied to student self-assessment, the possible implications are obvious for students' judgement of any work for which they hold a strong sense of ownership associated with its creation.

Failure to engage System 2

The literature on judgement and decision-making suggests several reasons why students adopt the kind of heuristics, with associated biases, discussed in the previous section and, in so doing, may fail to engage (or to engage adequately) with the desired analytical processes of evaluative judgement. A prime reason may lie in a general tendency to opt, unconsciously, for the cognitively less taxing System 1 processes. Simon (1955) coined the term "cognitive miser" to describe this tendency; later writers see this tendency as the basis for many of the heuristics and consequent biases that are now associated with System 1 (Tversky and Kahneman 1974; Stanovich 2010). The cognitive miser has been seen to be responsible for three kinds of failure, all of which could apply to students (West 2010). First, the student, having an overall sense of the quality of their work, may not even consider further analysis if it is not explicitly required. Second, they may engage in System 2 processing but focus only on some aspects of their work or of the analytic framework. Finally, the student may seek to engage analytically but still fail to overcome the judgement they have made intuitively.

One quite different factor in students' engagement in analytical judgement appears to be their "thinking disposition", which includes

> the tendency to collect information before making up one's mind, the tendency to seek various points of view before coming to a conclusion, the disposition to think extensively about a problem before responding, the tendency to calibrate the degree of strength of one's opinion to the degree of evidence available . . . the tendency to explicitly weigh pluses and minuses of a situation before making a decision, and the tendency to seek nuance and avoid absolutism.
>
> (Stanovich 2010, 36)

Stanovich's research suggests that dispositions, associated with what he terms "the reflective mind", are unrelated to other cognitive abilities, including what he calls "the algorithmic mind", which engages with the analytic processes of System 2. In other words, the *disposition* to engage in evaluative judgement, and the *quality* of that engagement, can be separated. This has important implications for both how we engage students in acts of evaluative judgement, and the issues that need to be addressed in helping them develop their capacity for, and disposition towards, such judgement.

Developing students' capacity for evaluative judgement

While dual system theory, and the specific heuristics and biases associated with it, make an important contribution to our understanding of student evaluative judgement, it is less clear how this understanding can be used in developing students' capacity for judgement. This is primarily due to the unconscious, and therefore invisible, nature of System 1 processes. Many are sceptical about ameliorating the influence of System 1 on judgement, following Kahneman in his conclusion that "System 1 is not readily educable" (Kahneman 2011, 416; see also Larrick 2004; Phillips et al. 2004).

Nevertheless, certain directions do emerge, including the need to explicitly develop students' understanding of evaluative judgement as a conscious, analytical process; the need to address dispositions as well as understanding; and the development of reflexivity as part of students' self-awareness, including the role of their beliefs, assumptions and biases. Becoming increasingly aware of the advantages of System 2, while recognising the dangers of an unknowing reliance on System 1, lies at the heart of developing students' capacity for evaluative judgement. The complexity and importance of this has been highlighted by the work at Alverno College, where acts of what they have long termed "evaluative judgment" (Alverno College Faculty 1994, 62) are applied by students to all assessment tasks, contributing to the development, over a whole programme, of their disposition and ability to judge their own performance. This ability has long been seen as "an important part and overriding outcome of their educational process" and, thus, a critical one which graduates should not be without (Loacker and Jensen 1988, 128).

This chapter commenced with two quotations highlighting the difficulty in applying careful analysis to the process of judgement once an initial position has been identified, and thus the complexity entailed in any act of evaluative judgement of one's own work. As these statements span a period from early in the seventeenth century to early in the twenty-first, it seems that there may be some intractable difficulties in human judgement, including students' evaluative judgement. By locating at least some of these difficulties within heuristics and biases, some of the challenges of evaluative judgement have been highlighted, while some promising ways of addressing them have been proposed. At the same time, an untapped field of research into students' evaluative judgement and its development has been identified.

References

Abercrombie, M. L. J. (1960) 1989. *The Anatomy of Judgment: An Investigation into the Processes of Perception and Reasoning.* London: Free Association Books.

Alverno College Faculty. 1994. *Student Assessment-as-Learning at Alverno College.* Milwaukee, WI: Alverno College Institute.

Baron, J. 2008. *Thinking and Deciding*, 4th edn. Cambridge, UK: Cambridge University Press.

Berner, E. S., and M. L. Graber. 2008. "Overconfidence as a cause of diagnostic error in medicine." *American Journal of Medicine* 121 (5): S2–S23. doi:10.1016/j.amjmed.2008.01.001.

Brooks, V. 2012. "Marking as judgment." *Research Papers in Education* 27 (1): 63–80.

Dunning, D. 2011. "The Dunning–Kruger effect: on being ignorant of one's own ignorance." *Advances in Experimental Social Psychology* 44: 247–296.

Dunning, D., C. Heath, and M. Suls. 2004. "Flawed self-assessment: implications for health, education, and the workplace." *Psychological Science in the Public Interest* 5 (3): 69–106.

Dunning, D., K. Johnson, J. Ehrlinger, and J. Kruger. 2003. "Why people fail to recognize their own incompetence." *Current Directions in Psychological Science* 12 (3): 83–87.

Ehrlinger, J., K. Johnson, M. Banner, D. Dunning, and J. Kruger. 2008. "Why the unskilled are unaware: further explorations of (absent) self-insight among the incompetent." *Organizational Behavior and Human Decision Processes* 105: 98–121.

Evans, J. St. B. T., and K. Frankish. 2009. *In Two Minds: Dual Processes and Beyond.* Oxford, UK: Oxford University Press.

Furnham, A., and H. C. Boo. 2011. "A literature review of the anchoring effect." *The Journal of Socio-Economics* 40 (1): 35–42.

Garry, J, M., A. McCool, and S. O'Neil. 2005. "Are moderators moderate? Testing the 'anchoring and adjustment' hypothesis in the context of marking politics exams." *Politics* 25 (3): 191–200.

Gilovich, T., D. Griffin, and D. Kahneman, eds. 2002. *Heuristics and Biases: The Psychology of Intuitive Judgment.* Cambridge, UK: Cambridge University Press.

Hammond, J. S., R. L. Keeney, and H. Raiffa. 2013. "The hidden traps in decision making." In *On Making Smart Decisions,* 1–19. Boston, MA: Harvard Business Review Press.

Joughin, G., P. Dawson, and D. Boud. 2016. "Improving assessment tasks through addressing our unconscious limits to change." *Assessment & Evaluation in Higher Education* 42 (8): 1221–1232. doi:10.1080/02602938.2016.1257689.

Kahneman, D. 2011. *Thinking, Fast and Slow.* London: Penguin.

Kahneman, D., and S. Frederick. 2001. "Representativeness revisited: attribute substitution in intuitive judgment." In *Heuristics and Biases: The Psychology of Intuitive Judgment,* edited by T. Gilovich, D. Griffin, and D. Kahneman, 49–81. Cambridge, UK: Cambridge University Press.

Kahneman, D., D. Lovallo, and O. Sibony. 2013. "*Before You Make That Big Decision . . .*" In *On Making Smart Decisions,* 21–40. Boston, MA: Harvard Business Review Press.

Kahneman, D., J. L. Knetsch, and R. H. Thaler. 1991. "The endowment effect, loss aversion, and status quo bias." *Journal of Economic Perspectives* 5 (1): 193–206.

Kahneman, D., P. Slovic, and A. Tversky. 2001. *Judgment under Uncertainty: Heuristics and Biases.* Cambridge, UK: Cambridge University Press.

Keren, G., and G. Wu, eds. 2015. *The Wiley Blackwell Handbook of Judgment and Decision Making.* Chichester, UK: Wiley.

Koehler, D. J., and N. Harvey, eds. 2004. *Blackwell Handbook of Judgment and Decision Making.* London: Blackwell.

Krueger, J, and R. A. Mueller. 2002. "Unskilled, unaware, or both? The better-than-average heuristic and statistical regression predict errors in estimates of own performance." *Journal of Personality and Social Psychology* 2 (2): 180–188.

Kruger, J., and D. Dunning. 1999. "Unskilled and unaware of it: how difficulties in recognizing one's own incompetence lead to inflated self-assessment." *Journal of Personality and Social Psychology* 77 (6): 1121–1134.

Laming, D. R. J. 2004. *Human Judgment: The Eye of the Beholder.* London: Thomson.

Larrick, R. P. 2004. "Debiasing." In *Blackwell Handbook of Judgment and Decision Making,* edited by D. J. Koehler and N. Harvey, 316–337. London: Blackwell.

Loacker, G., and P. Jensen. 1988. "The power of performance in developing problem solving and self assessment abilities." *Assessment & Evaluation in Higher Education* 13 (2): 128–150.

Mussweiler, T., B. Englich, and F. Strack. 2004. "Anchoring effect." In *Cognitive Illusions: A Handbook on Fallacies and Biases in Thinking, Judgement and Memory,* edited by R. F. Poll, 183–200. Hove, UK: Psychology Press.

Newell, B. R. 2013. "Judgment under uncertainty." In *The Oxford Handbook of Cognitive Psychology,* edited by D. Reisberg. New York, NY: Oxford University Press. doi:10.1093/oxfordhb/9780195376746.013.0038.

Norton, M. I., D. Mochon, and D. Ariely. 2012. "The 'IKEA effect': when labor leads to love." *Journal of Consumer Psychology* 22: 453–460.

Phillips, J., G. Klein, and W. R. Sieck. 2004. "Expertise in judgment and decision making: a case for training intuitive decision skills." In *Blackwell Handbook of Judgment and Decision Making,* edited by D. J. Koehler and N. Harvey, 297–315. London: Blackwell.

Sadler, D. R. 1989. "Formative assessment and the design of instructional systems." *Instructional Science* 18: 119–144.

Schlösser, T., D. Dunning, K. L. Johnson, and J. Kruger. 2013. "How unaware are the unskilled? Empirical tests of the 'signal extraction' counterexplanation for the Dunning–Kruger effect in self-evaluation of performance." *Journal of Economic Psychology* 39: 85–100.

Simon, H. 1955. "A behavioural model of rational choice." *Quarterly Journal of Economics* 69: 99–118.

Slovic, P., M. Finucane, E. Peters, and D. G. MacGregor. 2002. "The affect heuristic." In *Heuristics and Biases: The Psychology of Intuitive Judgment,* edited by T. Gilovich, D. Griffin, and D. Kahneman, 397–420. New York: Cambridge University Press.

Stanovich, K. E. 2010. *Rationality and the Reflective Mind.* Oxford, UK: Oxford University Press.

Stanovich, K. E., and K. R. F. West. 2000. "Individual differences in reasoning: implications for the rationality debate?" *Behavioral and Brain Sciences* 23: 645–726.

Suto, W. M. I., and J. Gatorex. 2008. "What goes through an examiner's mind? Using verbal protocols to gain insights into the GSCE marking process." *British Educational Research Journal* 34 (2): 213–233.

Thaler, R. 1980. "Toward a positive theory of consumer choice." *Journal of Economic Behavior and Organization* 1 (1): 39–60.

Thaler, R. 2015. *Misbehaving: How Economics Became Behavioural.* London: Alan Lane.

Tversky, A. and D. Kahneman. 1974. "Judgment under uncertainty: heuristics and biases." *Science* 185: 1124–1131.

Tversky, A. and D. Kahneman. 1981. "The framing of decisions and the psychology of choice." *Science* 211: 453–458.

West, R. F. 2010. "A taxonomy of rational thinking problems." In *Rationality and the Reflective Mind,* edited by K. Stanovich. New York: Oxford University Press. doi:10.1093/acprof:oso/9780195341140.003.0006.

CHAPTER 7

Understanding, assessing and enhancing student evaluative judgement in digital environments

Jason M. Lodge, Gregor Kennedy and John Hattie

Student evaluative judgements are seen as problematic in higher education because it is difficult for students to develop sophisticated understandings of quality work in their discipline (Cowan 2010). Much of the emphasis in the existing literature on student evaluative judgement has focused on judgements of artefacts (e.g., Boud and Soler 2016); that is, quality is determined through an evaluation of a product or output in relation to another product. While it is imperative that students are given a clear sense of what quality output looks like so that they can strive towards it, it is also important that they know what quality learning processes look like so that they can calibrate as they learn. As Sadler (2009) points out, evaluative judgements need to occur not only in relation to completed work but also during production of the work.

In this chapter, we deal with student evaluative judgements of their progress towards outcomes. In line with notions of "assessment for learning" and "learning-oriented assessment", we will particularly highlight the need to address successful student progress during a learning task. By "task" we here refer to an individual learning activity that could occur during a single lesson or over days or weeks. We seek to emphasise the process of learning, not just the outcome. When considering this process, "how good is this?" must also simultaneously incorporate "do I have sufficient knowledge, skill and ability to do this?" and "am I using an appropriate learning strategy to get it done?" Digital environments are well suited to both investigating and intervening while student work is being produced. The evolving translation of foundational psychological research to learning in digital environments is creating possibilities for interventions targeting student learning processes and strategies in real time. We will explore what these emerging technologies can contribute to student evaluative judgement in higher education.

The psychology of self-evaluation of learning

Broadly speaking, students are relatively accurate when asked to predict how they will do in terms of assessment performance and grades (Kuncel et al. 2005). Despite this, there is growing evidence that demonstrates a complicated association between student perceptions of learning and their actual quality of learning. At the macro-level, there is substantial evidence that student evaluation in formal evaluations of quality learning experiences in higher education does not correlate with how well they perform (Uttl et al. 2017). Cassidy (2007) found that many students, particularly less experienced students, also struggle to identify and select effective learning processes and strategies. Undergraduate students have been found to be broadly unaware of the most effective strategies for learning according to the accumulated evidence (McCabe 2011), despite the finding that there are strategies which have been reliably shown to enhance learning when adopted (Hattie and Donoghue 2016). The evidence for students' overall capacity to judge their own performance is therefore mixed, with many confounding factors. Understanding these factors will become more critical as students increasingly go about their learning in digital environments.

There is some difficulty in determining what underlying psychological factors contribute to the development of evaluative accuracy in learning. Numerous factors are implicated. One theoretical framework that provides a psychological basis for understanding how these judgements are made is the metamemory framework of Nelson and Narens (1990). In this framework, Nelson and Narens depict an ongoing flow of information from an "object-level" to a "meta-level". The object level is related to the cognitive task at hand (for simplicity, we refer to this as the task level), while the meta-level represents a "higher level", namely the metacognitive and executive functioning required to make judgements about progress and inform decision-making about what to do next. We suggest that this meta-level is where evaluative judgement occurs. Monitoring is the process whereby information from the task level flows to the meta-level. The process of control occurs when the meta-level impacts on the task level. In other words, control refers to the decisions a student makes in real time about how to progress.

When translating what this ongoing flow of information between the task level and meta-level might look like in relation to learning tasks, it is necessary to revise the framework. What is missing from the meta-level is the vital calibration of progress towards a goal. Calibration is a critical feature of the evaluative judgements students make as they progress, because these judgements need some benchmark against which they can be compared. While it is evident what this looks like when comparing one complete artefact with another, it is less clear how this calibration occurs in relation to real-time monitoring and decision-making. The importance of these calibration processes has been somewhat neglected in the past (Hattie 2013). The judgements that occur at the meta-level, on the basis of the ongoing monitoring and decision-making processes evident while students learn, need to be compared against an external benchmark, preferably a goal outcome. As has been highlighted in other chapters in this volume (Panadero and Broadbent, Chapter 8; Johnson & Molloy, Chapter 17), in order to make successful evaluative judgements, students need to have a clear sense of the gap between where they currently are and where they need to be (see also Sadler 1989). A graphical depiction of the relationship between evaluative judgements of learning progress and calibration against the external goal, based on the Nelson and Narens framework, is presented in Figure 7.1.

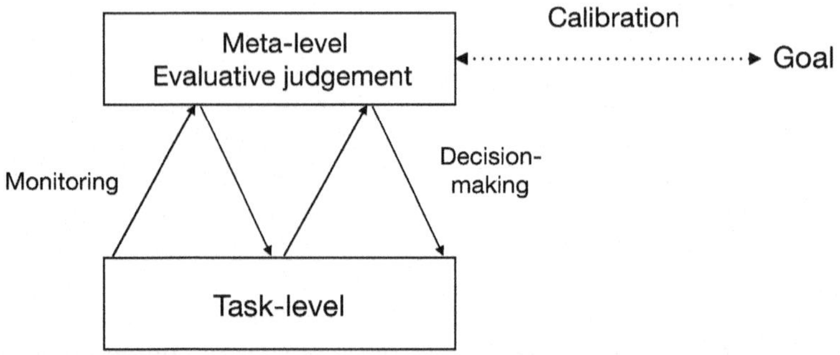

Figure 7.1 Framework for evaluative judgements of learning progress (building on Nelson and Narens 1990)

The framework articulates the mechanisms by which students make judgements about how they are progressing as they learn. Other psychological factors, such as self-efficacy, motivation and beliefs, also inevitably impact on the judgements students make about their progress while learning and undertaking assessment tasks (Nicol and Macfarlane-Dick 2006). However, we have focused here on monitoring and decision-making as the most critical processes informing and progressing judgement and calibration in real time. Over several decades, psychological scientists in particular have been examining the evaluative judgements that students make about their progress while learning (Soderstrom et al. 2016). For example, Kruger and Dunning (1999) found that unskilled learners are often unaware of being unskilled and are thus overconfident about their progress. As a result of inherent cognitive biases, it appears that humans are generally poor at evaluating their learning as it occurs, though this varies significantly between individuals (Maki et al. 2005). The key finding here is that students make evaluations about their learning progress on the basis of heuristics informing both the monitoring and decision-making processes. These heuristics do not always lend themselves to accurate evaluative judgements and vary between students, leading to a cycle where students perpetually make poor decisions about their progress based on these flawed judgements. Before discussing how it may be possible to assess and enhance these evaluations in digital environments, we will first survey some of the main findings in this area.

Understanding judgements of learning

Psychological research examining how people make judgements about progress in learning tasks has a long history (Rhodes 2016). The results of this research broadly indicate that, while human perceptions of memory and learning can at times be highly accurate in relation to actual performance, often these judgements are grossly misaligned (Soderstrom et al. 2016). As is evident in the classroom setting, these misalignments are problematic, particularly when the misalignment leads to an "illusion of competence" (Koriat and Bjork 2005). These illusions predominantly occur due to a subjective sense of fluency or an impression that remembering, comprehending and applying knowledge is easier than is really the case (Bjork et al. 2013). Another way of looking at this observation is that short-term learning experiences that feel fluent sometimes give a misleading impression of long-term learning progress (Soderstrom et al. 2016). Fallacies such as the illusion of competence, although mostly observed in the laboratory, do have implications for student evaluative judgements – particularly as their learning is increasingly mediated by digital technologies.

Illusions of competence are particularly evident in students who perform poorly. This observation has come to be called the "unskilled but unaware" or "Dunning–Kruger" effect (Kruger and Dunning 1999). What this effect suggests is that the students who are most in need of help to rectify the mismatch between their evaluative judgements of their progress and their actual progress are least likely to recognise that they need help. Illusions of competence are potentially compounded because of the easy access to information provided by the Internet and the fluency effects associated with multimedia and digital platforms for knowledge acquisition. Multimedia environments do seem to impact on the quality of learning, labelled "screen inferiority" (Ackerman and Goldsmith 2011). For example, highly produced multimedia resources tend to be processed fluently, leading to an illusion of competence. Carpenter et al. (2013) found that students who watched a fluent version of an instructional video thought that they had learnt more than students watching a less fluent version, despite performing no better on a test of their understanding. Students can be given an impression of understanding and progress in digital environments without having deeply encoded the material. While learning in these environments, students are therefore at risk of overestimating their level of understanding. The material feels like it is being adequately learnt and leads to overconfidence (Finn and Tauber 2015). Inadequate encoding of the material will in turn lead to substandard decision-making when applying the knowledge, and thus have a negative impact on performance.

Both the Dunning–Kruger effect and work examining the illusion of competence highlight the importance of considering learning as process rather than focusing on outcomes or artefacts (Soderstrom and Bjork 2015). This focus on process also aligns with the notion of assessment for learning (Boud 2000), in that students are better able to monitor and make better decisions about their learning and subsequent performance as it occurs. Learning is after all an ongoing process and, as Thompson (2016) contends, technologies have an increasing role to play in this process, particularly in relation to student self-assessment. So, while laboratory-based research is helping to shed light on the processes underpinning judgements about progress, these judgements are increasingly being mediated and moderated in educational environments by technologies. As more learning in higher education is occurring in digital environments, there are simultaneously opportunities to monitor and intervene on learning and performance as processes, not just as outcomes.

Assessing judgements of learning for calibration in digital environments

While technology may play a role in increasing illusions of competence, new technologies are also creating opportunities for enhancing evaluative judgements. In some cases, these opportunities are being created by a closer relationship between the science of learning and the use of educational technologies. For example, Shute (2011) highlighted the potential for technologies to assess student learning progress in real time as they go about the process of learning (see also Timms and Lodge 2015). Adaptive technologies that afford this kind of assessment continue to impact on higher education (Adams et al. 2016).

There are several advantages to using these adaptive learning environments. First, students can be given real-time feedback on their progress as they work towards a specified outcome. Referring back to the model presented in Figure 7.1, this means interventions that can more directly target students' monitoring, judgements and decision-making processes, on top of helping them to calibrate against a goal or artefact. Second, teachers can similarly receive real-time feedback on student progress, allowing them to intervene in a more nuanced, targeted way. This more nuanced intervention could also be tailored to assist students to make better evaluative judgements of their work. For example, adaptive technologies allow for differentiation between students on the decisions they make when they learn, the strategies they are using and what these indicate about their progress. In this example, pathways that students take through a flexible environment shed light on the decisions they make as they progress, which in turn provides an indication of the judgements that students are making about their progress. A student accurately judging that they do not have sufficient knowledge might decide to review material, while an overconfident student may plough ahead despite not having sufficient understanding. This could then form the basis of an assessment of the student's progress, as described by Shute (2011).

The assessment of differences in student progress in a digital learning environment is difficult but possible to determine. One example is that there are differences in how experts and novices approach problem-solving; for instance, experts notice deeper structures in problems and draw on tacit knowledge to solve them (Hmelo-Silver and Pfeffer 2004). These differences become apparent in discovery-based or more flexible learning environments. Laboratory-based studies using these environments provide clues as to the process by which emerging expertise can be developed, and how to track this development. For example, haphazard or non-systematic patterns of interaction in discovery-based environments can be a marker for substandard progress in learning (e.g., Dalgarno et al. 2014). This, in turn, may indicate poor judgement (particularly overconfidence) of students' own progress (Lodge and Kennedy 2015). Novices potentially do not have the required knowledge to effectively navigate discovery-based environments, which may be why these environments have been found to be ineffective (e.g., Mayer 2004). The distinct patterns of problem-solving strategies provide behavioural markers that can give an indication of the student's progress from novice to expert. These markers can then be used to provide students with instruction based on the progress they are making. This includes the provision of interventions, to enhance their capacity to judge their own progress.

While there is potential to develop evaluative judgement through assessing student progress as they learn, there are some unresolved issues to address before this becomes viable. In particular, discovery-based environments provide clues as to whether students are effectively deploying strategies that will most likely lead to them producing quality outcomes. The selection of strategy, in turn, provides an indicator of the judgements students are making about their progress. Determining exactly what these markers are is still a matter of debate (VanLehn 2015). Despite these challenges, the importance of helping students make better evaluative judgements about the processes by which they learn and work towards outcomes is growing. The challenges to be faced by graduates in the twenty-first century are complex systemic, social, economic, environmental and geopolitical problems which may not have clearly defined solutions. The overall goal or final product in these situations is not always apparent. While potentially difficult, assessing students on their processes – and assessing the capacity for students to monitor these processes themselves and make good decisions about their progress – is therefore also of increasing importance.

Enhancing judgements and decision-making through feedback

To conclude this chapter, we will focus on a more concrete example of how digital environments can be employed to assist students in making better judgements about their progress in real time. Given the dynamic and individualised nature of student learning, it is difficult for teachers to intervene in real time as students work towards a goal. This is partly why snapshots (in the form of artefacts) have traditionally been used as the primary evidence of student learning progress. One of the most obvious possibilities for the use of digital learning environments is to assist with this problem by providing hints or feedback in real time; that is, as students learn.

Another possibility is to determine what sort of feedback best assists students to develop their evaluative judgement, and how best to provide this. For example, with the possibility of monitoring and assessing student progress in real time, there is also potential for providing targeted, nuanced feedback that will best support metacognitive processes (Azevedo et al. 2013). One area in which this targeted feedback may have a particularly strong effect is in the development and application of conceptual knowledge. Prior knowledge, confidence and the strategy used to work through concepts have all been found to influence whether a student achieves meaningful conceptual change (Kennedy and Lodge 2016). While a teacher may be able to provide targeted feedback to students in a tutorial setting, this is increasingly difficult in mass education systems.

Work in the science of learning suggests that there are alternative forms of feedback which are more effective at helping students to overcome misconceptions (Van Loon et al. 2015). Just as Sadler (2010) has pointed out, there are shortfalls associated with feedback that consists of students simply being told what they did wrong. Evidence that students are using particular strategies or approaches to enhance their conceptual understanding also provides some benefit here. When feedback which targets the processes students engage in during learning can be provided, there is potential for this feedback to prompt students into making better evaluative judgements about how they are progressing. In other words, by picking up on the ways in which students use interactive learning environments, and drawing on algorithmic models to predict student progress and provide feedback, it will be possible to help them answer the questions "do I have sufficient knowledge, skill and ability to do this?" and "am I using an appropriate strategy to get it done?"

The science of learning is providing an enhanced understanding of the processes underpinning how students make evaluative judgements in real time as they learn. Advances in adaptive technologies can help inform interventions that may also be delivered in real time. While the focus in this example is the development of conceptual knowledge, interventions could target monitoring, calibration or decision-making, and therefore enhance the processes underpinning evaluative judgement in real time as students learn. As the problems that graduates will deal with become more complex, without straightforward answers, it will be increasingly important for students to develop the knowledge and skills to monitor their own progress as they work towards answering these problems. As discussed in this chapter, digital environments provide a means of monitoring markers suggestive of the ways in which students make evaluative judgements in real time. These can then be used to intervene and help students improve these judgements over time, by focusing on how students monitor their progress and make decisions about what to do next.

References

Ackerman, R., and M. Goldsmith. 2011. "Metacognitive regulation of text learning: on screen versus on paper." *Journal of Experimental Psychology: Applied* 17 (1): 18–32.

Adams Becker, S., M. Cummins, A. Davis and B. Yuhnke. 2016. *2016 NMC Technology Outlook for Australian Tertiary Education: A Horizon Project Regional Report.* Austin, TX: The New Media Consortium.

Azevedo, R., J. Harley, G. Trevors, M. Duffy, R. Feyzi-Behnagh, F. Bouchet, and R. Landis. 2013. "Using trace data to examine the complex roles of cognitive, metacognitive, and emotional self-regulatory processes during learning with multi-agent systems." In *International Handbook on Metacognition and Learning Technologies,* edited by R. Azevedo and V. Aleven, 427–449. New York: Springer.

Bjork, R. A., J. Dunlosky, and N. Kornell. 2013. "Self-regulated learning: beliefs, techniques, and illusions." *Annual Review of Psychology* 64 (1): 417–444. doi:10.1146/annurev-psych-113011–143823.

Boud, D. 2000. "Sustainable assessment: rethinking assessment for the learning society." *Studies in Continuing Education* 22 (2): 151–167. doi:10.1080/713695728.

Boud, D., and R. Soler. 2016. "Sustainable assessment revisited." *Assessment & Evaluation in Higher Education* 41 (3): 400–413. doi:10.1080/02602938.2015.1018133.

Carpenter, S. K., M. M. Wilford, N. Kornell, and K. M. Mullaney. 2013. "Appearances can be deceiving: instructor fluency increases perceptions of learning without increasing actual learning." *Psychonomic Bulletin & Review* 20: 1350–1356. doi:10.3758/s13423–013–0442-z.

Cassidy, S. 2007. "Assessing "inexperienced" students' ability to self-assess: exploring links with learning style and academic personal control." *Assessment & Evaluation in Higher Education* 32 (3): 313–330. doi:10.1080/02602930600896704.

Cowan, J. 2010. "Developing the ability for making evaluative judgements." *Teaching in Higher Education* 15 (3): 323–334. doi:10.1080/13562510903560036.

Dalgarno, B., G. Kennedy, and S. Bennett. 2014. "The impact of students' exploration strategies on discovery learning using computer-based simulations." *Educational Media International* 51 (4): 310–329. doi:10.1080/09523987.2014.977009.

Finn, B., and S. K. Tauber. 2015. "When confidence is not a signal of knowing: how students' experiences and beliefs about processing fluency can lead to miscalibrated confidence." *Educational Psychology Review* 27 (4): 567–586.

Hattie, J. 2013. "Calibration and confidence: where to next?" *Learning and Instruction* 24 (C): 62–66. doi:10.1016/j.learninstruc.2012.05.009.

Hattie, J., and G. M. Donoghue. 2016. "Learning strategies: a synthesis and conceptual model." *npj Science of Learning*. doi:10.1038/npjscilearn.2016.13.

Hmelo-Silver, C. E., and M. G. Pfeffer. 2004. "Comparing expert and novice understanding of a complex system from the perspective of structures, behaviors, and functions." *Cognitive Science* 28 (1): 127–138.

Kennedy, G., and J. M. Lodge. 2016. "All roads lead to Rome: tracking students' affect as they overcome misconceptions." In *Show Me the Learning. Proceedings ASCILITE 2016 Adelaide*, edited by S. Barker, S. Dawson, A. Pardo, and C. Colvin, 318–328. Adelaide: University of South Australia.

Koriat, A., and R. A. Bjork. 2005. "Illusions of competence in monitoring one's knowledge during study." *Journal of Experimental Psychology: Learning, Memory, and Cognition* 31 (2): 187–194. doi:10.1037/0278–7393.31.2.187.

Kruger, J., and D. Dunning. 1999. "Unskilled and unaware of it: how difficulties in recognizing one's own incompetence lead to inflated self-assessments." *Journal of Personality and Social Psychology* 77 (6): 1121–1134.

Kuncel, N. R., M. Crede, and L. L. Thomas. 2005. "The validity of self-reported grade point averages, class ranks, and test scores: a meta-analysis and review of the literature." *Review of Educational Research* 75 (1): 63–82. doi:10.3102/00346543075001063.

Lodge, J. M., and G. E. Kennedy. 2015. "Prior knowledge, confidence and understanding in interactive tutorials and simulations." In *Globally Connected, Digitally Enabled. Proceedings ASCILITE 2015 Perth*, edited by T. Reiners, B. R. von Konsky, D. Gibson, V. Chang, L. Irving, and K. Clarke, 178–188. Perth, Australia: Curtin University.

McCabe, J. 2011. "Metacognitive awareness of learning strategies in undergraduates." *Memory & Cognition* 39 (3): 462–476.

Maki, R. H., M. Shields, A. E. Wheeler, and T. L. Zacchilli. 2005. "Individual differences in absolute and relative metacomprehension accuracy." *Journal of Educational Psychology* 97 (4): 723.

Mayer, R. E. 2004. "Should there be a three-strikes rule against pure discovery learning? The case for guided methods of instruction." *The American Psychologist* 59 (1): 14–19. doi:10.1037/0003–066X.59.1.14.

Nelson, T. O., and L. Narens. 1990. "Metamemory: a theoretical framework and new findings." *The Psychology of Learning and Motivation, Advances in Research and Theory* 26: 125–173.

Nicol, D. J., and D. Macfarlane-Dick. 2006. "Formative assessment and self-regulated learning: a model and seven principles of good feedback practice." *Studies in Higher Education* 31 (2): 199–218.

Rhodes, M. G. 2016. "Judgments of learning." In *The Oxford Handbook of Metamemory*, edited by John Dunlosky and Sarah Tauber, Chapter 4. New York: Oxford University Press.

Sadler, D. R. 2009. "Transforming holistic assessment and grading into a vehicle for complex learning." In *Assessment, Learning and Judgement in Higher Education*, edited by G. Joughin, 45–64. Dordrecht, The Netherlands: Springer.

Sadler, D. R. 2010. "Beyond feedback: developing student capability in complex appraisal." *Assessment & Evaluation in Higher Education* 35 (5): 535–550. doi:10.1080/02602930903541015.

Sadler, R. 1989. "Formative assessment and the design of instructional systems." *Instructional Science* 18: 119–144. doi:10.1007/BF00117714.

Shute, V. J. 2011. "Stealth assessment in computer-based games to support learning." *Computer Games and Instruction* 55 (2): 503–524.

Soderstrom, N. C., and R. A. Bjork. 2015. "Learning versus performance: an integrative review." *Perspectives on Psychological Science* 10 (2): 176–199. doi:10.1177/1745691615569000.

Soderstrom, N. C., C. L. Yue, and E. L Bjork. 2016. "Metamemory and education." In *The Oxford Handbook of Metamemory*, edited by J. Dunlosky and S. Tauber, Chapter 11. New York, NY: Oxford University Press.

Thompson, D. G. 2016. "Marks should not be the focus of assessment: but how can change be achieved?" *Journal of Learning Analytics* 3 (2): 193–212. doi:10.18608/jla.2016.32.9.

Timms, M., and J. M. Lodge. 2015. "Assessment in interactive learning environments." In *Australian Council for Education Research Conference 2015*, edited by R. Leech, 45–53. Melbourne, Australia: ACER.

Uttl, B., C. A. White, and D. Wong Gonzalez. 2017. "Meta-analysis of faculty's teaching effectiveness: student evaluation of teaching ratings and student learning are not related." *Studies in Educational Evaluation* 54: 22–42. doi:10.1016/j.stueduc.2016.08.007.

VanLehn, K. 2015. "Regulative loops, step loops and task loops." *International Journal of Artificial Intelligence in Education* 26 (1): 107–112. doi:10.1007/s40593–015–0056-x.

Van Loon, M. H., J. Dunlosky, T. van Gog, J. J. van Merriënboer, and A. B. de Bruin. 2015. "Refutations in science texts lead to hypercorrection of misconceptions held with high confidence." *Contemporary Educational Psychology* 42: 39–48.

SECTION 3

Approaches to developing evaluative judgement

CHAPTER **8**

Developing evaluative judgement: a self-regulated learning perspective

Ernesto Panadero and Jaclyn Broadbent

Self-regulated learning (SRL) is defined as "self-generated thoughts, feelings, and actions that are planned and cyclically adapted to the attainment of personal goals" (Zimmerman 2000, 14). The attainment of SRL is nowadays considered a crucial educational goal because of its key impact on students' learning (Panadero 2017). The use of SRL strategies has been found to predict academic achievement in both face-to-face (Richardson et al. 2012) and online learning environments (Broadbent 2017; Broadbent and Poon 2015). SRL provides a framework to explain how students learn and what we, as teachers, can do to intervene in and promote student learning (Panadero 2017).

Evaluative judgement is the ability to assess a piece of work (one's own or that of others) while attending to the context, quality, standards and criteria built upon previous experience. That is, to make an accurate and appropriate judgement the student needs to: (1) consider the context in which the performance is to be evaluated (e.g., consider the audience, the required genre, etc.); (2) have an understanding of what a quality performance looks like; and (3) consider the different standards and (4) assessment criteria. Thus, evaluative judgement does not develop in a vacuum but is based in previous experience as an assessor and/or assessee, as from these two roles students gain more knowledge about the four above-mentioned aspects. Why is it important to develop evaluative judgement? As claimed by others, including the opening chapter of this volume, to be able to assess one's own work and that of others is a crucial skill, not only in higher education but also for lifelong learning capacity and the ability to become a capable and successful professional (Boud and Falchikov 2007; Cowan 2010; Nicol 2014; Sadler 2010). Therefore, developing evaluative judgement should be a major educational aim and, as a result, an outcome. For example, students who graduate from higher education programmes should enter the workforce having acquired such ability, which can be further developed in their workplaces.

Why is it then interesting to frame evaluative judgement from an SRL perspective? There are three basic shared tenets between the two theories: students' autonomy, expertise and interrelation. First, regarding autonomy (understood here as the ability to take care of one's own learning), both SRL and evaluative judgement promote it, and in turn both capacities develop as a consequence of autonomy. That is, students who know how to self-regulate and to judge their own work can be autonomous, and because they act autonomously, they have more opportunities to enhance their SRL and evaluative judgement capacities. A second tenet for the connection between SRL and evaluative judgement is that both aim at developing students' expertise within a given task or discipline. In other words, both require training through practice to develop expertise; however, as expertise is developed in one, so too is expertise developed in the other. In fact, to be fully effective in either capacity requires both capacities to be actualised. And third, SRL and evaluative judgements are highly interrelated; that is, to develop one the other must be present. To be able to self-regulate appropriately the student needs to be able to self-assess, to ensure strategies are being applied appropriately (Panadero and Alonso-Tapia 2013; Paris and Paris 2001), and to self-assess successfully and accurately, evaluative judgement is key. Similarly, to be able to develop evaluative judgement capacity over time, the student needs to activate a significant number of self-regulatory learning strategies. Students with self-regulated profiles that have high motivational regulation and high adoption of SRL strategies have been shown to benefit more academically. Moreover, those students with higher self-regulatory skills are able to produce better internal feedback, which amplifies their evaluative judgement capacity (Butler and Winne 1995). Because of these three shared tenets, it is crucial to analyse how, from SRL theory and models, we can help students develop their evaluative judgement capacity.

In this chapter, we will characterise the SRL concepts that can help us develop evaluative judgement in our students. Based on the multi-level model of SRL (Zimmerman and Kitsantas 2005), we will explore how such a model can be applied to enhance our students' expertise in evaluative judgement. The structure of the chapter will be as follows. First, the SRL multi-level model will be presented theoretically. Each level of the model will be analysed, while presenting specific examples of how we can promote the development of evaluative judgements through pedagogical practices. Second, as peer- and self-assessment are the classroom activities with the most potential to enhance evaluative judgement capacity (Nicol 2014), these will be analysed as a way to enhance students' evaluative judgement.

The development of SRL: a look at the multi-level model and its application to evaluative judgement

The attainment of SRL is nowadays considered a crucial educational goal because of its key impact on students' learning (Panadero 2017). For that reason, teachers need to design their learning activities to promote SRL. Paris and Paris (2001) developed a list of 12 principles that teachers can use to develop their students' SRL capacity. While these principles were created for a school setting, they are just as relevant in higher education. Principle 3a deals with direct instruction about SRL, and emphasises that reflection about the regulatory processes themselves will result in major gains in SRL capacity. The claim from assessment scholars for evaluative judgement is concordant (Boud and Falchikov 2007; Nicol 2014): the capacity to generate evaluations about one's own work (or that of a peer) is crucial to learning. Additionally, the model by Dreyfus and Dreyfus (2005) on how to gain expertise in real-world tasks has been applied in an evaluative judgement capacity (Nicol 2014). Here, we will present how the SRL field has visualised the development of regulatory skills.

Barry Zimmerman, a key SRL scholar, has developed three different SRL models, each with different foci (Panadero 2017). Of interest to this chapter, his multi-level model written with Anastasia Kitsantas explains how, through practice, students can master self-regulation in a given task (Zimmerman and Kitsantas 2005). There are two important aspects to point out before presenting the model. First, Zimmerman's work has been developed from his early collaboration with Albert Bandura (Zimmerman 2013). Therefore, socio-cognitive theory and vicarious learning are key elements in his multi-level model. Second, even though the model has several levels, this does not imply that students have to go through all of them to achieve self-regulation of the task; the levels are usually sequential but exceptions can occur. The main aim here is to adapt and apply the perspective of Zimmerman's SRL model to evaluative judgement, in order to explore a similar developmental approach to evaluative judgement. Next, we will present the four levels (observation, emulation, self-control, and self-regulated) with classroom examples to help visualise how they might apply to the development of evaluative judgement.

Zimmerman's multi-level model of SRL – Level 1 observation: in this level the student observes a model performing the activity. This observation is more beneficial if it is active; in other words, if the student pays attention to the model and tries to extract patterns and conclusions, or even attempts to visualise how s/he would perform it based on what s/he just observed.

How does it enhance evaluative judgement in the classroom?

In this level students are learning to make judgements about their understanding of the task requirements. Teachers can help students develop this capacity through classroom activities that explain the task and/or criteria used for evaluation, or by presenting exemplars to them. Exemplars help students to increase the knowledge, understandings and skills required to meet the demands of a task, and give students a clear indication of what is expected. This can be further enhanced if explicit links are given between the assessment task and the achievement standards that are being assessed. For example, the teacher might spend time unpacking the application of standards and criteria (e.g., a rubric) to the assessment, as well as their own notion of quality (e.g., "that is a good one, see how X, Y and Z stand out" or "this section needs work because of W"), with the student (see Broadbent, Panadero and Boud, 2018, for an example). This could be done in person, through classroom activities, or in written, audio- or video-recorded format.

Zimmerman's multi-level model of SRL – Level 2 emulation: in this level, the student will try to perform the task, keeping in mind the example seen in the observation. As presented by Zimmerman and Kitsantas, the learners do not completely imitate the model or the model's work, but typically it is the general pattern that is followed. In other words, the learner tries to perform similarly but it is (a) usually not possible because of the lack of expertise, and (b) it would not be beneficial because the learner needs to adapt his or her behaviour to his or her capacities.

How does it enhance evaluative judgement in the classroom?

Emulation occurs in order for students to determine what the standards are, what they look like in another's work, and how to meet those standards in their own work. Continuing with the previous example, students may do this by attempting to emulate the exemplar. They can use the exemplar to define a valid standard against which they can compare the development of their own work. Comparisons between their own work and that of the exemplar help students to calibrate their understanding of how their own work meets those same standards. Guidance and feedback are essential during these emulative experiences, and can lead to higher levels of understanding of what is required (Kitsantas et al. 2000). As the emulative level of SRL is often social in nature, involving students in assessment exercises where they peer assess other students' work in relation to defined criteria can enhance their judgements of quality. As will be discussed in the third section, peer assessment is the activity with most potential to enhance evaluative judgement capacity (Nicol 2014), and can be used in both formative and summative assessment and both in and out of class. During the emulative phase, students' ability to successfully and accurately peer and self-assess with a novel task are still at a technical and rudimentary stage with little flexibility in applying the standards.

Zimmerman's multi-level model of SRL – Level 3 self-control: here the learners practise in the absence of the model. Practice must be structured and reflexive to produce better results; if students just repeat an action without further cognitive processing, the chances to fully internalise patterns and extract practical conclusions decrease. A crucial process at this level is the achievement of automaticity. This is the ability to perform the task, reducing the cognitive load by the automatic activation of response patterns (Bargh 1994; Bargh and Williams 2007). By achieving mastery of this process, the learners decrease their cognitive load, freeing up cognitive resources which can then be used for other actions (Kirschner 2002).

How does it enhance evaluative judgement in the classroom?

As students further develop their self-regulation capacity, they enter the self-control level where they are able, to a higher extent, to compare their efforts against the standards. That is, they can begin to make sound evaluative judgements about the quality of their work through internally generated feedback. For example, at this level students are more automatically able to make evaluative judgements about their work against that of the exemplar because of repeated reflexive practice, and have moved to refine their understanding of the standards independent of the exemplar given to them. To foster independence, teachers could build self-assessment into their assessment practices, by asking students to assess their own work against the marking criteria before submission for grading. As described in the next section, being able to self-assess is instrumental to both SRL and the development of evaluative judgement. While self-assessment may also occur earlier in the emulation phase, this skill is refined further and becomes more sophisticated at the self-control level, as is the students' ability to assess peers' work against the standards. As students' ability to peer assess becomes more advanced, so does their ability to transfer and apply this learning to their own self-assessment of their work.

Zimmerman's multi-level model of SRL – Level 4 self-regulated: at this level the learners can, and should, practise in new and changing conditions to further develop the skill. Based on their repeated practice, at this point they are able to adjust the performance to achieve the desired results in more challenging and wide-ranging situations. At the self-regulated level, students: (1) reflect on prior similar performances and, based on this reflection, plan their future performance; and then (2) take the useful strategies from prior performance and (3) apply them to novel and/or more challenging situations. Here, they are able to identify the key contextual and personal factors that will influence the result, and they are able to adjust while performing the task to achieve their goals. In other words, they are able to act strategically at this point.

How does it enhance evaluative judgement in the classroom?

The ability to self-regulate in this way improves the student's evaluative judgement because of the enhanced capacity to judge what quality looks like against a set of standards. Metacognitive skills and associated monitoring allow students to repeatedly check and determine whether they are meeting those standards. The iterative nature of this process means that students are better able to understand and judge the gap between standards and performance and modify performance accordingly. To take advantage of these processes, teachers could employ iterative scaffolded assessment that allows students to reflect on performance and adjust their understanding of the standard required for the following assessment. In the same way, formative assessment allows students to reframe their appraisal quality in low-stakes tasks. Teachers can also draw clear links between the application of judgement to a different but similar situation/assessment. For example, this might be achieved by using a standardised rubric across a program of study for similar tasks (e.g., a psychology lab report).

Activities with most potential to enhance both SRL and evaluative judgement capacity: self- and peer-assessment

In this section, we will specifically focus on self- and peer-assessment as tools for enhancing students' evaluative judgement in the classroom. As has been shown in the section on "The development of SRL: a look at the multi-level model and its application to evaluative judgement", students have varying levels of ability to (1) self-regulate and (2) judge the quality of a piece of work. To enhance both their evaluative judgement capacity and ability to self-regulate, they need to be given plenty of opportunities to practise their assessment skills. Two crucial processes, through which both aims are achieved for students, are providing opportunities for self-assessment and peer assessment (Nicol 2014; Nicol and Macfarlane-Dick 2006; Panadero et al. 2016a).

Self-assessment involves "a wide variety of mechanisms and techniques through which students describe (i.e., assess) and possibly assign merit or worth to (i.e., evaluate) the qualities of their own learning processes and products" (Panadero et al. 2016b, 804). The connection between self-assessment and self-regulated learning has been largely supported theoretically (Nicol and Macfarlane-Dick 2006; Paris and Paris 2001) and also empirically (Brown and Harris 2013). By implementing self-assessment activities in the classroom, teachers promote students' self-generation of feedback, which is crucial for students' development (Andrade 2010). Most importantly for this chapter aim, self-assessment practice benefits the enlargement and consolidation of more advanced evaluative judgement. Through practice, students can apply their own understanding of evaluative judgement for a particular task, and test, with feedback from the teachers to reach full potential, whether they need to correct or have successfully self-assessed.

Peer assessment was claimed by Nicol (2014) as the activity with most potential to enhance evaluative judgement capacity, as it allows self-regulation and co-regulation to happen (Panadero et al. 2016a). By assessing a peer's work, the students (1) have access to another performance example that they can contrast with their own, and (2) have to apply their evaluative judgement in order to provide explicit feedback to that peer. This is especially true if the peer assessment is implemented with formative purposes, which has been shown to produce better interpersonal, motivational and emotional effects (Panadero 2016). Nonetheless, Nicol (2014) agrees with others (e.g., Dochy et al. 1999) that the biggest impact of peer assessment is on the assessor's capacity to self-assess. That is, the knowledge gained from peer assessment is, in turn, applied to enhance both one's own work and the ability to assess that work for quality. As argued by Andrade (2010), this ability is the definitive source of feedback.

In summary, by implementing self- and peer-assessment activities we are providing students with opportunities for practice. When self- and peer-assessment are implemented, students stop being just recipients of assessment and feedback; they become active agents in the process of creating and delivering both, and therefore their potential for learning increases. Additionally, and more importantly, by practising self- and peer-assessment students have the opportunity to reflect, practise and amplify their evaluative judgement capacity. As formulated in the previous section, the more students practise and develop this skill, the higher the chances are that they will become self-regulators of their own evaluative judgements.

As can be seen in the recommendations about peer- and self-assessment given by Panadero et al. (2016a), the activities of self- and peer-assessment need to be central parts of instruction and learning. For example, the teacher needs to provide feedback about the self- and peer-assessments themselves, rather than focusing just on the task characteristics. Such recommendations are important because they emphasise the potential for students to learn how to self- and peer-assess, which will unquestionably have an impact in the development of their evaluative judgement capacity.

Conclusions

As proposed here, by applying an SRL perspective to evaluative judgement we are promoting a developmental approach to the latter that will help clarify how students can acquire it. By looking more closely at each of the four SRL levels and providing examples, our intention was to help visualise how evaluative judgement can develop in a similar fashion to SRL. The key implications of this approach are that students need to practise to master a new skill, and that this practice should be deliberative and benefits from observing models and receiving feedback as it progresses. This approach, while not always applied (e.g., Panadero et al. 2016b), should be a major educational goal and a salient feature of all instructional designs. As the developmental approach has been proposed with success in SRL (Panadero 2017; Paris and Paris 2001), it is our belief that the evaluative judgement field would benefit from adopting a similar approach.

Acknowledgement

First author funded by the Spanish Ministry (Ministerio de Economía y Competitividad) via Ramón y Cajal programme (File id. RYC-2013–13469).

References

Andrade, H. 2010. "Students as the definitive source of formative assessment: academic self-assessment and the self-regulation of learning." In *Handbook of Formative Assessment*, edited by H. L. Andrade and G. J. Cizek, 90–105. New York: Routledge.

Bargh, J. A. 1994. "The four horsemen of automaticity: awareness, intention, efficiency and control in social cognition." In *The Handbook Of Social Cognition: Vol. 2. Basic Processes*, edited by R. S. Wyer and T. K. Srull, 1–40. Hillsdale, NJ: Erlbaum.

Bargh, J. A., and L. E. Williams. 2007. "The nonconscious regulation of emotion." In *Handbook of Emotion Regulation*, edited by J. J. Gross, 429–445. New York: Guilford Press.

Boud, D., and N. Falchikov. 2007. "Developing assessment for informing judgement." In *Rethinking Assessment for Higher Education: Learning for The Longer Term*, edited by D. Boud and N. Falchikov, 181–197. London: Routledge.

Broadbent, J. 2017. "Comparing online and blended learner's self-regulated learning strategies and academic performance." *Internet and Higher Education* 33: 24–32.

Broadbent, J., E. Panadero, and D. Boud. 2018. "Implementing summative assessment with a formative flavour: a case study in a large class." *Assessment & Evaluation in Higher Education* 43 (2): 307–322. doi:10.1080/02602938.2017.1343455

Broadbent, J., and W. L. Poon. 2015. "Self-regulated learning strategies and academic achievement in online higher education learning environments: a systematic review." *The Internet and Higher Education* 27: 1–13. doi:10.1016/j.iheduc.2015.04.007.

Brown, G. T. L., and L. R. Harris. 2013. "Student self-assessment." In *The SAGE Handbook of Research on Classroom Assessment*, edited by J. McMillan, 367–393. Thousand Oaks, CA: SAGE.

Butler, D. L., and P. H. Winne. 1995. "Feedback and self-regulated learning: a theoretical synthesis." *Review of Educational Research* 65 (3): 245–281. doi:10.3102/00346543065003245.

Cowan, J. 2010. "Developing the ability for making evaluative judgements." *Teaching in Higher Education*, 15 (3): 323–334. doi:10.1080/13562510903560036.

Dochy, F., M. Segers, and D. Sluijsmans. 1999. "The use of self-, peer- and co-assessment in higher education: a review." *Studies in Higher Education* 24 (3): 331–350. doi:10.1080/03075079912331379935.

Dreyfus, H. L., and S. E. Dreyfus. 2005. "Expertise in real world contexts." *Organization Studies* 26 (5): 779–792.

Kirschner, P. A. 2002. "Cognitive load theory: implications of cognitive load theory on the design of learning." *Learning and Instruction* 12 (1): 1–10. doi:10.1016/S0959-4752(01)00014-7.

Kitsantas, A., B. J. Zimmerman, and T. Cleary. 2000. "The role of observation and emulation in the development of athletic self-regulation." *Journal of Educational Psychology* 92 (4): 811–817.

Nicol, D. 2014. "Guiding principles for peer review: unlocking learners' evaluative skills." In *Advances and Innovations in University Assessment and Feedback*, edited by C. Kreber, C. Anderson, N. Entwistel, and J. McArthur, 197–224. Edinburgh, Scotland: Edinburgh University Press.

Nicol, D., and D. Macfarlane-Dick. 2006. "Formative assessment and self-regulated learning: a model and seven principles of good feedback practice." *Studies in Higher Education* 31 (2): 199–218. doi:10.1080/03075070600572090.

Panadero, E. 2016. "Is it safe? Social, interpersonal, and human effects of peer assessment: a review and future directions." In *Handbook of Human and Social Conditions in Assessment*, edited by G. T. L. Brown and L. R. Harris, 247–266. New York: Routledge.

Panadero, E. 2017. "A review of self-regulated learning: six models and four directions for research." *Frontiers in Psychology* 8: 422. doi:10.3389/fpsyg.2017.00422

Panadero, E., and J. Alonso-Tapia. 2013. "Self-assessment: theoretical and practical connotations. When it happens, how is it acquired and what to do to develop it in our students." *Electronic Journal of Research in Educational Psychology* 11 (2): 551–576. doi:10.14204/ejrep.30.12200.

Panadero, E., G. T. L. Brown, and J. W. Strijbos. 2016b. "The future of student self-assessment: a review of known unknowns and potential directions." *Educational Psychology Review* 28 (4): 803–830. doi:10.1007/s10648-015-9350-2.

Panadero, E., A. Jonsson, and J. W. Strijbos. 2016a. "Scaffolding self-regulated learning through self-assessment and peer assessment: guidelines for classroom implementation." In *Assessment for Learning: Meeting the Challenge of Implementation*, edited by Dany Laveault and Linda Allal, 267–281. Switzerland: Springer.

Paris, S. G., and A. H. Paris. 2001. "Classroom applications of research on self-regulated learning." *Educational Psychologist* 36 (2): 89–101. doi:10.1207/S15326985EP3602_4.

Richardson, M., C. Abraham and R. Bond. 2012. "Psychological correlates of university students' academic performance: a systematic review and meta-analysis." *Psychological Bulletin* 138 (2): 353–387. doi:10.1037/a0026838.

Sadler, D. R. 2010. "Beyond feedback: developing student capability in complex appraisal." *Assessment & Evaluation in Higher Education* 34 (5): 535–550.

Zimmerman, B. J. 2013. "From cognitive modeling to self-regulation: a social cognitive career path." *Educational Psychologist* 48 (3): 135–147. doi:10.1080/00461520.2013.794676.

Zimmerman, B. J. 2000. "Attaining self-regulation – a social cognitive perspective." In *Handbook of Self-Regulation*, edited by M. Zeidner, P. R. Pintrich and M. Boekaerts, 14–39. San Diego, CA: Academic Press.

Zimmerman, B. J., and A. Kitsantas. 2005. "The hidden dimension of personal competence: self-regulated learning and practice." In *Handbook of Competence and Motivation*, edited by A. J. Elliot and C. S. Dweck, 509–526. New York: Guilford Press.

CHAPTER **9**

Understanding self-regulated learning in open-ended online assignment tasks

Sue Bennett, Lori Lockyer, Gregor Kennedy and Barney Dalgarno

Contemporary university courses increasingly require students to navigate more open-ended, student-centred tasks, many of which are supported by digital technologies that supplement or replace face-to-face classes. To be successful, students must be able to interpret open-ended task requirements and independently regulate their own learning, either partly or solely online. At the same time, higher education teachers are expected to design high-quality tasks and provide effective support face-to-face and online. Although the situation is increasingly familiar to those who research and teach in higher education, there is much we do not fully understand about how to achieve the best outcomes for students in this context.

In this chapter we consider the role of self-regulated learning in open-ended online assignment tasks. We begin by describing a four-stage model of self-regulated learning which we then use to conceptualise how students approach these tasks, including the role of evaluative judgement. We then draw on findings from our study of university students which has investigated how students interpret tasks, monitor their progress, and adapt their approaches. Our findings draw particular attention to how students interpret cues from their peers' online contributions, and from the task descriptions provided by their teachers.

Self-regulated learning

Of the various conceptualisations of self-regulated learning, the one we adopt in this chapter includes four stages: (a) developing an understanding of a task,[1] (b) setting goals and planning, (c) applying study tactics and strategies, and (d) adapting study for the future (Winne and Hadwin 1998). Throughout each of the stages, metacognitive monitoring allows a student to determine whether he or she is meeting the requirements of the task and to decide whether to exercise metacognitive control to change conditions, if possible, or approach. Self-regulated learning has three important characteristics. First, the stages of this model are *recursive* in that the products of one stage feed into the same or any other stage. Second, the stages are *weakly sequenced*; therefore in practice they do not proceed as a linear sequence but are more loosely coupled, such that any given task may involve multiple iterations and include skipping over or revisiting a stage. Third, self-regulated learning is *contextual*, meaning that the extent to which an individual is self-regulated in his or her learning depends upon multiple individual and situational factors. These factors include, but are not limited to, individual motivation and domain knowledge and opportunities within the learning environment.

Thus, self-regulated learning is both an aptitude and an event. It is an aptitude in the sense that it is "a relatively enduring attribute of a person that predicts future behaviour" and an event in that it is "a transient state embedded in a larger, longer series of states unfolding over time" (Winne and Perry 2000, 534). This conceptualisation allows that individuals may be disposed to successfully self-regulating their learning but may not always do so, because of – for example – a lack of domain knowledge or motivation, or unfavourable conditions. Previous study experiences can be drawn on when applying and adapting self-regulated learning strategies and tactics in different contexts, helping individuals to develop a repertoire they can potentially use in future when faced with similar or new situations. Even an expert who is well equipped with self-regulated learning strategies and tactics within the domain of their expertise may find that the strategies and tactics they have used previously do not transfer to an unfamiliar task or domain. This conception is of self-regulated learning as developmental, in that we develop capacity for self-regulated learning in particular situations over time, often with the support of others (Hadwin and Oshige 2011). This means that self-regulated learning is not only important in the immediate context of the task at hand but is also a capacity which is developed over time through engagement in multiple, varying tasks.

Self-regulated learning during an assignment task

To understand self-regulated learning in the context of higher education we consider what students do when they work towards the completion of an assignment. Like all personal study activities, including routine weekly revision and preparation for an in-class assessment or exam, assignment preparation requires a response to a task set by the teacher – usually with limited intervention by a teacher, often as a solo activity (although it may involve collaboration or peer support), over multiple study sessions requiring that progress be self-monitored and adapted if necessary, and undertaken in a setting over which the student has a degree of control. Unlike other forms of personal study, however, assignments offer particular opportunities for students to be self-regulated. Let us consider those opportunities within the four-stage conceptualisation of self-regulated learning (Winne and Hadwin 1998) (see Box 9.1).

It is important to note again that the stages of self-regulated learning are not a stepwise sequence. Completing an assignment in personal study time is likely to involve iterations through various stages across multiple study sessions, as students' understandings of and approaches to the task evolve towards the final product: their submitted assignments.

Four-stage conceptualisation of self-regulated learning (Winne and Hadwin 1998)

In Stage 1, students develop an understanding of the task set by a teacher. Depending on the nature of the assignment, the task instructions may be very specific or they may be very open-ended. Open-ended assignment tasks require that students actively interpret the nature of the task they are being asked to address. Indeed, the rationale for many open-ended tasks is to encourage students to exercise choice and take responsibility for shaping what and how they learn. Such tasks are designed to be student-centred, with the aim of developing students as independent learners.

In Stage 2, students set goals and plan their approach to addressing the task. This is a process in which students form their own goals, which may align strongly or weakly to the goals set by the teacher for the task. The nature of goal-setting and planning may be highly variable, depending on the capacities of the students and their interpretations of what the task requires of them. For example, if students judge the task to be straightforward, they may spend limited time on goal-setting and planning. Likewise, goal-setting or planning may be limited when students themselves have limited capacity, because they lack the knowledge about how the task could or should be done.

In Stage 3, students apply self-regulated learning tactics and strategies that they believe are likely to help them to achieve their goals and plan. At this stage, students engage in study activities, such as summarising or concept mapping. These activities produce traces, such as notes and drafts, which reflect changes in understanding.

In Stage 4, students consider the outcomes of other stages and make adaptations for the future. In this stage, students engage in metacognition about the immediate task, which may result in adaptations in understanding of the task, goals and plans, and/or tactics and strategies to use. These adaptations are applied in future study sessions devoted to completing the assignment. Adaptations may also apply beyond the immediate task to influence future study.

Metacognitive monitoring and evaluative judgement

Self-regulated learning is guided by metacognition in that the products of each stage are evaluated against standards (Winne and Hadwin 1998). Metacognitive monitoring enables students to make judgements about how they are progressing in a task according to their understanding of what is required, their goals and plans, the success of their study tactics and strategies, and the appropriateness of any adaptations made. Evaluations are made on the basis of internally generated feedback, but may also involve feedback from external sources (Butler and Winne 1995). This aspect of self-regulated learning aligns most clearly with the notion of evaluative judgement (Ajjawi et al., Chapter 1; Panadero and Broadbent, Chapter 8).

Being able to make appropriate evaluative judgements about the quality of one's own work supports not only activities within that stage, but feeds into other stages of self-regulated learning. Considering each stage leads to the following observations:

- Students must evaluate their understanding of the task and the learning environment. Open-ended tasks particularly require students to make judgements about how they have interpreted the task requirements. It may be particularly important to revisit initial impressions as more information about a task is revealed, or when faced with alternative interpretations from a teacher or peer.
- Students need to make judgements about the appropriateness of their goals and plans. This includes making assessments of what they need to produce, based on standards and criteria set by a teacher which are reframed by the student. Goals, plans and standards may need to be adjusted and renegotiated.
- Students enact tactics and strategies to produce the work on which they will be judged. Associated monitoring by students seeks to determine whether the tactics and strategies in use are effective for the particular task.
- Students assess their progress towards their goals by judging the quality of their work. In deciding how to close the gap between their performance and the standards, they may revisit their understanding of the task, adjust their goals and plans, or change their tactics and strategies. These judgements have implications for future study sessions working on the same task, but can also be carried over to work on future tasks.

(Ellis, Chapter 13)

In sum, the concept of evaluative judgement appears to have a strong alignment with the role of the metacognitive monitoring that underpins self-regulated learning. It may be possible to develop a better understanding of the nature of evaluative judgement, the role it plays in learning, and how it can be developed, by considering how students can monitor their progress and success when working on tasks such as open-ended assignments, which offer scope for interpretation, self-evaluation and adaptation. Like evaluative judgement, metacognitive monitoring is not only important in determining how to tackle a task at hand, but also how to study and learn in the future.

Contextual factors

The contextual nature of self-regulated learning draws our attention to features of the learning environment that can support or hinder student learning. The "self" in self-regulated learning gives prominence to the internal cognitive processes of an individual, although most models of self-regulated learning acknowledge the social context in which learning occurs. This acknowledgement varies in extent, with an evolution from early models that included context as a component to more recent models that situate self-regulated learning within the social context (Hadwin and Oshige 2011). The social context of any given task includes interactions with: teachers who provide cues through their descriptions of the task and may be a source of formative as well as summative feedback; peers undertaking the same task, whose own interpretations and approaches can be important influences and sources of peer feedback; and peers outside the class, friends and family whose advice and experience may be drawn upon. All of these interactions offer possible avenues for help-seeking that may shape interpretation, approach and adaptation. Self-regulation of learning also extends to how students manage their study environment, including the locations in which they choose to study, the resources on which they can draw, and their management of their study time and schedule (Pintrich 2004).

If the task context includes online technologies there may be both new opportunities and additional challenges. Online communication may offer more opportunities for students to seek clarification about a task from their teachers, and for teachers to provide additional descriptions of a task to students based on the kinds of questions they receive. Self-paced flexible learning supported by online technology can give students more control over when and where they access resources and study material. To capitalise on these opportunities, however, students may need to take more initiative to seek help and organise their study than if they were participating in more structured face-to-face modes. If anything, blended and flexible approaches arguably make capacity for self-regulated learning even more critical to student success.

A case study

To develop a better understanding of students' self-regulated learning in the context of an open-ended online task, we draw on findings from a recent case study we conducted as part of a large-scale research project. This case provides insights into how task design and teaching practice interact with students' interpretations of a task and their approaches to completing it. Through this we will highlight conditions that support and hinder students' capacity to monitor their learning and exercise and develop evaluative judgement.

The task required students to post a 300-word critical commentary each week to an online discussion forum, in response to weekly study materials that included a film, associated readings and a lecture. The task comprised 35 per cent of the assessment for a second-year history unit that aimed to develop students' understanding of historical events through film. The unit was offered across five sites, including one main campus and four remote centres. Each week a film was screened at the main campus and made available on DVD at the remote centres and the main campus library. A weekly lecture was presented at the main campus, broadcast simultaneously by video conference to the remote centres, and recorded and made available shortly after through the learning management system.

All other materials were made available online. Face-to-face weekly tutorials were offered at all sites, with the unit coordinator and one tutor at the main campus and a tutor at each of the remote centres. Students were required to attend 80 per cent of the tutorials but otherwise could engage as flexibly as they wished. Posts were uploaded to a discussion forum specific to each tutorial group and due prior to the weekly tutorials, during which students would discuss the topic and draw on the posts contributed online. Students were able to view and comment on posts from other students across all tutorial groups, although this was not a requirement of the assessment task. The postings for each student were compiled and a mark was allocated at the end of the teaching session.

The unit coordinator and three of the tutors were interviewed prior to the teaching session. The unit coordinator, Graham, was responsible for the design of the unit and coordinating the team of tutors. He described the aim of the unit as "trying to get [students] to think about what constitutes truth, what constitutes an historical explanation . . ., [and] about why historians and why film-makers as historians have done what they've done". He described the rationale for the postings task as follows: "You want [students] to be reflective, you want them to be aware that other people have got views which might not agree with yours and you might want to comment on that but you might want to do it in a way which doesn't say 'You're an effing shit' ". The official description of the task in the unit outline was brief:

> For each of the tutorials in weeks listed above, post a 300-word commentary on one of the readings set for each of the tutorials marked as requiring postings to your tutorial slot on the unit's Moodle site. The readings will form the basis for tutorial discussion. Commentary means more than a summary of content and your tutors are familiar with the set readings. Respond to the material, the arguments put, the reasons for the argument and/or what might puzzle you. Postings received after the time specified for submission will not be marked.

Graham's approach to working with his team of tutors was to give them a high level of responsibility and ownership:

> They're all fantastic and they're all, well kind of, on the same page and I trust them implicitly and I don't touch them at all. I don't cross mark; they mark and I accept their mark. I might set them up, I might mentor them a little bit at the beginning and say "This is what I'm going to do today . . . It might be good if you looked at . . ." and that's about it.

He explained that each of the centres were "little tight communities" and he wanted each tutor to tailor their teaching according to the students' needs. In their interviews, the tutors described their initial understanding of the task in similar ways, aligning with both Graham's explanation and the official description.

Participation in the study was requested from the cohort of 85 students, with 16 students randomly selected from the pool of 54 volunteers. Each of these 16 students was interviewed three times: at the beginning of the teaching session, before commencing the task but after receiving initial information through the unit outline and initial lectures; after completing one or more postings; and after completing the last posting and receiving feedback. An analysis of the interview transcripts reveals the following key findings.

All of the students interviewed described the uncertainty they initially had when making their first postings. Reasons given included the openness of the task description and a lack of familiarity with the type of task. All understood the need to be critical and to go beyond mere description, and some found further explanations of the task by their tutors to be critical to developing their understanding of the task requirements. In the words of one student:

> The unit outline was pretty clear about it but I definitely think when [our tutor talked about it] in class . . . not just myself but a lot of people in the class were actually like "Oh, okay that's what we're meant to be doing" and it was not necessarily recounting the whole thing or even critiquing the whole thing; it was maybe drawing upon one theme in it.

Not only was the tutor explanation important in developing students' interpretations of the task, the interviews revealed that the distributed approach to teaching resulted in varied task descriptions as each tutor emphasised her distinctive perspective or approach. For example, one tutor took a strong feminist perspective, while another was focused more on developing students' writing skills. These differing descriptions further shaped each student's particular interpretation.

The online nature of the task also allowed students to judge the quality of their work in relation to postings by their peers in the class:

> I started off by reading a unit guide which was actually quite vague with what we had to do. The tutorials didn't particularly clarify it. [Our tutor] just said "You can basically talk about whatever you want in the postings". But you can actually view other people's postings so I was trying to write mine and I finished writing my own and I thought "Well, I could be completely on the wrong track so I'll just check out a few other people's postings, see what their opinions are". So I did that.

Not all students found this positive, however, with some feeling that the public nature of the posts was intimidating. One explained "I hate other people reading my stuff" and that the online nature of the task influenced what she wrote because "I don't want to sound like a know-it-all or an idiot". Furthermore, being able to view other students' posts revealed the variation in students' interpretations and approaches. One student summed this up: "It's been a bit sort of wishy-washy, we get different stories . . . that's my concern because there are some of us that are actually following the instructions and we're putting effort in and there's others that are clearly not".

The postings were used as stimulus material for tutorial cases and feedback was provided generally rather than individually. This reflected Graham's intention that students develop their understanding through successive postings. Some students found this approach frustrating: "I wasn't sure where I went right and where I went wrong with the postings". This went beyond the immediate task context too: "I'm always wanting to improve next time to do a different unit or whatever. I would probably do something [different] if I got feedback that was insightful. It might be able to change the way I approach a task."

The case study, though presented here briefly, shows how the task design and teaching and learning practices both promoted and hindered opportunities for metacognitive monitoring by students. As with all open-ended tasks, there was scope for interpretation and students could and did develop different perceptions of the task and the standards for performance. The task design of multiple postings over an extended time allowed for students to evaluate their progress and adjust their approach as their perceptions of the task changed. External feedback was offered by tutors, who used postings as the basis for tutorial discussions. Students' perceptions of the task were shaped by their tutor's further elaborations on the task design. These instructional cues were valuable, but the distributed approach to teaching amplified the variation in students' interpretations. Being online allowed students to see each others' work, making difference in interpretation and performance apparent. This led some students to express concerns about the lack of clarity in the task requirements and the implication that different standards were being expected. This was also complicated by the feeling from at least some students that they could not perform in an authentic way online because of exposure of their work on a public forum. In addition, the approach to feedback left some students unsure of how to interpret their final mark or how they might improve their approach to similar tasks in the future.

In sum, the case demonstrates that a well-intentioned, student-centred approach to designing an open-ended online task gave students scope to interpret what is required of them and seek support from the social context. However, the distributed approach to teaching and formative feedback, not uncommon in universities, challenged students' capacity to make effective judgements about current and future performance. This is not to suggest that ambiguity should be avoided, but that the framing and support for open-ended tasks may need particularly careful consideration, especially those undertaken online and across multiple physical sites.

Conclusion

In this chapter we have outlined some concepts common to self-regulated learning models, considered how they apply in higher education, and presented a brief case study that helps to demonstrate how the complex interplay between task design and teaching practice can support and hinder students' judgements about their performance. In doing so, our goal has been to highlight how the notion of metacognitive monitoring might inform the conceptualisation of "evaluative judgement". Further pursuit of this goal could provide new opportunities for theorising teaching and learning in higher education, in ways that bridge the gaps between parallel traditions of research – for example, in self-regulated learning and student approaches to learning (Pintrich 2004). Such developments could inform and be informed by empirical studies, with practical implications for higher education that could improve task design and teaching practice and suggest effective strategies to support metacognitive monitoring in current and for future tasks.

Note

1 We use the term 'task' to distinguish between the task that is set by the teacher and the activity undertaken by a student in response.

References

Butler, D. L., and P. H. Winne. 1995. "Feedback and self-regulated learning: a theoretical synthesis." *Review of Educational Research* 65 (3): 245–281.

Hadwin, A., and M. Oshige. 2011. "Self-regulation, coregulation, and socially shared regulation: exploring perspectives of social in self-regulated learning theory." *Teachers College Record* 113 (2): 240–264.

Pintrich, P. R. 2004. "A conceptual framework for assessing motivation and self-regulated learning in college students." *Educational Psychology Review* 16 (4): 385–407.

Winne, P. H., and A. Hadwin. 1998. "Studying as self-regulated learning." In *Metacognition in Educational Theory and Practice*, edited by D. Hacker, J. Dunlosky, and A. Graesser, 277–304. Mahwah, NJ: Lawrence Erlbaum.

Winne, P. H., and N. Perry. 2000. "Measuring self-regulated learning." In *Handbook of Self Regulation*, edited by M. Boekaerts, P. R. Pintrich, and M. Zeidner, 531–597. San Diego, CA: Academic Press.

CHAPTER **10**

Exemplars, feedback and bias: how do computers make evaluative judgements?

Phillip Dawson

For more than 50 years, researchers have been designing "automated essay scoring" systems which perform the classic evaluative judgement task of marking written student assignments (Page 1966). When compared with human markers, computers can be more reliable at arriving at the "right" score in some circumstances (Shermis 2014). However, beneath this accuracy lies a set of concepts, debates and open questions that may reveal much about the nature of evaluative judgement, and how we might support human students to develop it.

Automated essay scoring systems are part of the larger fields of artificial intelligence (AI) concerned with processing natural languages and classifying documents (Shermis 2014). These fields build systems that make judgements about quality: Google's PageRank algorithm makes quality judgements about webpages to list in search results; spam filters decide if an email looks legitimate; and tools like Grammarly judge the quality of writing.

In contrast with our understanding of the development of student evaluative judgement, which is largely theoretical, our knowledge of the development of computer evaluative judgement is both theoretical and empirical. Many billions of dollars have been invested in designing, comparing and refining approaches to computer evaluative judgement. Lessons have been learnt that are relevant to matters core to the development of human evaluative judgement, such as exemplars, bias and feedback.

This chapter examines what has been learnt from computer-based evaluative judgement and asks if these lessons can inform the development of student evaluative judgement. It focuses on lessons learnt and mistakes made, seeking to draw links between empirical learnings from AI and theory about evaluative judgement in education. It concludes with recommendations for developing evaluative judgement, based on these links.

An important caveat throughout is that students are not computers. We should not assume that approaches that work in artificial intelligence will work with human intelligence. However, just as the field of computer evaluative judgement was greatly inspired by human psychology and biology – artificial neural networks, genetic algorithms and deep learning, to name three dominant AI approaches –

studying the lessons learnt and mistakes made in AI may lead to insights and metaphors for research and practice with people.

The limitations of experts in describing evaluative judgements

Early approaches to teaching computers to make judgements focused on converting human knowledge into logical propositions, which were used to develop "expert systems" for domains such as medical diagnosis. Acquiring this knowledge was expensive and time-consuming. Worse still, these approaches were only capable of capturing some elements of expert decision-making. Explicit rules were acquirable, given enough time working with experts talking about how they made judgements, but expert intuition and experience proved very challenging for expert systems to acquire (Carroll 1987; Cooke 1992). The ways experts said they made judgements, with explicit rules, were different from the ways they actually made judgements; any system modelled on what they said they did was thus imperfect at best. As a result of this and other challenges, most of the work from the expert systems boom of the 1980s was abandoned, despite billions of dollars of investment (Gill 1995).

A key finding of the expert systems literature is that comprehensively articulating the ways an expert makes a judgement is very difficult. The same may apply to evaluative judgements. There are parallels between expert systems and evaluative judgement tools such as rubrics. Both are attempts to represent complex judgements in a logical, rule-based system. The expert systems research would suggest that developing an analytic rubric that can make a robust evaluative judgement should be an immensely difficult task, because it is not usually possible for experts to comprehensively articulate how they would make such a judgement. Sadler's (2009a) observations about indeterminacy with preset criteria similarly note that the criteria educators provide often cannot completely capture the decisions made when evaluating student work.

To better attempt to capture the full decision-making process, expert systems developers employed "knowledge engineers" who were very skilled at teasing out intuition and experience (Carroll 1987). As academic roles are becoming more specialised (Macfarlane 2011), perhaps there is need for a similar role to assist academics in communicating how they make evaluative judgements. Academics could seek help from an "evaluative judgement specialist" when constructing rubrics, and when working with students in other ways, to communicate how evaluative judgement works in a given domain. However, even with such assistance, the expert systems literature indicates that rule-based articulations of quality will likely fail to completely capture how experts really make evaluative judgements.

Feedback on evaluative judgements

In contrast to expert systems, which are explicitly taught how to make decisions, more modern machine-learning approaches learn to make decisions directly from real-world data. There are two broad categories of machine-learning approaches (Hastie et al. 2009). Unsupervised approaches view many examples and attempt to find common features among them. These systems are never told what quality looks like; they are just provided with many cases and left to come up with commonly occurring categories. In contrast, supervised approaches are provided with both examples and expert evaluations of those examples. Most supervised approaches learn by attempting to make an evaluation of the quality of an example, and comparing that attempt with an expert judgement. Through a feedback process, the system is either changed in response to a mistake, or reinforced if the correct judgement was made.

Unsupervised approaches can be useful for some problems where finding similar instances is helpful. Search engines use unsupervised approaches to group similar webpages; and businesses use unsupervised approaches to identify groups of customers with similar behaviour. However, measures of similarity are not in and of themselves evaluative judgements. As an example, an unsupervised machine-learning tool provided with videos of student presentations could cluster according to potentially useful features of quality, such as the pace of the speaker's voice or use of graphics; however, it would not know which cluster represented high quality. It could similarly cluster according to spurious features such as the colour of the presenter's clothing.

The implication of this for the evaluative judgements of humans is that – if we expect our students to move beyond identifying similarities between work samples, towards a calibrated evaluative judgement – they need some combination of instruction on what quality looks like, exemplars of work and corresponding expert evaluative judgements, or feedback on their evaluative judgements. This feedback may come in the same form as supervised learning approaches: summative feedback on the correctness of an evaluative judgement. However, although computers can engage in millions of cycles per second of making evaluative judgements and recalibrating based on feedback, it takes students minutes or hours per judgement. This suggests that students need to get the most out of the comparatively fewer cycles of evaluative judgement and feedback they can make, perhaps through formative dialogical approaches such as those used by Carless and Chan (2016). In the absence of dialogue, we could expect the development of evaluative judgement to require many more cycles of exemplar evaluation and feedback.

Analytic vs holistic may be a false dichotomy

Many supervised machine-learning methods used to develop computer evaluative judgement have their roots in understandings of biology and psychology. "Artificial neural networks" were an early attempt to re-create the brain in a computer, in the form of "neurons" connected to each other through "synapses". Where previous problem-solving approaches such as expert systems required a computer to be told the rules that led to a particular judgement, biologically inspired neural network models were able to learn from real-world data and feedback.

Neural networks have been applied to complex quality appraisal tasks. With respect to judgements about individual evaluative criteria, neural networks were able to move beyond the rule-based analytic judgements that expert systems were capable of, towards what Sadler (2009b) would call "qualitative judgements". For overall multi-criterion judgements, neural networks were able to move beyond analytic approaches (such as adding up the numbers in a rubric) towards holistic approaches (per Sadler 2009b) that incorporate complex judgements without articulable rules. Perhaps controversially for the field of human evaluative judgement, these approximations of qualitative and holistic judgements were realised mathematically through very large numbers of basic additions and multiplications (Kůrková 1992). This means that qualitative or holistic judgements may just be very complex analytic judgements; rather than being concerned with an analytic vs holistic binary, it may be more fruitful to instead consider evaluative judgements in terms of their complexity (Dawson 2015).

Scaffolding evaluative judgement

Learning evaluative judgement from complete, real-world examples is taxing – cognitively taxing for humans and computationally taxing for computers. It is only with recent advances in computing power that it has become feasible to provide machine-learning algorithms with raw data (such as a Word document or an audio file). A much more efficient approach is for a human to custom-develop programs that highlight the important parts of the raw data and conduct some preliminary processing. In the context of making judgements about the quality of an essay, this might involve developing algorithms to calculate readability scores or word counts for sections, which are then fed into the system. This process is termed "feature extraction" in the artificial intelligence literature (Guyon and Elisseeff 2006).

In a human context, feature extraction is very similar to the cognitive load theory principle of "signalling", which suggests that learning can be improved by explicitly pointing out the most important information (Clark et al. 2005). Experimental research indicates that students learn more effectively in signalled environments than in non-signalled environments, and that the mechanism behind this result is better management of cognitive load (Mautone and Mayer 2001).

Both the principles of signalling and feature extraction would suggest that annotated or abridged exemplars will better support the development of evaluative judgement than raw exemplars. This could be done through: highlighting aspects of the work most relevant to quality; focusing on excerpts of an item of work rather than the complete piece; and, where appropriate, constructing exemplar tasks that require students to apply one or two criteria at a time rather than simultaneously considering all criteria.

However, in humans the signalling principle is contingent on the "expertise reversal effect": the same scaffolds that support a novice to learn can hurt the learning of experts (Clark et al. 2005). As students build expertise over time, scaffolds such as annotation may need to be withdrawn. By graduation, it would be expected that students are able to make evaluative judgements on complete work samples without the scaffolds that will be unavailable to them in the world of work. In contrast, computational approaches become completely dependent on feature extraction and drastic changes are required for them to continue without it.

Making the right judgement for the right reasons

In the artificial intelligence field, some approaches are known as "black boxes", because although they may be accurate at making a judgement, they are completely unable to describe how that judgement was made. In contrast, "white box" approaches reveal the inner workings of both an individual judgement and the processes of making a judgement in that domain. White box approaches include decision trees, which break down complex judgements into a sequence of smaller judgements. Analytic rubrics could similarly be thought of as a white box approach to grading, although Sadler's (2009a) principle of indeterminacy suggests that this may be very challenging. Unfortunately, black box approaches tend to be more accurate than white box approaches (Kuhn and Johnson 2013), which leads to a difficult decision between accuracy and explainability. This raises an important issue for student evaluative judgement: is the ability to explain an evaluative judgement an important feature of evaluative judgement?

Many automated essay-scoring systems are able to explain how they make evaluative judgements. A recent review of all available automated essay-scoring tools found that most were as good as humans at arriving at the "correct" grade for essays, based on a comparison with an expert assessment (Shermis 2014). However, although the grades matched, the reasons for the grades were different. Automated essay-scoring systems placed little emphasis on aspects of the work thought by experts to represent quality, such as demonstration of essential cognitive skills, and a far greater emphasis on relatively trivial but easily computable aspects, such as word length (Perelman 2014). The quantitative evaluative judgement arrived at was still high quality, however, as the seemingly trivial indicators of quality the algorithms identified as meaningful tended to occur alongside writing constructs human experts valued.

Automated essay-scoring systems might still be of use if they make their judgements differently from experts, but does the same logic apply to the development of student evaluative judgement? Do we want our students to make correct evaluative judgements, or are we more concerned that they make their judgements in the right way?

It is difficult to completely avoid heuristics or cognitive shortcuts when making evaluative judgements (Joughin, Chapter 6). However, when we expect students to learn evaluative judgement exclusively through synthesising from exemplars, they may not find the same quality indicators that experts look for. Instead, they may learn shortcuts which are useful in the short term, but unsustainable in the long term.

The problem with developing an evaluative judgement capability based on shortcuts is that it may not generalise or transfer easily; it may be based on peculiarities of the exemplars. An example of the danger of overfitting judgement capability to exemplars can be found in early attempts by the US military to develop a system that could identify the presence of a tank in a photograph (Yudkowsky 2012). They trained an artificial neural network by showing it 50 pictures that had tanks, and 50 pictures without tanks. They then showed it 100 new pictures, and it was able to identify which of these pictures had tanks with perfect accuracy. However, when the system was trialled in practice it was no better than random chance at spotting tanks. Further investigation revealed that all of the photographs of tanks the system had learnt from were taken on cloudy days. All the examples of pictures without tanks were taken on sunny days. The system based its judgements on easily identifiable features that were peculiar to the exemplars provided, rather than generalisable features present in the real world.

Exemplar-based approaches that consist solely of university assignments risk developing similar blind spots to the tank-spotting neural network. The tank example would suggest that exemplar-based approaches should consider using authentic examples, generated from real practice-based environments, rather than just relying on samples of student work from university or artificially constructed exemplars. As insiders to the university context, some academics may not be well equipped to spot the peculiarities contained in exemplars that are artefacts from the act of assessment. Selection of exemplars to reflect real-world quality may thus need to involve consultation with practitioners, to avoid spurious quality features unique to academia. Both the tank-spotting and automated essay-scoring domains also suggest that explainability is vitally important to developing an evaluative judgement capability that is truly sustainable. To ensure explainability, students should be required to articulate not just a sound judgement, but also the reasons for that judgement.

Avoiding learning bias and prejudice

When artificial intelligence is trained on real-world data, it tends to reproduce biases present in that data. In 2016 the "beauty.ai" artificial intelligence system conducted an online beauty competition, rating contestants who uploaded pictures of themselves (Levin 2016). The algorithm trained itself on the set of pictures, without human oversight. Beauty.ai's final judgements led to claims that the algorithm was racist: of the 44 finalists judged most attractive, all were white except for six who were Asian and one who had dark skin. This was due to an underrepresentation of different groups within the dataset; the creators of the algorithm stated: "If you have not that many people of colour within the dataset, then you might actually have biased results" (Levin 2016). A similar result occurred when an AI system was trained to predict criminality based on photographs of faces; the system came to associate criminality with diversity, and non-criminality with faces that looked more homogeneous (Wu and Zhang 2016).

In response to the increasing power of algorithms in making important judgements, researchers have promoted the idea of algorithmic accountability (Diakopoulos 2015): that algorithms are not neutral, and contain biases based on their creators and the data with which they interact. It is possible to mount a similar argument with respect to the development of evaluative judgement in humans: when students develop evaluative judgement in a purely inductive manner from exemplars, they may take on biases inherent in those exemplars.

Existing AI judgement systems have tended to take a WYSIWYG (What You See Is What You Get) approach to instances of quality: that data accurately represent everything about quality (Friedler et al. 2016). Such systems learn any biases present in the data as useful, salient discriminators of quality. In response, AI researchers have recently proposed new mathematical approaches to adjust understandings of quality for inherent biases in datasets; these researchers label their alternative approach as We're All Equal (Friedler et al. 2016).

Is human evaluative judgement similarly biased by the exemplars humans have seen while forming their understandings of quality? Meta-analysis of marker bias has demonstrated an effect size of around 0.36 for factors such as unattractiveness and different racial/ethnic backgrounds (Malouff and Thorsteinsson 2016). If students are trained to conduct evaluative judgements in the same ways their teachers do, it is reasonable to expect that these biases may be perpetuated. This suggests that, in addition to exemplars needing to be sourced to represent the real world, they may need to be carefully sampled to ensure representation of a range of perspectives, cultures, epistemologies and traditions.

Learning from artificial intelligence: future directions for developing student evaluative judgement

Sadler (2013, 8) stated that "quality is something I do not know how to define, but I recognise it when I see it". Getting experts to articulate all the rules behind their understandings of quality, as is required for an expert system, may be a very challenging task. Fortunately, the AI literature has shown that some other approaches may be feasible – at least as far as computers are concerned. This section identifies three key principles for exemplar-based approaches, based on the artificial intelligence literature discussed in this chapter.

Principle 1: exemplars should be drawn from real-world practice, representing diversity and equality

Exemplars of student work are helpful in so far as they develop an understanding of work appropriate to the university context. Educators should ensure that their exemplars represent the breadth of real-world practice to avoid students "overfitting" their evaluative judgement to university-specific work. However, these exemplars need to be carefully curated to include the full range of quality, as too much homogeneity may develop bias.

Principle 2: exemplars should be scaffolded with annotation, signalling and abridging

Learning from exemplars is cognitively demanding. Rather than presenting complete, "raw" exemplars, forms of scaffolding should be used for novice students. The most relevant parts of exemplars should be shown to students, and the locations of salient features of quality should be highlighted. Worked examples of exemplar evaluative judgement tasks should be presented. This range of scaffolds should be more present in the first year, and gradually withdrawn so that graduates are able to operate without supports that are unavailable in real-world practice.

Principle 3: exemplars should be used in a dialogue, focusing on feedback and explainability

Learning from exemplars will likely be made more efficient and more effective through feedback. Such feedback should be dialogic, and focused on both the evaluative judgement made and the explanations for the evaluative judgement.

These principles should be considered as suggestions for practice and avenues for research, as although the evidence supporting them is extensive, the underlying research has been conducted with computers rather than people.

A core premise of this book is that the development of evaluative judgement should be built into university curricula. If this is achieved, there will very likely be further synergy between the fields of artificial intelligence and evaluative judgement. The AI field has a long-term goal that computers will be able to function indistinguishably from humans. One of the tests of this ability is that a computer will be able to pass the "Robot College Student Test", by enrolling in a university degree and completing all course requirements without any special human assistance (Goertzel et al. 2012). Progress towards this goal may see AI researchers very interested in how students develop evaluative judgement.

References

Carless, D., and K. K. H. Chan. 2016. "Managing dialogic use of exemplars." *Assessment & Evaluation in Higher Education* 42 (6): 930–941. doi:10.1080/02602938.2016.1211246.

Carroll, B. 1987. "Artificial intelligence expert systems for clinical diagnosis: are they worth the effort?" *Behavioral Science* 32 (4): 274–292. doi:10.1002/bs.3830320404.

Clark, R. C., F. Nguyen, and J. Sweller. 2005. *Efficiency in learning: Evidence-based Guidelines to Manage Cognitive Load.* San Francisco, CA: Pfeiffer.

Cooke, N. J. 1992. "Modeling human expertise in expert systems." In *The Psychology of Expertise: Cognitive Research and Empirical AI*, edited by Robert R. Hoffman, 29–60. New York: Springer.

Dawson, P. 2015. "Assessment rubrics: towards clearer and more replicable design, research and practice." *Assessment & Evaluation in Higher Education* 42 (3): 347–360. doi:10.1080/02602938.2015.1111294.

Diakopoulos, N. 2015. "Algorithmic accountability." *Digital Journalism* 3 (3): 398–415. doi:10.1080/21670811.2014.976411.

Friedler, S. A., C. Scheidegger, and S. Venkatasubramanian. 2016. "On the (im)possibility of fairness." ArXiv e-prints 1609. Accessed 1 September, 2016. https://arxiv.org/abs/1609.07236.

Gill, T. G. 1995. "Early expert systems: where are they now?" *MIS Quarterly* 19 (1): 51–81. doi:10.2307/249711.

Goertzel, B., M. Iklé, and J. Wigmore. 2012. "The architecture of human-like general intelligence." In *Theoretical Foundations of Artificial General Intelligence*, edited by Pei Wang and Ben Goertzel, 123–144. Paris, France: Atlantis Press.

Guyon, I., and A. Elisseeff. 2006. "An introduction to feature extraction." In *Feature Extraction: Foundations and Applications*, edited by Isabelle Guyon, Masoud Nikravesh, Steve Gunn and Lotfi A. Zadeh, 1–25. Berlin, Germany: Springer Berlin Heidelberg.

Hastie, T., R. Tibshirani, and J. Friedman. 2009. "Unsupervised learning." In *The Elements of Statistical Learning*, 485–585. New York: Springer.

Kuhn, M., and K. Johnson. 2013. *Applied Predictive Modeling*. New York: Springer-Verlag.

Kůrková, V. 1992. "Kolmogorov's theorem and multilayer neural networks." *Neural Networks* 5 (3): 501–506. doi:10.1016/0893–6080(92)90012–8.

Levin, S. 2016. "A beauty contest was judged by AI and the robots didn't like dark skin." *The Guardian*, 9 September. www.theguardian.com/technology/2016/sep/08/artificial-intelligence-beauty-contest-doesnt-like-black-people.

Macfarlane, B. 2011. "The morphing of academic practice: unbundling and the rise of the para-academic." *Higher Education Quarterly* 65 (1): 59–73. doi:10.1111/j.1468–2273.2010.00467.x.

Malouff, J. M., and E. B. Thorsteinsson. 2016. "Bias in grading: a meta-analysis of experimental research findings." *Australian Journal of Education* 60 (3): 245–256. doi:10.1177/0004944116664618.

Mautone, P. D., and R. E. Mayer. 2001. "Signaling as a cognitive guide in multimedia learning." *Journal of Educational Psychology* 93 (2): 377–389. doi:10.1037/0022–0663.93.2.377.

Page, E. B. 1966. "The imminence of . . . grading essays by computer." *The Phi Delta Kappan* 47 (5): 238–243.

Perelman, L. 2014. "When 'the state of the art' is counting words." *Assessing Writing* 21: 104–111. doi:10.1016/j.asw.2014.05.001.

Sadler, D. R. 2009a. "Indeterminacy in the use of preset criteria for assessment and grading." *Assessment & Evaluation in Higher Education* 34 (2): 159–179. doi:10.1080/02602930801956059.

Sadler, D. R. 2009b. "Transforming holistic assessment and grading into a vehicle for complex learning." In *Assessment, Learning and Judgement in Higher Education*, edited by G. Joughin, 1–19. Dordrecht, The Netherlands: Springer.

Sadler, D. R. 2013. "Assuring academic achievement standards: from moderation to calibration." *Assessment in Education: Principles, Policy & Practice* 20 (1): 5–19. doi:10.1080/0969594X.2012.714742.

Shermis, M. D. 2014. "State-of-the-art automated essay scoring: competition, results, and future directions from a United States demonstration." *Assessing Writing* 20: 53–76. doi:10.1016/j.asw.2013.04.001.

Wu, X., and X. Zhang. 2016. "Automated inference on criminality using face images." ArXiv e-prints 1611. Accessed 1 November, 2016. https://arxiv.org/abs/1611.04135.

Yudkowsky, E. 2012. "Friendly artificial intelligence." In *Singularity Hypotheses: A Scientific and Philosophical Assessment*, edited by H. Amnon Eden, H. James Moor, H. Johnny Søraker and Eric Steinhart, 181–195. Berlin, Germany: Springer Berlin Heidelberg.

CHAPTER **11**

Developing students' capacities for evaluative judgement through analysing exemplars

David Carless, Kennedy Kam Ho Chan, Jessica To, Margaret Lo and Elizabeth Barrett

Exemplars are defined as carefully chosen samples of student work used to illustrate dimensions of quality. The analysis of exemplars is a potentially powerful way of familiarising students with academic standards and supporting their capacities to make informed evaluative judgements. By producing accounts of strengths, weaknesses and how samples could be improved, students gain experience in making judgements and compare their appraisals with those of peers and the teacher (Sadler 2010). Analysing exemplars supports the development of student assessment literacy, and has potential to be a high-leverage strategy requiring relatively modest investment of time and resources (Smith et al. 2013). In short, when teachers and students analyse exemplars together, a number of important goals may be achieved: clarifying expectations and standards; enabling students to develop an evolving sense of what good work looks like; enhancing their capacities to make sound evaluative judgements; and potentially improving learning outcomes.

A theoretical rationale for exemplar use is based on the notion of tacit knowledge, aspects which are hard to transfer verbally or in writing (Polanyi 1958). Acquiring tacit knowledge has particular potential to emerge through student participation in observation, imitation and dialogue (Bloxham and Campbell 2010). A key aim of analysing exemplars with students is to support them in beginning to acquire tacit knowledge by making visible some of the expert thinking and judgements of the teacher. Knowing what is worth noticing is an essential element of a competent appraiser's tacit knowledge (Sadler 2010).

Exemplars appear to be commonly – but not universally – used in higher education. One of the main concerns about using exemplars lies in the risk that students may perceive them as model answers to be imitated (Handley and Williams 2011). Viewing an exemplar as a model may lead to a superficial or surface approach to learning, impede student ownership of the task, and inadvertently reduce some of the task's originality and intellectual challenge.

The aim of the chapter is to analyse implementation strategies for the principled use of exemplars. The co-authors were participants in a teaching enhancement project in which we all experimented with different ways of using exemplars. We see the incorporation of exemplars into the curriculum as a pedagogic tool to develop student capacities in evaluative judgement, as well as a means of clarifying assessment requirements. We embed our analysis within three varied accounts of practice involving co-authors Margaret, Elizabeth and Kennedy. We use the cases of Margaret and Elizabeth to address scaffolded use of exemplars, and Kennedy's case to illuminate the nature of productive dialogues around exemplars. The cases interweave, because dialogue is part of the scaffolding for students to develop their evaluative judgement capacities.

Scaffolded use of exemplars

Exemplars provide a form of scaffolding for students. Scaffolding refers to support provided during the learning process, focused on helping students achieve learning goals, and gradually reduced or faded according to the progress of the learner (Sawyer 2006). The intention is that the support not only assists learners in accomplishing tasks but also enables them to learn from the experience to improve performance in future tasks (Reiser 2004). There is an important social aspect to scaffolding, in which learning occurs through interactions with more capable others – primarily peers or teachers. Timing is a factor in scaffolding and the desirability of immediate or delayed forms of guidance depends on various contextual factors (Wise and O'Neill 2009).

The first strategy we discuss involves students in working on a task *before* analysing exemplars. We refer to this as scaffolded use of exemplars, to denote pedagogical sequences that combine: student work in progress; interaction with peers and teachers; and the support provided by high-quality exemplars. Requiring students to begin the act of production before analysing exemplars reverses the dominant trend in the exemplars literature, where students are exposed to exemplars and then work on the assessment task. Our thinking is that, through reversing the process, students may be more cognitively engaged and primed to develop skills in evaluative judgement through comparing their own work with exemplars. Conceptually, this use of exemplars resonates with Sadler's seminal article on formative assessment in that, for improvement, learners need to: possess a concept of the standard being aimed for; compare current performance with that standard; and engage in appropriate actions which lead to closing the gap (Sadler 1989).

Scaffolded use of exemplars is a particularly prominent theme in the teaching of Margaret and Elizabeth. One of their aims is to develop students' ownership and voice before they are exposed to exemplars. During the comparison of their own work with that of the exemplars, students see different ways of approaching the task. By first engaging students in assignment-related work, we aim to tackle the challenge that providing an exemplar at the outset might reduce student creativity or limit student aspirations to the kind of approach used in the exemplar.

Teacher education example

In one of Margaret's undergraduate teacher education units, part of the assessment involved pairs of students planning a lesson and developing a lesson plan, teaching the lesson in a local secondary school, and writing a reflection about the experience. There were two texts that students needed to write for this assignment: a lesson plan and a post-lesson reflection. Working with understandings of written texts as genres, and Vygotskian theories of language as mediating thought, students' writing of the lesson plan was developed through the following instructional stages. Students first wrote an outline of the main steps of the lesson and posted this on the learning management system (LMS). Second, students developed an initial draft of their lesson plan using a provided lesson-planning template. Third, students analysed an exemplar lesson plan, examining the relationship between the exemplar and the template material. The students worked in groups, which were each assigned a section of the plan to analyse. Each group then reported their analysis to the class, scaffolded by the teacher through questions, prompts and reformulations. On the LMS forum, students were invited to post comments on their peers' lesson plans. Students then revised the lesson plan based on this feedback and posted it on the LMS prior to teaching the lesson.

The second part of the assignment, a reflective piece of writing, was also scaffolded in similar ways. After the students taught their lesson, they met with Margaret to discuss their experiences. To facilitate their reflections, students were guided to explore what factors impacted upon the lesson events and to think about what they had learnt, both about the learners and about themselves. Students drafted their reflections and were then exposed to a strong written reflection by a senior student. Students were asked to post an evaluation of this exemplar reflection on the LMS before the next classroom session, but only a few students did so due to time and motivational constraints. In the next session, the discourse of the exemplar reflection was examined, including exploring how the student provided evidence from the lesson and how she theorised her practice. Finally, as the assignment also required students to reflect upon their developing identity as a teaching professional, students were exposed to a second exemplar reflection written by another previous student which wove her concrete experiences of teaching with her journey of becoming a teacher. In class, ways that she had expressed her developing teacher identity were examined, and students shared with each other their own drafts of their reflections on their professional development.

In terms of the student response, students were judged by the teacher to be engaged during the activities, and positive about both the use of exemplars and the scaffolding provided. In relation to the intended learning outcomes, all students produced satisfactory written reflections, with some students excelling in linking theory, practice and personal beliefs. They were less competent in relation to the peer review stage of the lesson planning because they did not have the teaching experience or depth of thinking to provide many useful suggestions.

In this case, exemplars are woven into the teaching and learning processes, which makes assessment firmly integrated into the unit pedagogy rather than a separate element. The focus on examining the discourse of exemplars and students' own written work helps students to understand the relationship between language, meaning and social purpose, and how written texts are embedded in wider professional practices. This aims to facilitate greater text awareness when students attempt other written assignments in their university study. The analysis of exemplars is interleaved with the development of student work in progress, so that there is interplay between student assignments and the exemplars. This may promote "noticing the gap" between student production and the target standard evidenced by the exemplar (Sadler 1989).

Problem-based learning example

Elizabeth is teaching a tutorial class, loosely based on problem-based learning (PBL), for a Bachelor of Science programme in Speech and Hearing Sciences. In her unit, the students are presented each week with a case description and some suggestions for possible readings. After the students carry out some reading, they submit a 500-word assignment (reading response) which relates key concepts from student reading to the PBL problem. Exemplars were introduced after the students received four rounds of written feedback from Elizabeth. This teacher-written feedback provided comments on the organisation of the writing, the logic of the arguments, and how well the ideas were supported by information from the readings. A key aim was for students to work independently to incorporate teacher feedback before comparing their work to the exemplars.

The exemplars were selected from the best work produced by the tutorial class, and each week two exemplars were chosen and discussed without the name of the student writer being revealed. Students reflected on the strengths and possible weaknesses of the exemplars individually. They were encouraged to identify what traits the exemplar demonstrated that their reading response lacked, reinforcing the need for students to compare exemplars with their own work. During tutorials all students, including the anonymous student writer, presented their comments on the exemplars. Elizabeth encouraged students to explain their points in detail and specifically identify useful aspects of the exemplars. A common student observation was that their reading response and the exemplars involved similar arguments, yet the organisation of ideas in the exemplars added clarity and logic. The writing style of the exemplars was also frequently identified as strong. After students shared their opinions, Elizabeth facilitated a discussion which highlighted how the two exemplars differed, yet achieved similar outcomes, and elicited from students how their reading response could incorporate some of the exemplar's strengths. The analysis and discussion took about 15 minutes each week.

From Elizabeth's point of view, it seemed that the students needed much prompting to identify qualities of the work beyond a surface-level description. One of the first qualities the students pointed out about the exemplars was that they used "good English". However, when encouraged to refer to the unit objectives and explain how the assignment achieved some of these, students highlighted other strengths. For example, many students were able to identify how the exemplars provided support from high-quality sources of information to justify clinical decisions.

Students expressed enthusiasm for the process because they felt they made significant improvements in organising ideas and using appropriate academic formats. Students also reported feeling more confident because they had a better understanding of what high-quality reading responses looked like. However, one area that remained difficult for several students was how to justify their ideas by integrating information from the reading. Students could identify this as a strength of the exemplars, but found it difficult to do so themselves. This highlights that exemplars may be an effective way for students to appreciate what constitutes quality, but translating this understanding into practice may remain a challenge.

The timing of sharing the exemplars seemed to be important. Before the exemplars were introduced, students used the teacher-written feedback to improve their first two reading responses but their performance then plateaued. However, after the exemplars were introduced, the students evidenced steady improvements to their reading responses. The students explained that seeing how other students wrote up their reading helped them to better understand and use the teacher's written feedback. This suggests that there may be positive relationships between exemplar use and student uptake of feedback.

Pedagogical insights from these two cases

These two cases evidence interplay between student production of assessed work, analysis of exemplars, peer interaction and teacher scaffolding. Students were afforded ample opportunities to compare their views on the exemplars with those of their peers. In Margaret's class, student participation was promoted by extensive use of pair and group work. In Elizabeth's class, students took turns to express their views, which were scaffolded by the teacher. Both teachers incorporated peer review into the exemplar analysis process, by creating a collaborative learning environment which allowed students to learn from peer comments. By critiquing exemplars and/or the work of peers, students may benefit from taking a somewhat detached perspective to evaluate a piece of work and then using insights to monitor their own work – which is the cornerstone of developing evaluative judgement (Nicol et al. 2014).

Excellent samples were chosen for analysis in both cases. Although there are often advantages of analysing exemplars along a quality continuum, which enables useful comparisons of standards, we tend to believe that there is more to be learnt from an excellent sample than a mediocre one. Excellent samples also embody the standard being aimed for (Sadler 1989).

Students developed their own ideas and work prior to analysing exemplars. They then had opportunities to refine their own work after analysis of the exemplars. In Margaret's case, students could transfer insights from the exemplars process to improve their own lesson plan and post-lesson reflections, whereas in Elizabeth's case students had opportunities to apply what they had learnt from the exemplars to their future reading forms. Both teachers provided feedback and managed dialogues, which highlighted important qualities embedded in the exemplars and indicated connections between the assignment and wider program-level learning outcomes. The crucial aspect of dialogue is explored in more detail below, in terms of: its rationale; in relation to Kennedy's teaching; and on the basis of our team's wider discussions.

The role of dialogue in analysing exemplars

Dialogue is an important aspect of university education because learning is a dynamic and mediated process in which meaning is constructed through social interaction with others (Ashwin et al. 2015). Dialogic approaches involve an exploratory constructivist pedagogy, through which students think and reason together and develop critical, divergent perspectives (Burbules and Bruce 2001). Dialogue is a key aspect of analysing exemplars in that, through sharing their perceptions, students: develop a vocabulary for articulating their judgements; practise expressing their views; listen to the responses of others; and then may reconsider their judgements in light of the interaction. The purposeful conduct of the dialogue phase of analysing exemplars encourages students to move beyond the idea of a model and notice different ways in which quality can be manifested. Discussion of exemplars is consistent with the idea that tacit knowledge is hard to communicate and needs to be experienced through interaction. The nature of the dialogue around exemplars has been a focal point of our project and is a primary focus of the work done by David and Kennedy (Carless and Chan 2017).

Through video-taping and coding how Kennedy orchestrated an exemplars dialogue, with undergraduate teacher education students majoring in science, we analysed how dialogue was carried out. Kennedy emphasised eliciting students' views, while withholding his own judgement until the student voice had been extensively shared. Our analysis of the classroom talk revealed that this exemplars dialogue:

- Prioritised elicitation of student opinions and airing of divergent viewpoints;
- Privileged student thinking and reasoning about the exemplars;
- Developed links between peer talk and whole-class discussion;
- Evidenced some development of student views; and
- Scaffolded some key qualities of the exemplars.

(Carless and Chan 2017)

We have also tried, individually and collectively, to explore what a good exemplars dialogue might look like. We have some consensus that an exemplars dialogue should: involve full student participation in articulating their views; support the development of student ability to analyse the exemplars critically; show the relationship between the exemplars discussion and the wider learning outcomes for the unit; and encourage reflection on students' own work. Through dialogue, tacit knowledge may gradually start to be acquired.

Other elements of exemplars dialogue identified by one or more of us include: the exemplification of how abstract assessment criteria are operationalised into a specific assignment; going beyond surface features of the exemplars to a wider picture of quality; reaching some form of consensus in evaluating exemplars; and student learning from exemplar processes which can be transferrable to other future units. A challenge is that it is not always easy to convince the students of distinctions between an overall judgement of a sample and aspects of its constituent parts. For example, surface features may sometimes distract students from more holistic judgements.

Productive exemplars dialogue seems to share similarities with other forms of dialogue in higher education, but may be even more complex because of the tacit knowledge that is involved. Students seem to have strong motivation to engage in discussing exemplars because they carry implications for assessment and grading. The grading elements can, however, result in power dynamics becoming especially salient, in that students are likely to perceive teachers as the gatekeeper of assessment and this hierarchical relationship may present a challenge for student-centred exemplars dialogues.

Implications

To draw out wider implications for evaluative judgement, we discuss three interrelated themes: the timing of exposure to exemplars; peer feedback as part of the judgement process; and the role of exemplars dialogues in supporting students to decode teacher feedback.

First, scaffolded use of exemplars – whereby students attempt a task or part of a task, interact with peers and the teacher, and then benchmark their work against exemplars – has several advantages. The risk of unproductive copying from an exemplar is reduced, because students are engaged in production prior to exposure to samples. Student cognition is potentially enhanced, because there is a two-stage process of engagement with the task followed by dialogue around exemplars. In this way, students are involved in reflecting on task compliance: the congruence between the response stipulated in the assessment specifications and that produced by themselves (Sadler 2010). By benchmarking their work against that of an exemplar, students may generate internal feedback or inner dialogue in analogous ways to those described by Nicol et al. (2014) in relation to peer review. Using the terminology of Tai et al. (2016), there is an internal application of evaluative judgement through student self-evaluation of their own work and an external application through judging the quality of exemplars.

Second, the processes of student discussion of exemplars involve some similarities and differences with peer feedback or peer review processes. Students are evaluating the work of someone else through the exemplar, as well as comparing that performance with their own; but, in contrast with peer feedback, the work has usually been produced by someone other than the immediate interlocutor. Carrying out numerous, purposeful peer evaluations represents the crucible through which task compliance, quality and criteria interact to extend students' tacit knowledge (Sadler 2010). Acquiring tacit knowledge is a key strand in the development of evaluative judgement as it relates to the visibility of expert reasoning. Whereas in some forms of peer feedback students sometimes miss the voice and expertise of the teacher, in exemplar dialogues the teacher generally mediates the discussion and is able to scaffold learning transfer or adjudicate differing student judgements. In our cases of practice, student evaluative judgement is mediated through peer and teacher–student exemplar dialogues.

Third, dialogue about exemplars carries implications for feedback processes (To and Carless 2016). By developing capability in making complex judgements, students are being equipped to decode feedback (Sadler 2010). Through obtaining access to the processes by which teachers make and justify judgements, students gain insights into expert thinking. Only after students have acquired a sufficient basis of appropriate tacit knowledge can they understand the content and implications of teacher feedback (Sadler 2013). Importantly, when the exemplars process facilitates students' generation of internal feedback, this may help decrease their reliance on teacher feedback. It may also increase student understanding and engagement with the teacher feedback they do receive. Students probably do not need more teacher feedback, or more detailed explanation of it, but enhanced capacities to make their own evaluative judgements.

There are, of course, a range of unresolved issues requiring further research. For example, an issue currently being investigated by Kennedy and Jessica involves tracing students' transfer of insights from exemplar discussion to their own assignments. Preliminary analysis of student assignments, and interview data collected shortly after their submission, evidences some student perceptions of how their work is influenced by exemplars. Dialogue around exemplars seems to enable students to develop cognitive skills in aspects such as in-depth analysis, reflective thinking, and connections between assessment criteria and wider learning outcomes. This ongoing research, in line with the experiences of Margaret and Elizabeth, is suggestive of the value of incorporating exemplar use into pedagogy for developing students' evaluative judgement. An even more challenging future research and development endeavour could explore how exemplars might help learners carry out future unrelated tasks and how they contribute to medium-term refinements of capacities for evaluative judgement.

References

Ashwin, P., D. Boud, K. Coate, F. Hallett, E. Keane, K-L. Krause, B. Leibowitz, I. MacLaren, J. McArthur, V. McCune, and M. Tooher. 2015. *Reflective Teaching in Higher Education.* London: Bloomsbury.

Bloxham, S., and L. Campbell. 2010. "Generating dialogue in assessment feedback: exploring the use of interactive cover sheets." *Assessment & Evaluation in Higher Education* 35 (3): 291–300.

Burbules, N., and B. Bruce. 2001. "Theory and research on teaching as dialogue." In *Handbook of Research on Teaching,* 4th edn, edited by V. Richardson, 1102–1121. Washington, DC: American Educational Research Association.

Carless, D., and K. K. H. Chan. 2017. "Managing dialogic use of exemplars." *Assessment & Evaluation in Higher Education* 42 (6): 930–941.

Handley, K., and L. Williams. 2011. "From copying to learning: using exemplars to engage students with assessment criteria and feedback." *Assessment & Evaluation in Higher Education* 36 (1): 95–108.

Nicol, D., A. Thomson, and C. Breslin. 2014. "Rethinking feedback practices in higher education: a peer review perspective." *Assessment & Evaluation in Higher Education* 39 (1): 102–122.

Polanyi, M. 1958. *Personal Knowledge: Towards a Post-critical Philosophy.* London: Routledge and Kegan Paul.

Reiser, B. 2004. "Scaffolding complex learning: the mechanisms of structuring and problematizing student work." *Journal of the Learning Sciences* 13: 273–304.

Sadler, D. R. 1989. "Formative assessment and the design of instructional systems." *Instructional Science* 18 (2): 119–144.

Sadler, D. R. 2010. "Beyond feedback: developing student capability in complex appraisal." *Assessment & Evaluation in Higher Education* 35 (5): 535–550.

Sadler, D. R. 2013. "Opening up feedback: teaching learners to see." In *Reconceptualising Feedback in Higher Education: Developing Dialogue with Students*, edited by S. Merry, M. Price, D. Carless, and M. Taras, 54–63. London: Routledge.

Sawyer, R. 2006. *The Cambridge Handbook of the Learning Sciences.* New York: Cambridge University Press.

Smith, C., K. Worsfold, L. Davies, R. Fisher, and R. McPhail. 2013. "Assessment literacy and student learning: the case for explicitly developing students' 'assessment literacy'." *Assessment & Evaluation in Higher Education* 38 (1): 44–60.

Tai, J., B. Canny, T. Haines, and E. Molloy. 2016. "The role of peer-assisted learning in building evaluative judgment: opportunities in clinical medical education." *Advances in Health Sciences* 21 (3): 659–676.

To, J., and D. Carless. 2016. "Making productive use of exemplars: peer discussion and teacher guidance for positive transfer of strategies." *Journal of Further and Higher Education* 40 (6): 746–764.

Wise, A., and K. O'Neill. 2009. "Beyond more versus less: a reframing of the debate on instructional guidance." In *Constructivist Instruction: Success or Failure?*, edited by S. Tobias, and T. Duffy, 82–105. New York: Routledge.

CHAPTER 12

Designing for technology-enabled dialogic feedback

Michael Henderson, Michael Phillips and Tracii Ryan

In an age of increasingly computer-mediated higher education, there are fewer opportunities for personal and individualised rich communication between students and educators. When such interactions do occur, they can develop students' evaluative judgement; however, this development is supported by feedback processes that, for many students, only occur in relation to assessment. Even then, it has been shown that the comments students receive are often ineffectual and rarely stimulate a process of reflection and dialogue with peers or educators. Nicol (2010) argues that the widespread dissatisfaction with written feedback from both students and teachers is a symptom of "impoverished dialogue", which is exacerbated by the increasing prevalence of poorly designed online and digitally mediated education.

Within this context, this chapter describes a design for dialogic feedback processes surrounding assessment, enabled by both multimodal (such as video, audio and screencasting) and social media platforms (such as forums), with the goal of strengthening student evaluative judgement. In this design, these media are used to enable and enhance multiple feedback loops both pre- and post-assessment submission, in which educators and students explicate their evaluative thinking.

The chapter begins with a description of relevant research, with the goal of identifying potential design principles for the planning and implementation of a course. These include principles relating to evaluative judgement, dialogic feedback, exemplars and digital technologies.

Evaluative judgement

Evaluative judgement needs to be purposefully fostered through course design and instruction. At its core, evaluative judgement is a process in which students use explicit and tacit knowledge to judge quality and to explain that judgement. Other chapters within this book (e.g., Ajjawi et al., Chapter 1) describe evaluative judgement in greater detail, including the complex thinking involved and the fact that it is developed through experience. Indeed, Boud et al. (2013, 944) suggest that students need their "judgements to be calibrated against those who might be regarded as experienced judges of the kind of work being considered". Logically, then, evaluative judgement is something that needs to be built up over time, through multiple opportunities or iterations, to produce and compare evaluations. Such evaluations may occur with a teacher, but could also occur with peers or others.

This need to gradually develop evaluative judgement suggests three potential design considerations. First, the instructional design should engage students in planned activities that help develop their explicit and tacit knowledge relating to interpreting task specifications, making judgements of quality and the explanation of the criteria behind that judgement. Second, evaluative judgement is developmental and contingent, and therefore students need multiple and diverse opportunities to engage in the process. Third, evaluative judgement is most effectively developed in negotiation with others, including experts such as teachers as well as peers.

Dialogic approach to feedback

It has been argued that a dialogic process involving students, their tutors, or others such as peers can reduce misconceptions, calibrate judgements, and better sensitise evaluative reasoning. As Nicol (2010, 507) points out, "the meaning of feedback comments is not transmitted from the teacher to the student; rather meaning comes into being through interaction and dialogue". Feedback is more than an isolated one-way commentary on student performance and, as such, we need to find ways to stimulate an ongoing conversation in the negotiation of meaning.

Individual student–teacher feedback consultations are often held to be the gold standard of a dialogic approach. However, very few universities have the student-to-teacher ratios to make this option a frequent experience. Indeed, individual consultations are a significant workload concern that is unlikely to be recognised in labour models that value efficiency – often found in contemporary mass higher education. As a consequence, individual consultations are likely to be optional, such as during consultation hours, or would be severely constrained if conducted during class time. Even if such consultations are an option, it is likely that the students who are most in need of the support may not be able to access it. For example, Bloxham and Campbell (2010) noted that students who had limited understanding of staff expectations and the assessment standards were limited in their ability to initiate meaningful dialogue with their tutors. In addition, the highly personal nature of such sessions appears to heighten the perception of a power dynamic, which inhibited some students from "a 'real dialogue' that might involve questioning and challenging the tutor" (Blair and McGinty 2013, 471). It is also argued that, due to the richness of communication, students are likely to remember only some of the topics discussed and, even then, some nuances and points from the interaction may be lost (Henderson and Phillips 2015). As Nicol (2010) concludes, we need to shift the focus from teacher-centred feedback to what some describe as co-constructed feedback. One such approach may be the use of peer feedback.

Peer feedback increases the opportunities for feedback dialogue to occur, and can lighten the burden on tutors. Peer feedback can be enacted in many different ways; however, there are concerns that need to be considered, such as the potential for peer feedback to focus on less important issues or even reinforce incorrect practice or knowledge. For example, Bloxham and West (2004) reported that, even when tutors provide written and verbal explanations, students still varied in their understanding of the assessment standards. In addition, Rust et al. (2003) found that inexpert students were more likely to focus on the form of the work, such as structure or referencing, rather than the more complex and often tacit criteria such as analysis and coherence. Peer feedback processes need to be carefully designed, and student confidence and skills built up over time. Arguably, students "must feel comfortable and trust one another in order to provide honest and constructive feedback" (Burke and Pieterick 2010, 64). Nicol (2010) suggests that the judicious use of combined student and teacher feedback may help build students' confidence with the peer feedback process.

In summary, several instructional design principles can be drawn from research surrounding dialogic processes, including those of individual consultations and peer feedback: first, that we need to find a way to ensure all students have equitable access to, and experience in, feedback dialogue; second, that we should be sensitive to power relationships and performance anxiety, and find ways to build student confidence and skills; third, that individual consultation or even in-class discussions are likely to be rich in difficult-to-remember detail and, consequently, systems should be put in place to aid memory and meaning-making; fourth, that there may be value in leveraging peer feedback to increase the frequency and variety with which students experience the production and interpretation of evaluative judgements; and fifth, that students are likely to need, at least initially, carefully planned guidance from expert assessors. An approach which may incorporate these principles is the use of exemplars as a way of bridging the gap between student and teacher knowledge, especially in the case of tacit or hard-to-define criteria.

Exemplars

The careful selection and discussion of examples of past or analogous work can offer a valuable opportunity for students to develop their capacity for evaluative judgement (for example, see Blair and McGinty 2013; Carless and Chan 2016; Handley and Williams 2011; Rust et al. 2003; To and Carless 2016). Carless and Chan (2016) argue that tacit knowledge of quality and standards is hard to communicate and needs to be experienced. Even if exemplars include teacher annotations, it is not enough to simply offer exemplars for students' consumption. Instead, students should be actively involved in the discussion of exemplars, with teachers, peers or others, so that they can negotiate and test meaning (Carless and Chan 2016; To and Carless 2016). In particular, "teacher guidance serves to explicate the characteristics of good quality work and to increase students' critical awareness of the differences between exemplars and their own writing" (To and

Carless 2016, 746). Carless and Chan (2016) argue that teachers need pedagogic sensitivity to know when and how to elicit, facilitate and sustain student engagement. They report that one such technique is for the teacher to withhold their comments until the student has thoroughly explored an exemplar. However, "teachers need to plan various forms of discussion around exemplars and also react adroitly to on-going interaction with students" (To and Carless 2016, 761).

Exemplars are useful as a point of dialogue around standards, as they are based on a concrete elaboration of the work. While some researchers have taken this to mean that exemplars should be selected to demonstrate a range of quality from high to low (for example, Sadler 1989), it is argued here that the judgement of quality, particularly in response to complex topics and tasks, is contingent on a wide range of explicit and tacit knowledge. Therefore, it would seem a more fruitful approach to engage students in a process of evaluative judgement in response to an exemplar, chosen for its potential to stimulate conversations around issues of quality, rather than trying to find stand-alone examples of differing quality. Furthermore, the exemplar could be selected to represent specific elements or criteria, rather than a whole work.

The literature surrounding the use of exemplars for developing evaluative judgement suggests three design considerations. First, exemplars need to be negotiated in meaning, in which students are guided by teachers. Second, multiple and analogous exemplars may be useful to demonstrate the variety of possible responses and the contingent nature of evaluative judgement. Third, exemplars can be chosen to stimulate engagement with specific standards or aspects of the work.

Technology-mediated feedback

A growing body of literature has reported on the use of digital, recorded assessment comments over the past decade. This literature primarily refers to audio, video and, more recently, screencast recordings of the assessor commenting on students' work. All three modes of recordings have been reported in the literature as affording, in comparison with text-based comments: greater detail; sustainability, by being just as efficient or faster to create than written feedback; clearer meaning, facilitated by richer cues such as tone and gesture; more individualisation; and stronger connections between students and teachers (Henderson and Phillips 2015; Ryan et al. 2016). The success of audio, video and screencast feedback mechanisms can be explained in part by media richness theory (Daft and Lengel 1986), which posits that communication cues such as tone, pace, gesture and expression significantly enhance our ability to convey meaning and reduce ambiguity, especially in complex and stressful situations. With this in mind, it is not surprising that students tend to prefer audio-visual recordings to either audio-only or text-only feedback (Marriott and Teoh 2012).

In relation to dialogic feedback processes, Nicol (2010) and more recently Woodcock (2016) note that audio feedback appears to be a promising avenue for richer and more detailed comments and can be perceived as being closer to dialogue than written feedback. Woodcock (2016) goes on to suggest that the more personal experience of audio comments prompts students to be more receptive to the feedback. Yang and Carless (2013) offer an explanation for this dynamic: audio recordings allow more detailed and nuanced feedback and more effectively convey the teacher's concern for student progress, thereby helping to strengthen the teacher–student relationships which they argue are a key concern in any feedback process. These conditions arguably support the likelihood of students acting on the comments. The authors have come to similar conclusions with regards to video-based feedback. In their research, video-based comments were found to be: more individualised (specific) and personalised (valorising identity and effort); more supportive, caring and motivating; clearer, more detailed and unambiguous; prompting of reflection; and constructive, which led to future strategising (Henderson and Phillips 2014).

While simply using technology to record feedback does not automatically make feedback effective, the modality offers potential affordances. For instance, students report that they appreciate the ability to pause and replay the feedback (Henderson and Phillips 2014). Being able to revisit feedback is not afforded by face-to-face meetings unless they are recorded in some way. Students also indicate that recorded video allows time to "absorb and think reflectively rather than focus on a two way conversation and what you are going to say next" (Henderson and Phillips 2014, 61). As such, video-based feedback may increase the richness of the message, while at the same time avoiding challenges of performance anxiety.

Interestingly, a criticism of video feedback is that some students report difficulty in matching comments to the specific parts of the assignment to which they refer. However, this issue can be resolved through the use of screencasting. Screencasts are video recordings of a computer screen, but they can also simultaneously include a video image of the speaker, thereby leveraging all of the affordances described above. Screencasts also allow for a split screen approach that simultaneously presents multiple pieces of information, such as the educator's face and voice, the student's work, and a marking rubric. The use of screencast may be particularly appropriate for certain disciplines, particularly those in which there is a significant visual component to the work, or when written work is being "simultaneously evaluated on theoretic, empirical, compositional, stylistic, and research design components" (Anson 2015, 376). Nevertheless, it should be noted that from the perspective of multimedia learning theory and cognitive load theory, we should be cautious of too many simultaneous inputs.

Despite technology-mediated feedback provision being a relatively recent phenomenon, valuable advantages can be synthesised from the literature. First, rich media such as video and screencasts can offer time-efficient mechanisms for providing detailed and individualised comments that are less ambiguous than written comments. Second, rich media can facilitate a sense of dialogue, despite being asynchronous in nature, strengthening students' rapport with their teacher and thereby their openness to receiving feedback. Third, screencasting may provide an advantage over video and audio feedback by always showing which part of the work the speaker is engaging with; it may also be used to visually demonstrate alternatives.

A design for online or blended contexts

Bringing all of the above considerations into a single instructional sequence can be achieved in a number of ways. Figure 12.1 depicts one such design, used in a graduate class of both on-campus and online students. It acknowledges the need for multiple and diverse opportunities to engage in evaluative judgement, the need for experienced teachers to guide those experiences, especially initially, and the importance of dialogue in negotiating meaning.

In this design, exemplars were used in different ways to stimulate evaluative judgement. At the beginning of the course, students were provided with exemplars that were annotated by the teacher with regards to strengths and weaknesses. Students were then invited to post questions via an online forum. Later in the course, exemplars were provided without comments and students were invited to make – and explain – their own evaluative judgements with regards to specific assessment criteria. Students were also encouraged to respond to and build on each other's explanations. Critically, the teacher's role was to elicit explanations from students, strengthen students' evaluative judgements by identifying how their explicit or tacit understandings differed from the teacher's, and to then explain that difference. In this context, the use of video or screencast technologies by students and teachers was particularly useful, by facilitating the quick exchange of complex thinking. For many educators, the thought of using video or other media to record a response may seem to be a lengthy and arduous task. However, in this case, and as described in the authors' previous work with teachers (Henderson and Phillips 2015), video and screencast feedback has been found to be as fast as, if not faster than, preparing written comments. It also offers the

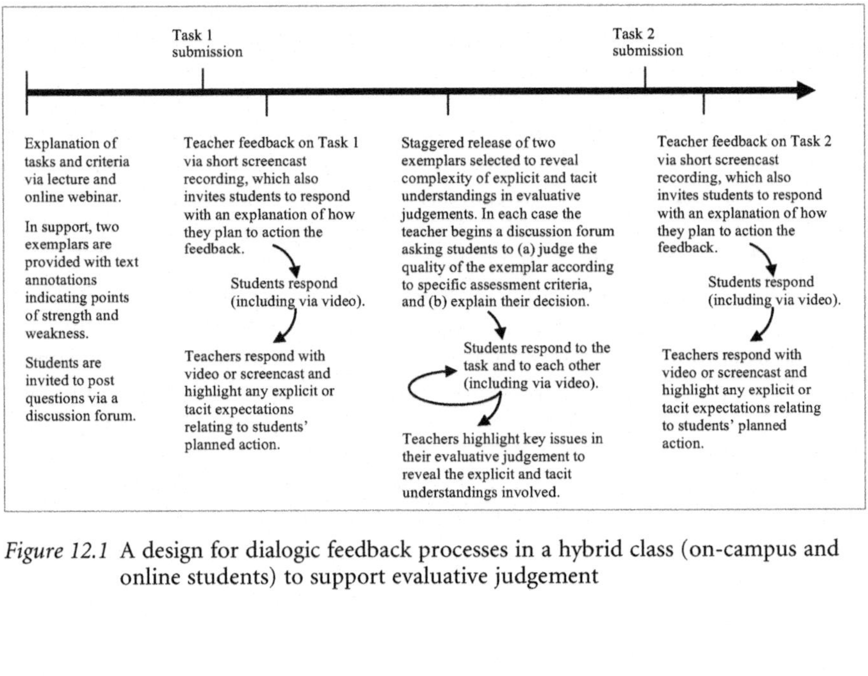

Figure 12.1 A design for dialogic feedback processes in a hybrid class (on-campus and online students) to support evaluative judgement

considerable additional value of greater volume of content and clearer communication through richer auditory and visual cues. In this case, 38 per cent of the class posted evaluative judgements; but 92 per cent of the class observed, with 81 per cent accessing the forums between two and twenty times. The majority of students reported that they found the exemplar activity to be useful because it clarified assignment expectations.

An additional design feature was the use of video and screencast technologies by teachers to provide detailed comments to students after their assignments. These videos replaced the written feedback comments, and since they were just as quick to produce, they were sustainable as a work practice as well as scalable to a large number of students. In this instance, the post-submission feedback included an invitation for students to continue the dialogue with their teacher by responding to the feedback, preferably using similarly rich media to share understandings more efficiently. This process was positively received by students, who explained that verbalising their responses had deepened their reflections on their own work, and that the teacher's subsequent response provided a clearer understanding and impacted on what they did in the next assignment.

The sustainability of this design, as well as the scalability, is dependent on the encouragement and scaffolding of student dialogue with one another, coupled with the efficiency of recorded media which allows teachers to explain complex thinking in a short amount of time. This design offers one response to the need for richer dialogue to support the development of students' evaluative judgement.

Conclusion

As the trend of massification and online delivery in higher education spreads, it is not uncommon for students to find themselves in large classes with overstretched educators. Such situations potentially limit the opportunities for students to engage in and develop evaluative judgement. With this in mind, this chapter has outlined literature on evaluative judgement, dialogic feedback, peer feedback, exemplars and technology-mediated feedback, and has identified several design considerations that may inform online or blended courses, whether small or large. This is not to suggest that these are the only considerations; the field of evaluative judgement, and feedback more broadly, is extensive. However, this chapter does argue that the key design considerations outlined here can be achieved through the judicious use of online systems and instructional design.

The evaluative judgement literature clearly indicates that any such instructional design needs to offer students multiple and diverse opportunities to develop their explicit and tacit understandings of quality in relation to task specifications. Moreover, the literature suggests that evaluative judgement is most effectively developed in negotiation with others, including expert others (such as teachers) and peers. Arguably, in meeting these needs, online systems have an advantage over the physical classroom context. Physical classrooms are typically limited in the time available for each student to have multiple opportunities to observe – *and practise* – making judgements in relation to assessment criteria, let alone to engage in a process of negotiation of meaning with their teachers or even peers.

The literature has also shown that evaluative judgement may be supported through a dialogic process in which students can engage in an ongoing conversation that helps to clarify and make sense of explicit and tacit understandings. However, most students are unlikely to have such opportunities in large classes where access to teachers is limited. In contrast, well-designed use of social media (such as discussion forums) can provide a platform for all students to observe and participate in feedback dialogue and, importantly, this can take place not only with their teachers but with each other. Indeed, in a massified context, the careful use of peer engagement is arguably the most logical way to increase opportunities for all students to engage in ongoing dialogue.

Individual consultations and in-class feedback conversations require students to perform "on the fly", and are likely to contain such rich information that it is unlikely to be fully processed or remembered. Asynchronous communication such as forums can give students the opportunity to construct a carefully considered response. In addition, recorded media such as video and screencasts can offer efficient mechanisms for providing detailed and individualised comments that are clearer (less ambiguous) than written feedback. They can also be replayed and stored for later reference. Screencasting may provide a particular advantage over other recorded media by always showing which part of the work the speaker is engaging with; screencasts can also be used to demonstrate alternatives. Additionally, it is useful to note that recorded feedback has been reported to facilitate a sense of dialogue, despite being asynchronous in nature.

The literature also indicates that exemplars can be useful as models of teacher evaluative judgement, as well as common reference points for students to negotiate meaning as they further develop their own evaluative judgement. Online platforms can support the staggered provision of exemplars, as well as scaffolded opportunities to negotiate meaning with others. Indeed, these experiences can even be sequenced according to cohort or individual progression through the curriculum or according to individualised performance indicators, such as via diagnostic assessment. Most social media also support the embedding of media such as documents, images, audio and video files. This provides a simple mechanism to share a variety of exemplars, as well as to explicate evaluative judgements in rich ways – whether by teachers or students.

This chapter describes one possible feedback design that has successfully brought these considerations together. Future work still needs to be done to track the impact on student performance, particularly in relation to different forms of technology-enabled dialogic experience. Nevertheless, despite pressures of massification and the increasingly technology-mediated instruction of students in higher education, it is clear that there are ways we can maintain – and even increase – students' opportunities to engage in dialogic processes to develop their evaluative judgement.

References

Anson, I. G. 2015. "Assessment feedback using screencapture technology in political science." *Journal of Political Science Education* 11: 375–390. doi:10.1080/15512169.2015.1063433.

Blair, A., and S. McGinty. 2013. "Feedback-dialogues: exploring the student perspective." *Assessment & Evaluation in Higher Education* 38 (4): 466–476. doi:10.1080/02602938.2011.649244.

Bloxham, S., and L. Campbell. 2010. "Generating dialogue in assessment feedback: exploring the use of interactive cover sheets." *Assessment & Evaluation in Higher Education* 35 (3): 291–300.

Bloxham, S., and A. West. 2004. "Understanding the rules of the game: marking peer assessment as a medium for developing students' conceptions of assessment." *Assessment & Evaluation in Higher Education* 29 (6): 721–733.

Boud, D., R. Lawson, and D. G. Thompson. 2013. "Does student engagement in self-assessment calibrate their judgement over time?" *Assessment & Evaluation in Higher Education* 38 (8): 941–956.

Burke, D., and J. Pieterick. 2010. *Giving Students Effective Written Feedback.* Maidenhead, UK: Open University Press.

Carless, D., and K. K. H. Chan. 2016. "Managing dialogic use of exemplars." *Assessment & Evaluation in Higher Education* 42 (6): 930–941. doi:10.1080/02602938.2016.1211246.

Daft, R. L., and R. H. Lengel. 1986. "Organizational information requirements, media richness and structural design." *Management Science* 32 (5): 554–571.

Handley, K., and L. Williams. 2011. "From copying to learning: using exemplars to engage students with assessment criteria and feedback." *Assessment & Evaluation in Higher Education* 36 (1): 95–108. doi:10.1080/02602930903201669.

Henderson, M., and M. Phillips 2014. "Technology enhanced feedback on assessment." Paper presented at the Australian Computers in Educational Conference 2014, Adelaide, Australia, October. http://acec2014.acce.edu.au/session/technology-enhanced-feedback-assessment.

Henderson, M., and M. Phillips. 2015. "Video-based feedback on student assessment: scarily personal." *Australasian Journal of Educational Technology* 31 (1): 51–66. doi:10.14742/ajet.1878.

Marriott, P., and L. K. Teoh. 2012. "Using screencasts to enhance assessment feedback: students' perceptions and preferences." *Accounting Education* 21 (6): 583–598. doi:10 1080/09639284.2012.725637.

Nicol, D. 2010. "From monologue to dialogue: improving written feedback processes in mass higher education." *Assessment & Evaluation in Higher Education* 35 (5): 501–517.

Rust, C., M. Price, and B. O'Donovan. 2003. "Improving students' learning by developing their understanding of assessment criteria and processes." *Assessment & Evaluation in Higher Education* 28 (2): 147–164.

Ryan, T., M. Henderson, and M. Phillips. 2016. " 'Written feedback doesn't make sense': enhancing assessment feedback using technologies." Paper presented at the Australian Association for Research in Education Conference 2016, Melbourne, Australia. www.aare.edu.au/publications-database.php/11095/written-feedback-doesnt-make-sense-enhancing-assessment-feedback-using-technologies.

Sadler, D. R. 1989. "Formative assessment and the design of instructional systems." *Instructional Science* 18 (2): 119–144.

To, J., and D. Carless. 2016. "Making productive use of exemplars: peer discussion and teacher guidance for positive transfer of strategies." *Journal of Further and Higher Education* 40 (6): 746–764.

Woodcock, P. 2016. "Towards dialogue: audio feedback on politics essays." *European Political Science* 16 (2):193–205. doi:10.1057/eps.2015.101.

Yang, M., and D. Carless. 2013. "The feedback triangle and the enhancement of dialogic feedback processes." *Teaching in Higher Education* 18 (3): 285–297.

CHAPTER 13

The practicalities of using assessment management to develop evaluative judgement

Cath Ellis

Helping students to develop their capacity to make good evaluative judgements about the quality of their own and others' work is clearly an important and worthy endeavour, if we are to produce graduates with the lifelong learning skills required for the twenty-first century. Boud and Molloy (2013, 23) go so far as to say that having "the ability to 'accurately' judge one's own work and the work of others is arguably one of the fundamental competencies required in the workplace" (see also Beckett and Hager 2000). Assuring this capacity presents a compelling value proposition, not only for prospective and current students, but also for graduate employers and their customers/clients, and indeed the taxpayers who contribute to the cost of higher education. All of these stakeholders are entitled to expect graduates to have the knowledge required in their discipline area and chosen professions, alongside the ability to evaluate the quality of their own and others' performance (Boud and Falchikov 2007).

Elsewhere in this book, there are chapters that speak to the pedagogical benefits of evaluative judgement. However valuable these principles are, they are worthless unless they are also practicable. It is to these practical issues that this chapter attends. In this chapter I draw extensively on the work of Boud and Falchikov (2007), who argue for the development of assessment for informing judgement, and of Boud and Molloy (2013), who offer new ways of thinking about feedback. Boud, Falchikov and Molloy all acknowledge the challenges of putting their ideas into practice. Here I suggest how we might harness the affordances of new technologies to approach those challenges, such that the principles of evaluative judgement are both genuinely meaningful and manageable for teachers and their students.

Evaluative judgement

Evaluative judgement is not something that comes naturally to most people; as Boud and Falchikov (2007, 188) explain, it "does not come fully formed and [. . .] staging is needed to develop expertise". It is something that students therefore need time and support to develop. As Boud and Molloy (2013, 22) point out, "this very tendency to lack objectivity when it comes to 'self' is why external feedback is so important for learning". Arguably, an ability to undertake evaluative judgement is something that distinguishes graduates from non-graduates in many people's minds. Students need several iterative opportunities to test and develop their skills in evaluative judgement – first by relying on external information from their teachers (who have already developed their expertise) and from their peers (whose expertise is developing alongside their own) – to finally be in a position to draw effectively on internal information (specifically, understanding criteria and standards in relation to personal performance) to make evaluative judgements about their own performance. There is simply not enough time or space available in the length of a typical university term for enough iterative cycles to take place (Boud and Falchikov 2007). To be most effective, therefore, the development of evaluative judgement "cannot solely reside in a single course unit or even group of units", and instead needs to be understood as a "notion that crosses every programme" across a whole programme of study (Boud and Falchikov 2007, 191).

Barriers to implementation in practice

In order for students to develop the capacity for evaluative judgement, Boud and Molloy (2013, 16) emphasise the importance of maintaining a "reasonable continuity of the educator–learner relationship". This is becoming more challenging as the higher education sector copes with the twin pressures of massification and modularisation. In large institutions there can be upward of a thousand students enrolled in a single unit, and each individual student's enrolment in and completion of a particular unit may be the only time they encounter and engage with a specific teacher, and vice versa. Large units are usually delivered by a team of teachers, each responsible for assessing scores of students; at this scale, keeping a "record of knowledge of student work [in order to] observe subsequent performances" (Boud and Molloy 2013, 16) is difficult to manage. When thinking about the educator–learner relationship in this context, it is clear that the role of "the educator" is necessarily a responsibility that must be shared across a teaching team.

In all institutions, even smaller ones, there is some amount of modularisation, whereby degree programmes are "atomised" into individual units of study. This means that any individual unit can potentially be a component of any number of degree programmes. In these situations, teachers have little alternative but to approach the management of these units with a kind of "tunnel vision". In many instances, tutors design, develop and deliver units with little awareness of other units running before, alongside or after their own. The complexity and flexibility of many programmes – particularly those with few or no core units and large numbers of electives or general education requirements – mean that few students undertaking any particular unit are likely to have completed exactly the same units prior to, alongside or after it. The tunnel vision approach is also true of the "view" tutors have of the performance of individual students. Even in highly structured degree programmes, teachers are rarely aware of what students have achieved or struggled with in prior or concurrent units, and are rarely able to pass information about student performance on to the teachers of units that students subsequently attempt. From the student point of view, this "atomisation" of programmes can mean they experience both duplication and gaps in the curriculum, as well as a general feeling of disjunction – that their teachers are not talking to or working with each other, or taking a long-term interest in them as they progress through their programme of study. Ultimately, it is the programme-level learning outcomes that are important and need to be consistent; these can therefore provide a point of focus around which students' and teachers' attention can cohere.

Any aspirations of implementing the principles of evaluative judgement in practice are also hampered by the way that assessment and feedback tend to be designed and implemented (Boud and Falchikov 2007). Just as programmes are atomised into units of study, so too are units further atomised into assessment tasks. The rigidly unidirectional way that assessment and feedback is typically understood – i.e., as something that teachers do to students and in which students are constructed as passive subjects – is a key barrier. In order for students to develop their own capacities for evaluating their own performance, feedback must move beyond the "monologic" structure that now prevails to incorporate self-assessment and to become dialogical, whereby students and teachers have conversations with each other *and* among themselves. It is important that this conversation be about more than just the quality of the piece of work itself; it should also address the accuracy of students' evaluative judgements of their own work and of areas that need development and refinement. Assessment also needs to move beyond the focus on task and content that currently dominates; this often leaves students and tutors struggling to explain how individual assessment tasks are connected to the curriculum and, ultimately, to the final performance standards that each student is expected to meet prior to graduation. Students need to be able to accept and value external feedback in order to take action on it and move to a point where they can see the development of their capacity to judge their own and others' performances as the most valuable outcome of their programme of study.

The pressing question that remains is: how can we achieve in practice the worthy ambition of developing students' evaluative judgement in a modularised and massified higher education industry? In the first instance, of course, it is vital that the learning context is designed to support and encourage the kinds of nested, iterative opportunities for developing evaluative judgement that Boud and others are calling for. This work needs to be done at all levels: from teaching and learning activities at the unit level right up to the whole-programme level, with teachers looking beyond "tunnel vision" to how the units they are teaching work together to deliver programmes as a whole. While it is important that teachers rethink how assessment and feedback is generally understood, it is equally important that institutions rethink how assessment and feedback are managed. Technology is a crucial part of this solution.

Electronic assessment management

While progress towards electronic assessment management (EAM) is being made in an increasing number of higher education institutions, many institutions still rely on paper-based systems to manage assessment and feedback. Apart from seeming, at best, quaintly old-fashioned and, at worst, frustratingly anachronistic to students, paper-based assessment management systems are severely limiting. The way that marking tends to occur in paper-based systems (i.e., with pen on paper) means that it is virtually impossible to "harvest" detailed and valuable information relating to expert judgements of students' performance against the standards of the discipline. In any case, this information is lost to the institution for further analysis at the point that the assessment is returned to students. This loss of data seems enormously wasteful given its value and importance, and the time it takes teachers to produce it. Paper-based assessment management systems are also cumbersome to manage for things such as self- and peer-evaluation, and students can struggle to collate all of the judgements they receive, from an array of teachers and peers, into a coherent whole. From a teacher's point of view, paper-based marking systems mean they have limited oversight of the information that they and other teachers are providing to students, and there are no easy or obvious ways students can identify to subsequent teachers or peers any plans they have for improving their work.

It is clear that students and teachers need new tools and procedures to support the development of evaluative judgement effectively and efficiently in large units and across complex programmes. While there are some very good EAM and eMarking tools available, they all remain limited in their effectiveness. This is largely because these tools have been built based on the needs of paper-based marking and assessment management processes. Clearly new tools are needed. Just as we argue and advocate for the benefits of developing evaluative judgement in our students, so too should we advocate for the design and development of tools that enable us to manage and facilitate it. This falls within the scope of what I have elsewhere referred to as "assessment analytics".

Assessment analytics

I have previously proposed assessment analytics to be a valuable subset of learning analytics (Ellis 2013). In terms of building appropriate tools, Martinez-Maldonado et al. (2015, 10) have taken established methods used in software engineering design processes and adapted them to meet the requirements of learning analytics by adding the vital component of taking "account of the learning context". They propose a new approach which offers a "workflow for designing and deploying awareness tools for technology-enabled learning settings" (Martinez-Maldonado et al. 2015, 11). They call the first stage of their workflow "problem identification", and they offer a series of useful questions as a guide. While it is beyond the scope of this chapter to consider this broad range of questions in detail, it is useful to address seven of them as a starting point.

The first question Martinez-Maldonado et al. pose is: "What are the requirements?" I argue that these requirements fall into two key areas: communication and data management. The requirement of communication prompts us to consider another of Martinez-Maldonado et al.'s questions: "Who are the stakeholders?" In other words: what conversations need to take place, and between whom? At the most fundamental level, these tools need to allow multilateral conversations between students and teachers that move beyond the monologic transmission of information from teachers to students – i.e., what is generally understood to be "feedback". These tools must support two-way conversations between students and their teachers, such that students are in a position to respond to information, provided to them by their teachers, relating to the expert evaluative judgements made on their work. Conversations also need to take place between students and their peers; alongside these conversations, teachers need to be able to have meaningful interactions with each other –including those outside the institution, such as external examiners, and outside the academy, such as work-based tutors – about the performances of students. Importantly, conversations between peers need to be able to take place both across and along the curriculum, such that student progression, development and performance are meaningfully considered throughout each student's programme of study. Boud and Falchikov (2007, 186) make the point that "judgement capability does not build linearly but through cycling through different tasks and returning to previous tasks when confronted with new domains of learning". Therefore, finally, students need to engage in reflective conversations with themselves; this, importantly, includes their former and future selves as well as their (con)current selves. As outlined above, all of these conversations – between students, their peers, their teachers and industry – need to be able to take place in meaningful ways, synchronously and asynchronously, between and not just within individual units.

Perhaps the most intriguing of the questions posed by Martinez-Maldonado et al. (2015) is: "What are the (unexplored) possibilities?" This question reminds us that the advent of new technologies brings new opportunities that have the potential to fundamentally reshape how teaching and learning takes place in educational institutions and, therefore, to reshape the pedagogy that drives it. The advent of EAM makes possible what has previously been unthinkable; the onus is on us as teachers to explore these possibilities. One unexplored area is to consider what might be possible if the evaluative judgements that stakeholders make on the quality of student work were able to be shared beyond the boundaries of a unit.

This prompts us to consider a fourth, and arguably the most important, of Martinez-Maldonado et al.'s questions: "What is the intended pedagogy?" To address this question, I return to the work of Boud and Molloy (2013), in which they identify two models of feedback. The first model (what they call Feedback Mark 1) moves the focus beyond "improving the information-imparting ability of the educator" to focusing "on what this information is used for" (Boud and Molloy 2013, 18). The innovation of this model is that the concept of what constitutes "feedback" changes – from the information that teachers provide to students to what the student subsequently does, as a result of that information, to improve their future work. While admirable, and clearly aligned with the pedagogical principles of evaluative judgement, the Mark 1 model is necessarily limited by the fact that it is envisaged as operating primarily *within* a unit, rather than as working across and between units. Boud and Molloy then go on to introduce a second model (which they call Feedback Mark 2), which departs from the first "because it is based on the notion that learners are necessarily active and volitional" and "sees students as having significant agency and choice" (Boud and Molloy 2013, 21). Importantly, one of the premises of Mark 2 is that it "has a role in developing students' continuing evaluative judgement", in that it is "seen not only as having an influence on immediate tasks but of building students' capability for making judgements about their subsequent work'" (Boud and Molloy 2013, 22). Feedback Mark 2 comes with two important expectations: that students "take more of an initiatory role" and that they "follow through and actively utilise the information they have solicited in subsequent work" (Boud and Molloy 2013, 23). Once again, this model is necessarily limited by the fact that it is envisaged as operating only within a unit and, to be reasonably practicable, with a relatively small number of students; it would present a challenge for students, but especially for teachers, to manage and keep track of the large volume of information and conversations that need to take place in order for Mark 2 to work at scale both within and across units. To identify the limitations of these models is not a criticism of them *per se*, but rather to agree with something that Boud and Molloy themselves acknowledge: that "with the increasing fragmentation of programs where experts deliver discrete topics/modules", the conditions required to enable appropriate iterative opportunities for students is "becoming harder to meet" (Boud and Molloy 2013, 16).

To consider how this might work beyond the level of the unit, I propose some approaches that allow for the practical application of Boud and Molloy's feedback models at scale, both within and across units of study, in modularised programmes. The first approach is that information that has been made available to a student in one unit is also shared with teachers of both concurrent and subsequent units studied by that student, so that they can identify and then evaluate the responses this student has made to information provided to them by other teachers. Obviously, not all information provided to a student within a unit is useful when shared in this way, and this approach also depends heavily on the consistency and alignment of such things as learning outcomes, criteria and standards across a programme. It is not necessary or useful for things such as information relating specifically to the content and material of a particular unit or task to be shared, and nor is it useful to share "basic material that can be demonstrated as learned through a single iteration" (Boud and Molloy 2013, 20). As Boud and Molloy explain,

> this leaves such things as core or threshold concepts i.e. key ideas that are challenging to appreciate but fundamental to further study; academic skills such as writing and other forms of communication; and discipline-specific material that requires continuing practice to fully learn.
>
> (2013, 20)

The second approach is that stakeholders have the environments they need to engage in conversation with each other, both within units (regardless of their size) and between units (regardless of the complexity of the degree programme). As an example, information that has been given by a teacher to a student about an essay in one unit, say in history, would be recorded and stored so it is available to the teacher as they mark this student's second essay for that unit. Because this information is shared, it is also available to the teacher of other units that the student is studying concurrently. This allows the student to take the information provided by the history teacher and put it to work at the next available opportunity, which may be in another unit that they are taking concurrently, say a philosophy unit. So, as this student prepares work for submission, they do so in the full knowledge that the philosophy teacher is aware that a particular issue has already been pointed out to the student by their history teacher. This leads to how another aspect of Boud and Molloy's Mark 2 model can be put into practice: specifically, how students can use this expert judgement to inform and develop their own evaluative judgement. The provision of peer evaluation tools, accompanied by the channels for conversation and dialogue (as outlined above), allows students to be actively involved in the process by practising making judgements of both their own work and that of their peers. To use the same example: all students can turn to their peers in both the history and philosophy units to ask each other for specific feedback, while simultaneously providing peer evaluation of the work of others and responding to requests for specific feedback. Each student would simultaneously have an opportunity to undertake self-evaluation by recording a judgement of their own work, which they would be able to compare to that of their peers. Lastly, an individual student would be able to submit a final essay to both the philosophy and history teachers and use the communication tool to inform the teachers of judgements made against standards, actions undertaken to improve on previous work, and to ask again for specific feedback. When both teachers come to evaluate this student's work, they have access to all of this information: the information previously provided by the other teachers, the student's self-evaluation, the peer evaluation that has been provided, and the actions that have resulted from all of this feedback information. Crucially, the iterative cycles can continue on beyond these two units to units this student takes in the subsequent term.

Two other useful questions posed by Martinez-Maldonado et al. (2015) are: "What are the available data sources?" and "How can the data be captured?" This turns our attention to the second requirement: data management. Clearly what is needed for the above scenario to work is for self-, peer- and teacher-evaluation all to take place in the same environment: thus, the judgements made and recorded about student work constitute the main data sources. To best inform decision-making, these judgements need to be easy to record and the information needs to be easy to harvest. This information then needs to be easily connected to (i.e., compared to and added to) other information, such as external standards, and to each student's previous performances. In order for both students and teachers to see, record and measure progress and attainment against a set of standards within all units – regardless of size, across even the most complex programmes and in the largest institutions – this information and these conversations need to be commensurate and interoperable. Again, this is highly dependent on a well-aligned curriculum, thus bringing the question of curriculum organisation and management into consideration. It is clear that all of these data needs to be centrally managed. This brings us, finally, to consider the last question posed by Martinez-Maldonado et al. (2015): "How is the data to be collected, used, shared and stored?" It stands to reason that institutional information technology infrastructure and enterprise architecture need to be able to accommodate and support these requirements. Siemens et al. (2011) have offered a proposal to design, implement and evaluate an open platform for learning analytics techniques, in which they outline what the technical strategy might be for managing data at an institutional scale. They suggest data marts or warehouses, analytics engines, student- and teacher-facing dashboards, learning adaptation and personalisation engines, and intervention engines that could provide automatic interventions for common problems such as grammar and punctuation.

Conclusions

If we agree that developing students' evaluative judgement is a fundamental part of every higher education programme, then we must acknowledge and address the challenges this presents in practice. Developing evaluative judgement should not be confined to students in small units and institutions; it must be available regardless of the complexity of the programme of study. Students are entitled to this "joined up" approach: they need to be given the time, space and opportunity to be actively involved in the process, to practise making judgements of their own and to work together to undertake the multiple iterative cycles required to develop their skill. They also deserve to understand that their teachers are working with them and with each other, across a teaching team, and are passing them hand-to-hand across and along their programmes of study. To achieve this requires a radical rethinking about how assessment and feedback is understood, but also about how it is managed and the technology needed to do this efficiently and effectively. We must move beyond the restrictions imposed by paper-based marking and into the previously unexplored possibilities that EAM offers.

References

Beckett, D., and P. Hager. 2000. "Making judgements as the basis for workplace learning: towards an epistemology of practice." *International Journal of Lifelong Education* 19 (4): 300–311. doi:10.1080/02601370050110365.

Boud, D., and N. Falchikov. 2007. "Developing assessment for informing judgement." In *Rethinking Assessment in Higher Education: Learning for the Longer Term*, edited by D. Boud and N. Falchikov, 181–197. London: Routledge.

Boud, D., and E. Molloy. 2013. "Changing conceptions of feedback." In *Feedback in Higher and Professional Education: Understanding It and Doing It Well*, edited by D. Boud and E. Molloy, 11–33. London: Routledge.

Ellis, C. 2013. "Broadening the scope and increasing the usefulness of learning analytics: the case for assessment analytics." *British Journal of Educational Technology* 44 (4): 662–664. doi:10.1111/bjet.12028.

Martinez-Maldonado, R., A. Pardo, N. Mirriahi, K. Yacef, J. Kay, and A. Clayphan. 2015. "LATUX: an iterative workflow for designing, validating, and deploying learning analytics visualizations." *Journal of Learning Analytics* 2 (3): 9–39. doi:10.18608/jla.2015.23.3.

Siemens, G., D. Gasevic, C. Haythornthwaite, S. Dawson, S. Buckingham Shum, R. Ferguson, E. Duval, K. Verbert, and R. S. J. D. Baker. 2011. "Open learning analytics: an integrated and modularized platform." Society for Learning Analytics Research. https://solaresearch.org/core/open-learning-analytics-an-integrated-modularized-platform/.

CHAPTER 14

Strategies for fostering the development of evaluative judgement

Darrall G. Thompson and Romy Lawson

It has been established for decades that assessment defines what students regard as important, how they spend their time and how they come to see themselves as students and then as graduates (for example, Boud 1988; Brown et al. 1997). If the system of assessment does not value students' judgements about aspects of their own work or performances, they are unlikely to consider such processes to be part of their educational development. Given the predominance of certification through marks and grades, there is minimal incentive for academic staff to include learning activities and assessment tasks that encourage the development of evaluative judgement.

Cowan highlights the issue in describing the dilemma for assessors who are required to produce marks as a measure of student performance: "The challenge for the assessors is thus to arrive at a valid and meaningful single judgement, having somehow conflated relevant but disparate elements and criteria" (Cowan 2010, 324). The significance of this conflation cannot be overstated when the crucial educational value of assessors' judgements against criteria is lost as they become subsumed within a total mark or grade. The conflation of assessments by connoisseurs may be valid in the context of subject experts (Ecclestone 2001), but we consider that such conflation is detrimental when attempting to develop the important capability of evaluative judgement.

While there are many guidelines to inform broader approaches to assessment design (McDowell 2006; Higher Education Academy 2012; Price et al. 2008), the accumulation of marks into a final grade for certification has remained a persistent and predominant practice. Unfortunately, this focus on final marks tends to relegate students' own evaluative judgement attempts to mere grade-guessing. However, we believe that whole-of-degree curricula and assessment within institutions, if supported at all internal levels, has great potential for the development of students' capabilities, including evaluative judgement.

In this chapter we propose three strategies that together can support an environment that fosters evaluative judgement:

Strategy 1: alignment to whole-of-degree outcomes
Strategy 2: software-enabled engagement
Strategy 3: communication with all stakeholders

These strategies are based on our involvement in previous studies (Bamford and Thompson 2005; Kamvounias and Thompson 2008; Lawson et al. 2012; Boud et al. 2013, 2015; Lawson 2015; Thompson 2016).

Strategy 1: alignment to whole-of-degree outcomes

Aim: to develop whole-of-degree learning outcomes, aligned through learning activities to assessment tasks, which foreground a capability development framework that spans individual unit boundaries.

There has been an international focus on graduate attributes or capabilities (Barrie 2004), and accreditation agencies now require universities to measure the learning outcomes of students against a specific set of programme-level learning goals (Hall and Kro 2006). For example, the Australian Tertiary Education Quality and Standards Agency states that assessment tasks for a course of study and its units must provide opportunities for students to demonstrate achievement of the expected degree-level learning outcomes (TEQSA 2015).

Recognising student achievement in relation to degree-level learning outcomes can have advantages in terms of student achievement. Haynes (2007) presented evidence that, where there is a greater sense of the holistic programme, students are likely to achieve higher standards than on more fragmented programmes.

However, a whole-of-degree approach, without the adoption of a framework that gives feedback to students about their capability development aligned to assessment, provides minimal motivation for them to engage in making and refining their own judgements. The framework may relate to university graduate capability statements, but needs to include degree-level learning outcomes that foreground these capabilities in such a way that students appreciate their value for lifelong learning and employability (Thompson 2016).

Whole-of-degree curriculum design has three key elements that must be aligned – learning outcomes, learning activities and assessment tasks – using the degree learning outcomes to drive design. This holistic design approach removes the silo effect of developing units in isolation to develop an integrated and scaffolded approach to the curriculum. When units relate and build on each other in a progressive way, students can see how each element of the degree relates to the overall degree-level learning outcomes.

If they are constructed well, the degree-level learning outcomes will encompass a range of requirements, for example: degree-level descriptions; discipline-based standards statements; professional-body requirements; university themes; current/future professional contexts; and graduate employability.

To ensure that assessments foster the development of degree-level learning outcomes and provide valid information in regards to student achievement, it is effective to embed these outcomes directly into units. The context and level for the degree-level learning outcome is expressed through the design of assessment tasks, using subject-specific knowledge and skills and setting the task at an appropriate level of complexity for the stage of the degree. The consistent use of the same degree-level learning outcomes throughout the course helps students understand what the aims of the degree are and helps them make connections throughout their learning. This strategy has the potential to inform the use of previous feedback for majors/unit selection as students progress through their degree.

We propose that a consistent, degree-focused curriculum and assessment framework is essential in fostering the development of evaluative judgement. As Sadler (2005, 177) writes, "Assessment and grading do not take place in a vacuum. Professional judgements about the quality of student work together with interpretations of such judgements are always made against some background framework or information".

However, engagement is key to the effectiveness of any framework for both staff and students. To engage students with judgements about the standards of their work or performances, within a framework that gives them context, is no small achievement. This leads us to Strategy 2, which employs online software systems to encourage and facilitate this engagement.

Strategy 2: software-enabled engagement

Aim: to integrate software-enabled marking and feedback that makes visible the links to both general capabilities and degree-level outcomes while facilitating student self-assessment against related criteria.

There is an increasing array of marking and feedback systems for assessing student work, and many universities are encouraging digital assessment wherever possible. The systems are designed with a plethora of purposes in mind, often leading academics to question their educational value. It is time-consuming for academics to gain understanding of the various systems and how they can function together, in their particular context, to support student learning. However, evidence from our previous studies has highlighted several advantages in using software to facilitate marking and feedback while providing students the opportunity to self-assess their work as part of normal assessment processes (Thompson and McGregor 2009; Lawson et al. 2012; Boud et al. 2013).

The sustainable integration of any software system demands a great deal of interaction and negotiation with IT departments and teaching and learning units, which each need to validate and approve purchases and support schemes. The complexity of available systems has increased the reliance of academics on learning technologists and centralised units, who need evidence that a system will be used extensively before it can become part of a university's official suite of software.

In this chapter, we are referring to a system used in three of our previous studies on self-assessment and assurance of learning. *REVIEW*™ has been developed at the University of Technology Sydney for the express purpose of reducing the focus on marks and grades, in favour of developmental feedback about whole-of-degree learning outcomes and meta-categories of attributes/capabilities while enabling student self-assessment.

The retention of detailed, criterion-referenced judgements linked in *REVIEW*™ facilitates longitudinal feedback of both whole-of-degree outcomes and meta-

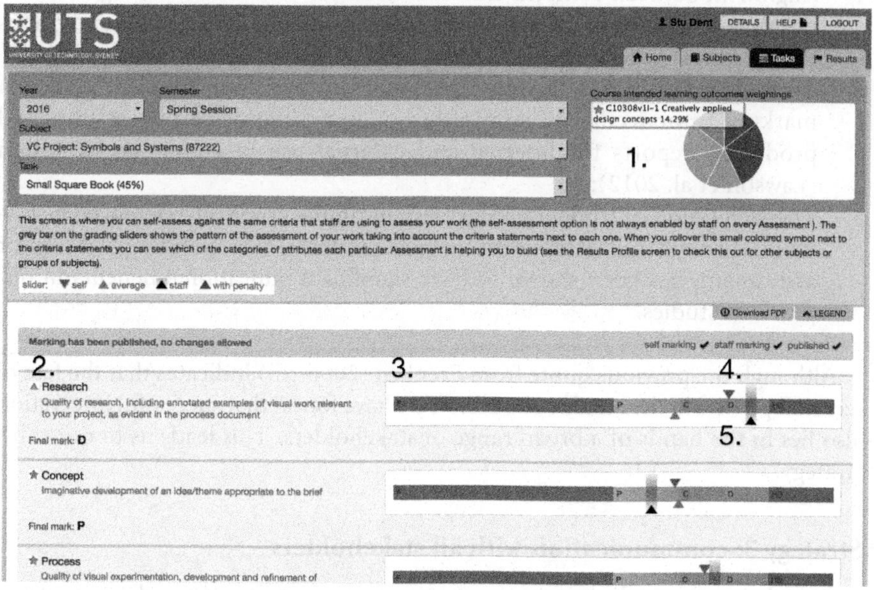

Figure 14.1 Student view of their marking screen from *REVIEW*™ for a first-year design subject, showing student self-assessment against criteria

Key to Figure 14.1

1 Pie chart showing percentages of the whole-of-degree learning outcomes covered in the task (shown on rollover)
2 Assessment criteria linked to degree outcomes and attribute/capability framework
3 Visual marking slider (configurable), used to allocate marks in a database by dragging triangle markers
4 Student self-assessment marker, which is displayed to staff only after they have made their own judgements against the criteria
5 Staff triangle marker, only shown to students after they have been published by the subject coordinator (the small grey triangle is the average composed of all students in the class)

categories of attributes across subjects or units of study. This occurs in the form of line graphs or bar charts, and the collation of related comments.

To suggest that a software intervention is actually causative of an educational benefit would be naïve in any context; as Frenken (2006, xii) observes, "Technological artefacts are the result of careful design. The fate of technology, however, lies in the hands of its users". However, the *REVIEW*™ software, accessed through the *Blackboard Learning Management System*™, has sustained student engagement over an extended period, with students voluntarily making criterion-referenced judgements about their own work prior to submission (Boud et al. 2013, 2015).

The ubiquitous, embedded use of this or similar software to engage both staff and students in the day-to-day marking of student work has a number of advantages:

1 Alignment between complex curricula levels can be clarified through colour–number–symbol coding and the use of dropdown menus, pie charts and graphs to make these links visible in longitudinal feedback and course mapping;
2 There is a significant timesaving element in marking, monitoring/bench marking tutor feedback, administering/compiling/delivering results, and producing reports for internal and external use in course accreditation (Lawson et al. 2012);
3 The facilitation of student engagement in online criterion-referenced assessment through self-assessment, which students can compare with tutor assessment, has been shown to have significant educational benefits in our previous studies.

Although the previous quote from Frenken (2006, xii) indicates that the fate of technology "lies in the hands of its users", we have found that successful integration also lies in the hands of a broad range of stakeholders. This leads us to our third strategy.

Strategy 3: communication with all stakeholders

Aim: to design and implement communication strategies that target students, academic teaching staff and other stakeholders, explaining the benefits of assessment focused on student capabilities and outcomes rather than final marks and grades.

Our experience with the first two strategies has revealed this third strategy to be a vital key that is often missed and almost always underfunded.

The task of communicating to students the importance of developing capabilities such as evaluative judgement relies on contextual supporting material, such as animations, videos and consistent course documentation. However, given that student focus is on assessment, the feedback that students receive in the day-to-day assessment of their work and performances forms the key communication strategy. Guidance can be provided in the form of degree-level rubrics that identify criteria for each degree learning outcome, along with the expected standards for different stages of the degree. However, it should be noted that too much descriptive detail can lead to the adoption of a surface approach by students (Marton and Saljo 1976; Ramsden 1992). We have found that the use of colour-coding and visual presentation through assessment software has been an important strategy to clarify communication to students about the alignment between curriculum levels and criteria.

A consistent approach to feedback about degree-level learning outcomes, when applied throughout the whole course, helps students appreciate what is needed to perform well, providing more awareness and control of their learning experience. This approach begins to address the focus on assessment that merely provides marks for individual pieces of work, which are then conflated into an overall final grade.

With a scaffolded approach based around each degree learning outcome and linked to broader generic attributes/capabilities, students can receive consistent feedback about achievement in relation to two layers above feedback for individual tasks. This approach can also communicate to students ongoing information about their performance in relation to their endpoint for each degree-level learning outcome. For example, in Figure 14.1 the pie chart has colour divisions for three of the five generic attribute categories applied across 17 undergraduate and postgraduate degrees. In this case, green represents Innovation and Creativity, red indicates Practical and Professional Skills, and grey signifies Research and Critique. The sub-category divisions inside these coloured areas relate to discipline-specific program learning goals (in this case, "Creatively applied design concepts" is a Course Intended Learning Outcome as part of a Creativity and Innovation attribute). With this approach students can be marked, not only on their progress for an individual piece of work, but in relation to the degree standards as a whole and the more generic attributes to which they relate.

We are suggesting that, in the process of marking and feedback engagement with criterion-referenced self-assessment, students begin to develop evaluative judgement. Self-assessment can be presented to students as an aspect of their engagement in a shared language with teaching staff, and the enhancement of their development of graduate attributes in readiness for the real world (UTS 2014).

The task of communicating with academic teaching staff about degree-level approaches and changing the focus of assessment requires a multifaceted approach. Top-down instructions to academics about changes to teaching and assessment can sometimes be counterproductive. It is well established that the pressure on academics to research has detrimentally impacted their tolerance for teaching and learning initiatives. Support through teaching and learning units and clear, consistent degree/subject mapping are essential in this degree-level approach. However, this can present a complexity that may lead to a surface, "tick-box" approach by staff. Sadler (2005) suggests that, together with documentation, allowance for discussion and dialogue among staff about assessment criteria and standards is essential. We have found that academics responsible for subject development need support in writing descriptive assessment criteria which both value specific aspects of a task and align with degree-level outcomes. Criteria-writing workshops are key to ensuring that the language used is accessible for students and consistently linked to the relevant degree learning outcomes.

In engaging staff we have found that the timesaving benefits of accessible, well-designed, easy-to-use and reliably integrated software have been key to adoption. However, academics also need to be convinced that there is educational value through published evidence and endorsement by colleagues (Thompson 2009).

Academic teaching staff accustomed to the extensive use of exams and tests often struggle with assessment that reveals the ways in which the questions relate to criteria. The ability to reproduce memorised information within a time constraint should clearly not be a predominant criterion if assessment is to support the development of evaluative judgement. The process of linking exams to degree learning outcomes and graduate capabilities has highlighted the low-level learning elucidated by many exam questions. Communication with staff about converting exam questions to criterion-referenced marking schemes has had the effect of increasing the number of scenario-based questions. For example, two criteria that relate to research and critical thinking have been used in a subject for a tax accounting exam: (1) Ability to develop appropriate strategies evident in your answers for the scenarios given in questions 11 and 12; and (2) Research references and citations integrated into your text to support your arguments (not just a list bolted on at the end). A staff communication strategy in this context requires exemplars, one-to-one assistance and staff champions who understand the importance of developing students' capabilities – including evaluative judgement. Because of staff turnover and casualised exam marking, communication needs to be continuous, consistent and ubiquitous.

Communication strategies for other stakeholders are also important; for example, ongoing communication with: university and faculty leaders; teaching and learning units; student support units; faculty boards; course administrators; and an increasing number of casual tutors and markers. University administrators and IT departments can also be crucial; for example, they may not understand the need to support the implementation of software that seems to replicate similar functions in existing systems. There is also communication needed with external professional bodies, external course advisory committees, and the business community of employers in general. The most important communication elucidated in this third strategy is clearly with students and academic teaching staff; but we have found that communication with these other stakeholders can have significant impacts on the success and sustainability of any intervention. These other stakeholders often appreciate the time taken to include them, and one approach we have successfully used is to extract and curate versions of the same media and documentation presented to academic staff and students. It is important to take the time to arrange suitable venues for meetings/workshops/presentations, and to ensure these opportunities take place well in advance of changes being announced where possible.

Conclusion

Based on our previous studies, we believe that the three interdependent strategies described above are all important to encourage the development of evaluative judgement as a capability to be valued by both students and academic teaching staff. The key message from this work is about the integration of curriculum design and assessment focused on whole-of-degree outcomes, through clear consistent communication to all concerned, with rich data on performance as a student progresses. These strategies shift the focus of assessment from certification towards a more developmental role, and help students and staff to understand what they are both trying to achieve at a degree level. This in turn provides an educational environment in which the development of evaluative judgement can be fostered.

References

Bamford, A. K., and D. G. Thompson. 2005. "Transforming student assessment to liberate pedagogy." *Snapshots – Journal of Innovation in Education* 3 (2): 17–21.

Barrie, S. C. 2004. "A research-based approach to generic graduate attributes policy," in "Generic Graduate Attributes: Citizens for an Uncertain Future," special issue, *Higher Education Research & Development* 23 (3).

Boud, D. 1988. "Moving towards autonomy." In *Developing Student Autonomy in Learning*, 2nd edn, edited by D. Boud. London: Kogan Page.

Boud, D., R. Lawson, and D. G. Thompson. 2013. "Does student engagement in self-assessment calibrate their judgement over time?" *Assessment & Evaluation in Higher Education* 38 (8): 941–956.

Boud, D., R. Lawson, and D. G. Thompson. 2015. "The calibration of student judgement through self-assessment: disruptive effects of assessment patterns." *Higher Education Research & Development* 34 (1): 45–59.

Brown, G., J. Bull, and M. Pendlebury. 1997. "Peer- and self-assessment." In *Assessing Student Learning in Higher Education*, 170–184. London: Routledge.

Cowan, J. 2010. "Developing the ability for making evaluative judgements." *Teaching in Higher Education* 15 (3): 323–334.

Ecclestone, K. 2001. "I know a 2:1 when I see it: understanding criteria for degree classifications in franchised university programmes." *Journal of Further and Higher Education* 25 (3): 301–313.

Frenken, K. 2006. *Innovation, Evolution and Complexity Theory*. Cheltenham, UK: Edward Elgar.

Hall, O. P., and K. Ko. 2006. "Learning assurance using business simulations applications to executive management education." *Developments in Business Simulation and Experiential Learning* 33: 1–6.

Haynes, A. 2007. "What can feedback practices tell us about variation in grading across fields?" Paper presented at the ASKe Seminar Series, Oxford Brookes University, Oxford, UK, September.

Higher Education Academy. 2012. "A marked improvement: transforming assessment in higher education." *Higher Education Academy Project Report*. Accessed 19 February 2017. www.heacademy.ac.uk/resource/marked-improvement.

Kamvounias, P., and D. G. Thompson. 2008. "Assessing graduate attributes in the business law curriculum." *Journal of the Australian Law Teachers Association* 1 (1): 181–195.

Lawson, R., T. L. Taylor, D. G. Thompson, L. Simpson, M. Freeman, L. Treleaven, and F. Rohde. 2012. "Engaging with graduate attributes through encouraging accurate student self-assessment." *Asian Social Science* 8 (4): 1–12.

Lawson, R. 2015. "Curriculum design for assuring learning – leading the way." *OLT National Teaching Fellowship Final Report*. Sydney, Australia: Office for Learning and Teaching. www.olt.gov.au/resource-curriculum-design-assuring-learning-leading-way-2015.

McDowell, L. 2006. "Assessment for learning." *Assessment Working Group, 14 November*, Teesside University, UK. Accessed 27 November 2014. http://nrl.northumbria.ac.uk/1325/.

Marton, F., and R. Saljo. 1976. "On qualitative differences in learning: I – outcome and process." *British Journal of Educational Psychology* 46 (1): 4–11.

Price, M., B. O'Donovan, C. Rust, and J. Carroll. 2008. "Assessment standards: a manifesto for change." *Brookes eJournal of Learning and Teaching* 2 (3). Accessed 19 February 2017. http://bejlt.brookes.ac.uk/paper/assessment_standards_a_manifesto_for_change-2/.

Ramsden, P. 1992. *Learning to Teach in Higher Education.* London: Routledge.

Sadler, D. R. 2005. "Interpretations of criteria-based assessment and grading in higher education." *Assessment & Evaluation in Higher Education* 30 (2): 175–194. doi:10.1080/0260293042000264262.

TEQSA (Tertiary Education Quality and Standards Agency). 2015. *Higher Education Standards Framework.* Canberra, Australia: Australian Government. www.teqsa.gov.au/teqsa-contextual-overview-hes-framework.

Thompson, D. G., and I. M. McGregor. 2009. "Online self- and peer assessment for groupwork." *Education & Training* 51 (5/6): 434–447.

Thompson, D. G. 2009. "Successful engagement in graduate attribute assessment using software." *Campus-Wide Information Systems* 26 (5): 400–412.

Thompson, D. G. 2016. "Marks should not be the focus of assessment – but how can change be achieved?" *Journal of Learning Analytics* 3 (2): 193–212. doi:10.18608/jla.2016.32.9.

UTS (University of Technology, Sydney). "Graduate attribute animated explanation for students." YouTube video, 1:38. Posted May 2013. https://youtu.be/_SBZOi5G21A.

SECTION 4

Evaluative judgement for practice and work

CHAPTER **15**

Prefigurement, identities and agency: the disciplinary nature of evaluative judgement

Margaret Bearman

> Evaluative judgments play an important role in everyday activities. They represent a central component of any choice process, because the decision-maker has to evaluate alternatives, attributes . . . Evaluative judgments, however, are not restricted to decision-making. They are made in the context of personal preferences (I like this wine) or religious, aesthetic, social, or other values or in connection with attitudes. . . .
>
> (Zysset et al. 2002, 938)

The process of evaluative judgement may be part of everyday life from a neuroscience perspective (Zysset et al. 2002), but that does not mean that evaluative judgement itself is a generic skill. Complex appraisals of everyday experiences – such as drinking wine, eating cheese or critiquing art – take place routinely in many people's lives, but none of these are context-free processes. Wine-tasting is clearly not the same as discussing the merits of contemporary painting. In other words, evaluative judgement is inextricably related to a particular domain. Notions of quality and associated evaluative judgements in higher education are likewise not domain-free. In this chapter, "evaluative judgement" is considered to be the construct underpinning a range of learning tasks, which ask students to make judgements about the quality of work. These learning tasks are most frequently formative and summative assessments. They require evaluative judgement to be exercised through students applying rubrics or criteria to their own and others' work. As Ajjawi et al. note (Chapter 1), evaluative judgement is not a "generic" professional skill of the sort sometimes conceptualised as a graduate attribute. This makes sense at a surface level, but what are the implications of this for assessment?

Assessment design is also not generic. At one level, this is self-evident. The sciences have customarily held examinations; the humanities have a tradition of setting essays. However, these assessments may also be operating at another, deeper disciplinary level, as indicated by recent publications, including Carless' (2015) study of expert educator assessments and Bearman et al.'s (2017) study of how university teachers design assessment. These studies suggest that, for educators, a tacit purpose of assessment may be to introduce a sense of the discipline or profession. For example, a history lecturer discusses his assessment task: '"It's an attempt to give students an opportunity to showcase their abilities; master the discourse of history; see the past is alive and that participants are reshaping it; and *see themselves as historians*"' (Carless 2015, 969, emphasis mine). Likewise, a lecturer describes their assessment requirements: . . . because *journalism being journalism*, deadlines are vital. So we don't give extensions. Unless a meteorite's fallen on their house or they're carried off to hospital in an ambulance" (Bearman et al. 2017, 56, emphasis mine). These quotes illustrate the entangled nature of disciplinary identity and assessment design. They also raise the question: what is the relationship between disciplinary identity and the discipline-specific nature of evaluative judgements in assessments?

This chapter explores the intersections between notions of disciplinary assessments, evaluative judgement and identity formation. It introduces the concept of signature pedagogy (Shulman 2005), and considers what can be learnt from this work with respect to the disciplinary nature of evaluative judgement in assessments. Extending these ideas further, Holland et al.'s (1998) work on identity and agency is used to explore some of the implications surrounding the act of evaluative judgement for both students and assessors. Finally, these theoretical notions are drawn together into a series of practical suggestions for assessment design.

Habits of mind, heart and hand

Shulman's exploration of signature pedagogies (2005) is possibly the best-known conceptualisation of disciplinary teaching in higher education. His work focused on programmes that lead to professional qualifications, such as law, medicine and teaching degrees. Shulman suggests that specific pedagogies are particular to individual professions. This makes intuitive sense: a teaching approach such as the mock trial or moot is a signature pedagogy of law, while bedside teaching is a signature pedagogy of medicine. Shulman (2005, 59) goes further and suggests that such signature pedagogies "form habits of the mind, habits of the heart, and habits of the hand".

Shulman (2005) identifies three dimensions to a signature pedagogy: *surface structures*, or the operational genres including assessments; *deep structures*, which include how to communicate tacit knowledge and know-how; and *implicit structures*, which are the core values or morals of the profession. The latter is a slippery concept, partly because its manifestations are often very implicit. To give Shulman's (2005, p. 55) illustration of an implicit pedagogical structure: in the United States, law students may be told that they are "there to learn the law, not to learn what [is] fair".

Shulman's original work is based on professional courses. Ideas of interwoven learning and "becoming" are most often associated with professional practice (e.g., Dall'Alba 2009) rather than disciplinary learning. For the purposes of this discussion, I take disciplines and professions to be more similar than different from the perspective of assessment design. That is to say, while the students may be undertaking an arts course, the teachers sees themselves as historians or journalists or linguists, and it is this understanding that drives assessment design (Bearman et al. 2017).

Shulman (2005) notes that not every pedagogical approach is a signature pedagogy, and it may be inferred that not every discipline has a particular signature pedagogy with particular associated evaluative judgements. This is not the value of Shulman's work to this discussion. Rather, Shulman's underpinning concepts of the relationship between a pedagogy and a profession may illuminate how we think about evaluative judgements.

Applying signature pedagogy dimensions to evaluative judgement

The connections between signature pedagogies and evaluative judgement have been noted within the literature, particularly within the arts and design disciplines. Most notably, the 2016 edition of *Arts and Humanities in Higher Education* explores the role of "critique" in the arts and humanities, and its relationship to signature pedagogies (Motley et al. 2016). The editors provide the following commentary on the issue:

> Essentially the 'rubric' becomes a living thing for students. The mystery is removed as the criteria for good or bad are debated live during the session . . . To me, it makes it all visible. Students understand why something works or doesn't. They receive multiple views from peers and instructor. And yes, there's surely a community and social dynamic: students have to communicate and even defend their assertions to others. . . . Critique is one way students learn the disciplinary frameworks—one of the requirements of expertise.
>
> (Motley et al. 2016, 4)

It is clear here that "critique" is strongly related to the phenomenon I am calling "evaluative judgement". More than this, "critique" is seen to have a strongly disciplinary form.

Applying Shulman's original dimensions to our understanding of evaluative judgement is revelatory. As previously discussed, if evaluative judgements are inextricably linked to a particular discipline, then making an evaluative judgement also engages the discipline's *surface structures* (or external markers of quality, such as might be captured in a rubric), *deep structures* (tacit understandings about what quality might mean within the discipline) and *implicit structures* (how the notion of quality reflects the core values of the discipline). Thus, for an architect student to make appropriate evaluative judgements regarding the merit of architectural drawings, that student must be able to understand quality from the standpoint of an *architect*, not a draftsperson or an engineer. With that understanding comes deeper knowledge of an architect's concerns, traditions and values.

These dimensions, which underpin signature pedagogies, illustrate how making evaluative judgements may both explicitly and implicitly guide students to a notion of disciplinary quality. In other words, learning to make evaluative judgements "prefigures" a discipline, to use Shulman's terminology (2005). Through learning to make judgements about the quality of their own and others' work, novices come to understand surface, deep and implicit structures – the higher-order and practical notions that do (or don't) underpin disciplinary practice. To provide a concrete example, if a chemistry student can identify what constitutes a well-written laboratory report against a sloppy laboratory report, this gives the student an understanding of: how scientific language works (surface); what makes "good" and "bad" lab reports (deep); and what constitutes a "good" or "bad" chemist (implicit). At a surface level, the student can identify and therefore come to know rules of lab reports. At a deep level, the student can identify the value of meticulous and accurate reporting. At an implicit level, the student comes to understand some of the values of being a chemist: that experimentation is a disciplinary foundation, and that beliefs, intentions and desires are less important than empirical facts. In short, identifying the merits of a piece of work is far more than a cognitive notion of quality.

Shulman (2005) notes that habits of mind, heart and hand are neither always stable nor always productive. For example, 50 years ago, a doctor might have considered it quality practice to withhold information from a patient. While this is a crude example, it suggests how evaluative judgements can, in certain instances, build implicit structures that are not desirable. Making evaluative judgements does not take place in a vacuum. Disciplines are complex social constructions and as educators we need to take account of this. Considering disciplinary values takes this chapter to more complex territory: a theoretical examination of social construction of identity, its relationship to agency and its relevance to evaluative judgement.

Identity, agency and evaluative judgement

Many different ways of theorising identity formation can be seen within the higher education literature (Trede et al. 2012). For the rest of this discussion, I will draw from Holland et al.'s 1998 work on identity formation, sometimes referred to as "figured worlds" (e.g., Bennett et al. 2017). Like many other theories of identity formation used in higher education, figured worlds is a practice theory. The work is eclectic, drawing from diverse theorists such as Vygotsky, Bourdieu and Bakhtin. It is particularly useful because its core concerns are *agency* and *identity*, and the inter-relationship between the two. Agency is particularly pertinent to this chapter as providing evaluative judgement opportunities is fundamentally a learner-centred pedagogy. Moreover, thinking about agency provides a counter to the dangers of the "habitual" undertakings of a profession or discipline.

There are four contexts to identity formation within the theoretical framework of figured worlds. The first is the "figured world" itself – that is, the imagined and idealised stories of a cultural identity, which individuals align with, or depart from, as their identities shift and change. The second context is "positionality", which draws from the relative status and power of individuals within these cultural identities. The third is the "space of authoring", which is both personal and public, as individuals "self-author" or improvise individual histories across these cultural traditions. The final context is that of "making worlds", which is the considerations of social play – to develop "new social competencies in newly imagined communities" (Holland et al. 1998, 272). Taken together, this theory suggests identities are multiple, shifting and continually constructed through individual and social improvisation within cultural traditions. Developing evaluative judgement can be seen as an opportunity for a student to learn to improvise within the constraints of the figured world. It is worth exploring these concepts a little further.

Signature pedagogies and figured worlds share an important concept: prefigurement. This is the notion that pre-existing stories, traditions and hierarchies (including pedagogies) foreshadow a particular sociocultural landscape. Thus, asking students to make evaluative judgements within a discipline is not neutral. By inducting the learner into notions of quality – with its necessary emphasis on "good" and "bad" practice – educators are also providing them with passage into professional narratives and hierarchies. Students will align to a greater or lesser degree with these figured worlds of the discipline or profession, partly through learning to "talk the talk" (Holland et al. 1998).

The use of language is particularly noteworthy as engagement with the language of the discipline is a key feature of making evaluative judgements. As Bakhtin notes: "All words have the 'taste' of the profession, a genre, a tendency . . ." (Bakhtin 1981, cited in Holland et al. 1998, 171). Assessments by their nature introduce the language of the discipline, whether it be history or chemistry or accounting. Engaging with the language of quality, which is required for making evaluative judgements, is complex. These words carry the burden of implicit value: useful/worthless, important/peripheral, good/bad. Articulating and applying notions of quality to work requires the student to position others and themselves within the figured world of the discipline. This echoes the positionality of assessment: a student who writes an essay that is judged "excellent" or "outstanding" is necessarily positioned differently within the discipline than those whose work is "poor" or "below standards". The higher-performing student has opportunities that come with their status; the "failing" student will not be able to continue with the course as planned and is marginalised from the discipline. By making evaluative judgements, the students are learning about the disciplinary hierarchy and also gaining a sense of their own position within it.

In summary, prefigurement and positionality suggest that an assessment, with associated evaluative judgements, is an influential contributor to identity formation through providing access to the traditions and hierarchies of the discipline. This comes to somewhat the same point as Shulman's emphasis on habits of mind, heart and hand, albeit with more emphasis on language and social capital. However, the figured world and associated positionality is only one part of the figured world equation. The other part is concerned with agency. The students, both individual and collective, author their own histories, which are co-produced by their interactions with the diverse figured worlds.

Agency is the necessary twin to identity: we want professionals who can raise the bar on what constitutes quality practice in a changing world. As with any participation in a cultural setting, students come to their assessment task with their own agencies, derived from their prior histories, and their own ways of engaging with the activity. Self-authoring can be seen as a pervasive, constant and essential part of living. Holland et al. (1998, 272, emphasis mine) write: "... authorship is a matter of orchestration: of arranging the identifiable social discourses/practices that are one's resources . . . in order to *craft a response in a time and space defined by others' standpoints in activity* . . .". The act of making an evaluative judgement is necessarily defined by others' "standpoints" – whether it be through the criteria that are written in the rubric, or through the social interaction of others' judgements. But at the same time, the student will be bringing a range of their resources to bear on this moment. Indeed, evaluative judgement's strength is its capacity to promote independent, agentic practice. We want professionals who will be able to appropriately make calls that may not be popular, or possibly against disciplinary tradition, when there is good reason to do so. This is the promise of evaluative judgement activities: that they explicitly allow the student to navigate their own way through holistic and tacit notions of quality.

The theoretical framework provided by figured worlds underlines the value of making an evaluative judgement. Making evaluative judgements requires assessing the value of one's work; with this comes positionality. As students engage with the act of evaluative judgement – such as critiquing other's designs, using a rubric to mark another's laboratory report, self-assessing their own history essay against criteria – they will be extending their practices "to operate in such a diverse yet powerful social universe" (Holland et al. 1998, 272). These assessment designs afford identity formation within a particular discipline or profession; however, the student themselves, in their constant work of self-authoring, may individually or collectively interpret or even re-imagine the disciplinary world in light of their own experiences.

Implications for assessment

This exploration of the disciplinary nature of evaluative judgement leads to the following surmises. First, when a teacher designs assessments and learning tasks, they do so as a tacit – and sometimes explicit – induction into the discipline. Second, when a student makes an evaluative judgement as part of these learning tasks, they are entering into a disciplinary space with the surface, deep and implicit layers discussed by Shulman. Next, the whole process of making an evaluative judgement as part of an assessment may be viewed as a piece in the broader landscape of identity formation, whereby students are constantly and agentically co-producing their identities between and across a variety of figured worlds. The figured world of the discipline – with its language, its traditions (pedagogical or otherwise) and its hierarchies – is made accessible to the student through engaging with the assessment task. Finally, making evaluative judgements allows the student to recognise and contest markers of worth, and hence both understand and contest the language of positionality within a discipline.

Why does all of this matter? The take-home message is that asking students to make evaluative judgements is not generic or neutral. As academics, we should be mindful of the broader cultural domain which we inhabit and which we must therefore always share with our students, through our language as well as our ideas. This has implications for assessment design and student support.

At the start of this chapter I suggested that, even at an "everyday" level, making an evaluative judgement requires an understanding of notions of quality within a particular domain. This examination of signature pedagogies and figured worlds suggests that a notion of quality is more than the "surface" structure of the task content; it also derives from deep and implicit structures which underpin the discipline. The practical implication is that evaluative judgements should be sought about work arising from activities central to the discipline – that is, "authentic assessment". At a simple level, these are those tasks that bear resemblance to a real practice environment and therefore appear relevant and meaningful to students (Gulikers et al. 2004). Work produced through completing these tasks is ideal for learning rich, holistic understandings of practice. Extending tasks to include making evaluative judgements will develop learners' nascent grasp of disciplinary quality and hence disciplinary identity.

As mentioned previously, identity is only one part of the equation; evaluative judgement tasks can be deliberately designed to develop students' agencies. An alternate definition of "authentic assessment" is useful: those tasks that allow students "an opportunity to become who they endeavour to be" (Vu and Dall'Alba 2014, 797). As noted by Vu and Dall'Alba, this type of assessment may assist in overturning assumptions; but it requires a supportive environment, with the appropriate resources of time and space to conduct the necessary "meaning making", which may include rejection of disciplinary assumptions and habits. Figured worlds suggest that there is value in a social interaction around overturning assumptions and habits, and that social play is one way that hierarchies can be changed. The assessment design and associated evaluative judgement should, therefore, deliberately give opportunities for the student to critically examine the disciplinary norms. This may involve specific tasks around markers of quality such as co-production, critique or application of multiple criteria.

Presenting opportunities for evaluative judgement may offer the teacher the opportunity to role-model reflexivity. That is, in considering how students will engage with notions of quality within the discipline, it may be worth teachers reflecting on how designing the task affects their own practice. If these musings are made explicit to students, then teachers can model a deeper understanding of the discipline, as well as the type of professional behaviours that we would wish for our graduates.

Thus far, the implications have focused on the work of the educator. What about the student? From a student perspective, it is important to remember the strengths and limitations of their notions of quality. It would not be fair or reasonable for students to believe that evaluative judgement is transferable – that the capacity to make good judgements in one environment may transfer to another discipline. However, the processes around co-producing such judgements may be more general to professional working: tools such as reflexive engagement with the "habits of heart, mind and hand", surfacing notions of quality and recognising the embedded nature of education. These critical thinking tools perhaps represent the "figured world" of our own academic practice and, through our educational designs, we are inviting students to participate within it.

Conclusions

This chapter suggests that making evaluative judgements in higher education is inextricably tied to the academic discipline of the assessment. Making evaluative judgements is linked to a holistic and tacit understanding of the discipline, including its stories, hierarchies and values; it supports students' development of disciplinary identity. However, students also bring individual and social self-authorship to this task and may align, alter or re-imagine the discipline. I regard this agentic approach to understanding disciplinary quality as a positive enabler of independent professional practice. There are many practical ways to promote agentic engagement with evaluative judgements – for example co-production of criteria and teachers role-modelling reflexivity. It may be that these types of approaches to teaching represent the figured world of our own discipline of higher education.

References

Bearman, M., P. Dawson, S. Bennett, M. Hall, E. Molloy, D. Boud, and G. Joughin. 2017. "How university teachers design assessments: a cross-disciplinary study." *Higher Education* 74 (1): 49–64. doi:10.1007/s10734–016–0027–7.

Bennett, D., Y. Solomon, C. Bergin, M. Horgan, and T. Dornan. 2017. "Possibility and agency in figured worlds: becoming a 'good doctor'." *Medical Education* 51 (3): 248–257. doi:10.1111/medu.13220.

Carless, D. 2015. "Exploring learning-oriented assessment processes." *Higher Education* 69 (6): 963–976. doi:10.1007/s10734–014–9816-z.

Dall'Alba, G. 2009. "Learning professional ways of being: ambiguities of becoming." *Educational Philosophy and Theory* 41 (1): 34–45. doi:10.1111/j.1469–5812.2008.00475.x.

Gulikers, J. T. M., T. J. Bastiaens, and P. A. Kirschner. 2004. "A five-dimensional framework for authentic assessment." *Educational Technology Research and Development* 52 (3): 67. doi:10.1007/bf02504676.

Holland, D., W. J. Lachiocotte, D. Skinner, and C. Cain. 1998. *Identity and Agency in Cultural Worlds.* Cambridge, MA: Harvard University Press.

Motley, P., N. L. Chick, and E. Hipchen. 2016. "A conversation about critique as a signature pedagogy in the arts and humanities." *Arts and Humanities in Higher Education* 16 (3): 223–228. doi:10.1177/1474022216652773.

Shulman, L. S. 2005. "Signature pedagogies in the professions." *Daedalus* 134 (3): 52–59. doi:10.1162/0011526054622015.

Trede, F., R. Macklin, and D. Bridges. 2012. "Professional identity development: a review of the higher education literature." *Studies in Higher Education* 37 (3): 365–384. doi:10.1080/03075079.2010.521237.

Vu, T. T., and G. Dall'Alba. 2014. "Authentic assessment for student learning: an ontological conceptualisation." *Educational Philosophy and Theory* 46 (7): 778–791. doi:10.1080/00131857.2013.795110.

Zysset, S., O. Huber, E. Ferstl, and D. Y. von Cramon. 2002. "The anterior frontomedian cortex and evaluative judgment: an fMRI study." *NeuroImage* 15 (4): 983–991. doi:10.1006/nimg.2001.1008.

CHAPTER **16**

The role of peers in developing evaluative judgement

Joanna Tai and Samantha Sevenhuysen

Peer-assisted learning (PAL) is defined as "[p]eople from similar social groups, who are not professional teachers, helping each other to learn and by so doing, learning themselves" (Topping and Ehly 1998, 1). PAL has been shown to equal educator instruction within health professions education, especially in the classroom, where basic sciences and anatomy are taught (Santee and Garavalia 2006; Secomb 2008). PAL can also contribute to gains in students' practical knowledge and skill (Burgess et al. 2014; Yu et al. 2011). There has been a longstanding focus on the accuracy of peer assessment (Speyer et al. 2011; Falchikov and Boud 1989). However, PAL also has a role to play in enhancing learning and developing students' capacity to make reasonable judgements of their own and others work, also known as "evaluative judgement" (Tai et al. 2016).

In this chapter, we review the literature with respect to types of PAL and settings which contribute to the development of students' evaluative judgement within higher education. We then present two case studies from our own research and practice, which more closely detail the circumstances by which forms of PAL can contribute to students' development of evaluative judgement.

Types of PAL that contribute to developing evaluative judgement

The literature on PAL infrequently uses the term "evaluative judgement"; nevertheless, there is a body of literature which describes how PAL is used to help students come to understand quality work. Though it is likely that evaluative judgement can be developed through many PAL activities in a range of settings, evidence falls largely into the categories of peer discussion, peer observation, and peer assessment (encompassing the close synonyms review, evaluation, and feedback). Peer discussion might vary in format from face-to-face interactions to online asynchronous discussion. It involves students co-constructing their understandings of a particular task, assignment or other piece of work, both in terms of the product and what the standards are for the production of that work. Peer observation refers to a student actively scrutinising a peer's work or performance of a task to discern its constituents and elements of quality. Peer assessments involve a judgement being made on a piece of work or task, with the potential for feedback and/or the return of a mark, derived through application of criteria. All of these activities require interaction with and application of criteria; that is, allowing students to practise making evaluative judgements, and therefore helping them to develop their evaluative judgement. To understand which types of PAL may be most appropriate in different environments, we group evidence into three settings: classroom, practical, and simulation.

Classroom

In-class PAL that contributes to evaluative judgement mostly involves peer discussion or assessment of work – whether it be students' own work or exemplars from a previous class. In these cases, there is an explicit intention for students to transfer the learning from that activity to a later piece of work which students must produce (To and Carless 2015; Nicol 2014; Wimshurst and Manning 2012). The incorporation of in-class exemplar analysis and peer feedback into an assignment preparation activity is discussed by Carless et al. (Chapter 11). Peer-to-peer teaching may include elements of feedback-giving and assessing others. A recent review of peer-to-peer and reciprocal teaching by Stigmar (2016) covered studies published from 2010 to 2013. Stigmar concluded that this form of PAL contributed to the development of "generic skills" such as providing feedback, along with critical thinking, self-regulation, increased student participation and engagement with the materials. Increased academic performance was not detected in the quasi-experimental studies included in this review. Included study designs focused on improvement in scores, which were unlikely to indicate an improvement in evaluative judgement; however, findings on improved critical thinking and self-regulation may hint at developing evaluative judgement, given the link argued by Panadero and Broadbent (Chapter 8).

Practical

Practical learning environments are frequently used to provide authentic learning experiences for students in environments that they are likely to work in one day. These may occur within university settings (e.g., science laboratory) or real workplaces (e.g., school placements for initial teacher education). Of course, PAL is only likely to occur where there is more than one student attached to a placement. Lamb (2015) implemented reciprocal peer review, observation and feedback in teacher training, where students developed their ability to critique and improve lesson plans through working with their peers.

A significant body of work on the benefits of PAL within health professions education exists. The clinical placement affords a variety of learning situations, including peer observation, peer feedback, peer assessment and peer discussion. Medical and allied health students have been placed in pairs or groups on wards for many years (Ladyshewsky 1995; Sevenhuysen et al. 2017). Within clinical medical education, students have reported that, through engaging in peer assessment and/or feedback activities, they were able to make judgements on the quality of others' work, thereby gaining a better understanding of quality (Burgess et al. 2013). Explicit criteria also helped the students to develop this ability (Bennett et al. 2012).

Simulation

Simulated settings can bridge the gap between classroom and practical or clinical learning, and may provide a safer learning environment. Again, simulation-based education frequently occurs in healthcare settings, and peer observation has been suggested to optimise learning (O'Regan et al. 2016). Facilitator-guided debriefings commonly contain feedback from co-participants, who are likely to be peers. More recently, scaffolded or guided peer observation has also been included, using a checklist or scoring sheet to attune students to indicators of quality (Stegmann et al. 2012; Livsey and Lavender-Stott 2015). In both of these studies, students who had an opportunity to observe and score their peers' performance performed better than those who did not have the same opportunity. This scaffolded peer observation, or vicarious learning, is likely contributing to students' understandings of quality through exposure to explicit forms of standards and the requirement to apply those standards. The experience therefore enables students to perform similar tasks at a higher standard than those who have not had the opportunity to observe a peer's performance.

We now present two case studies where interactions with peers, or peer learning, have contributed to the development of evaluative judgement. The first case identifies how informal peer learning opportunities for same-level peers in a clinical setting develops evaluative judgement. The second case contrasts formal opportunities for PAL.

Case study 1: informal peer learning

This case study is drawn from an investigation of PAL in undergraduate clinical medical education. The student participants were in their first clinical year, after spending two years in classroom-based, on-campus learning environments. In these prior years, students participated in various forms of PAL with weekly problem-based learning tutorials and clinical skills tutorials, including working with peers and providing formative feedback on performance. Students were encouraged to form peer study groups, both within the same year level and with students in other levels. Thus, students were already attuned to the idea of learning with and from each other, rather than solely from tutors and lecturers. However, the clinical environment is different from the structured on-campus classroom: instruction is much less direct; there is an expectation that students will be self-directed in learning; and the responsibility for students is shared among teams of doctors, whose primary concern is patient care. The transition to this type of learning environment can be difficult (see Rees et al., Chapter 18), for a description in the postgraduate environment). It was hypothesised that PAL might assist in easing the transition by providing psychological support and shared learning opportunities.

Mixed methods were used to examine the role of PAL within this setting. Students were surveyed about the benefits of types of PAL activities, while observations and reflective interviews aimed to capture where and how PAL was used, along with the benefits of PAL. Within this setting, informal PAL interactions contributed to two elements of developing evaluative judgement: "understanding notions of quality" and "making comparisons".

Understanding notions of quality

The vicarious observation of peers performing tasks helped students to understand notions of quality. This occurred within group tutorials:

> I try and concentrate on the person whose turn it is, and then so I can also see the feedback they get. There were some really good tips that I sort of noticed from someone else doing it, and then them getting feedback that I could apply to my own performance that day. – Interview participant

By attending to their peers' performance and subsequent feedback, students received with further information points which they could integrate into their understanding of what quality is. Receiving feedback from peers in a PAL feedback activity was also helpful to confirm students' understandings of quality:

> Very useful in knowing where I was going wrong and also reinforcing what I was doing right. – Anonymous survey

> Peers tend to give good critique in terms of mistakes and what was forgotten. – Anonymous survey

Students are here referring to having a peer observe their performance on a task (such as taking a history from a patient), and receiving feedback from that peer on their performance. The requirements for such tasks were usually not made explicit in the form of a checklist. Though there is typically professional consensus as to what a patient history or examination should contain, the expected level of performance for a junior medical student is less well-defined. Consequently, discussion and comparison between students was seen as useful for individuals to establish what these standards might be.

Forming judgements about quality: making comparisons

Students were also required to form judgements about quality by making comparisons in relation to the standards in PAL. This was achieved through discussing, observing, comparing, giving and receiving feedback on their performance.

Students reported that, in addition to making a decision about a performance, they had to articulate that decision in the form of feedback.

> Makes you think about what you would do, and you have to give [a] proper rationale as well. – Anonymous survey

> Gave me an idea of what being an examiner is like and what they look for. – Anonymous survey

Students were particularly focused on replicating examination conditions and thus took on perceived standards for their end-of-year examination. Through judgement-making, students became more familiar with the criteria, and therefore had a better understanding of standards. This facilitated their ability to self-monitor in subsequent situations. At the conclusion of the year, the students reflected on their improved evaluative judgement:

> At the start, it's difficult, mostly with trying to think of something positive, trying to think of something how to improve. But now, it's a lot easier, because we know [the subject matter] a lot better ourselves. – Interview participant

In this case study, informal PAL was found to be a useful resource. Formal PAL opportunities were also observed during the study, and reported by students as contributing to the development of evaluative judgement. Informal PAL was situated within a broader framework of activities designed to build judgement, which also included self-evaluation and expert feedback against (and modelling of) the standards of practice. Case Study 2 now exemplifies some formal instruments that can be incorporated within a practical setting.

Case study 2: formal peer learning

This case study is drawn from a randomised, controlled trial conducted with physiotherapy students undertaking five-week rotations. Students were placed in pairs for two rotations: one in a traditional educator-led model, and the other in a facilitated PAL model. The placement was evaluated both quantitatively (performance measures and daily activity statistics) and qualitatively (surveys and focus groups) (see Sevenhuysen et al. 2014; Sevenhuysen et al. 2015 for further details).

Although paired student placement models have been evaluated in clinical education, previous research has focused on qualitative review and/or comparison to the 1:1 student-to-educator model. The specific aim of this research was to evaluate the impact of deliberate facilitation of PAL *within* the paired student placement model, compared with an educator-led paired model. A range of standardised PAL activities were implemented within the PAL placement: peer observation (utilising a structured tool to record observations); verbal and written peer feedback; and structured peer collaboration on tasks using the SNAPPS (Wolpaw et al. 2003) and Complexity Risk Matrix (Kneebone et al. 2007) tools. In addition, students undertook typical learning activities such as involvement in patient care, team meetings, tutorials and administration.

Daily activity statistics demonstrated that the structured PAL placement increased the frequency of PAL activities such as peer observation, feedback and assessment – which may influence development of evaluative judgement – compared to the educator-led placement. Students and educators reported that the structured placement provided a framework for PAL to occur which "forced" students to observe and give feedback to their peers.

> We got used to giving each other feedback and now we still do that even though we don't have to. I guess we had to give feedback in the beginning. So I guess sometimes you might think you don't want to tell them, offend them but because we had to in the beginning now we just keep giving each other feedback. – Student, focus group

> I think it [the PAL model] pushed them to reflect more on each individual experience . . . they were forced to think about what they were doing and why, what they did well or not so well. – Clinical educator, focus group

The structure of the formal PAL model meant that students were required to make judgements about the quality of each other's performance in order to give feedback. The requirement to perform this activity may help to initiate, and enable further development of, evaluative judgement capacity. It may also help to establish positive habits for the future as students become more comfortable with these activities. The requirement for students to observe and appraise the quality of each other's work meant that students spent more time reflecting on the detail of aspects of their own performance, which has the capacity to positively influence the development of evaluative judgement skills.

Clinical educators reported that students' abilities to make judgements and deliver feedback improved throughout the PAL placement:

> I think [the students'] ability to give feedback to each other improved in the PAL model. That has to be an advantage. Feedback from week 1 certainly was much different to week 5. – Clinical educator, survey

Students reported that PAL was particularly beneficial early in the placement, while their (clinical and evaluative judgement) skills were rapidly developing.

> I felt like I learnt a lot from [my peer] in the beginning. In the beginning she would watch me, you know you're doing a lot of things wrong because it's the first time you've done it. You're doing so much stuff and can't pick up everything. Having her watch me and let me know, it would make me realise yeah, that was something I did wrong. – Student, focus group

> At the beginning it was useful to see how my partner was doing and being able to compare to my own performance. Also beneficial to see how the supervisor felt my partner went. – Student, survey

Providing a structured framework for PAL activities that may contribute to evaluative judgement may initiate the development of these skills early in the placement. The requirement of students to provide each other with feedback and collaborate on tasks influenced their ability to make judgements of the quality of their own performance and that of their peers.

Discussion and summary

PAL is a key process by which students' evaluative judgement can be developed in a range of learning situations, from the classroom to practical settings. PAL activities which particularly contribute to the development of evaluative judgement include peer discussion of work, peer observation, and peer assessment and feedback. Other chapters in this volume (Rees et al., Chapter 18; Carless et al., Chapter 11) also demonstrate the value of peer learning in both classroom and workplace settings.

PAL occurs to varying degrees when students are learning alongside one another, and a difference between informal and formal PAL has been identified (Henning et al. 2008). Informal PAL occurs due to the presence of a peer and results in opportunities for sharing ideas and practical skills. Formal PAL refers to specific teaching activities assigned to the pair or student group. Case study 1 identified which informal PAL activities contributed to the development of evaluative judgement. Case study 2 then described the facilitated and structured PAL activities which can foster students' positive peer learning behaviours. It is currently unclear which activities – formal or informal – might develop students' evaluative judgement more effectively, or if there are other unintended consequences of these types of PAL. Drawing from the literature and case studies, further suggested activities are detailed in Table 16.1. The common feature across these activities is that students are working with other students and participating directly in activities which require them to interact with standards and/or criteria, allowing them to practise using their evaluative judgement.

To successfully participate in PAL, students require other skills, including teamwork, communication and interpersonal skills. Depending on prior exposure to PAL, students may need support, development and structure to maximise the benefits of this learning approach. This could range from overarching guidance at the beginning of a course, unit or module to worksheets, timetabled activities and educator-led sessions as seen in case study 2.

The effect of PAL on skill development is likely to be influenced by many factors, including how peer-assisted learning is actively facilitated, the readiness of learners to engage, and how the environment enables peer collaboration (Boud 1999). "Experts" can also provide a benchmark against which students can evaluate their own performance and the performance of others, contributing to the

Table 16.1 Suggested PAL activities to develop students' evaluative judgement

PAL typology	*Setting*	*Example activities*
Peer review	Classroom	Students review exemplars prior to completing a similar task to discuss standards of work and elements of quality Students review final work (group or individual task) and make qualitative judgements against standards
Peer review with feedback	Classroom	Students review others' work, then make a judgement and provide feedback that can be incorporated into a future version of the task. Concomitant self-assessment may also identify focus for improvement
Peer observation and feedback	Practical/ Simulation	Student peers observe one another completing practical tasks and provide feedback against performance (may be enhanced with the use of criteria/tools/checklists) – e.g., teaching a lesson (education), taking a medical history from a patient (health professions), dissecting a specimen (science), constructing an argument (arts/law)
Peer discussion	Any	Students discuss an experience or performance. This provides additional information to peers on what standards might be expected for a given task. Discussion should be directed towards comparison of experiences, and strategies or elements which could be incorporated in the future

performance improvement cycle. Furthermore, self-assessment must be inherent in the PAL process: students are unlikely to be able to identify their foci for improvement, in order to make comparisons with peers and standards, without some self-assessment.

In this chapter, we have identified empirical work which suggests that PAL contributes to evaluative judgement, and illustrated this link through two case studies. Further work is required to understand in more detail which PAL activities most contribute to developing students' evaluative judgement, and in which settings certain activities are most successful.

References

Bennett, D., M. Kelly, and S. O'Flynn. 2012. "Framework for feedback: the peer mini-clinical examination as a formative assessment tool." *Medical Education* 46 (5): 501. doi:10.1111/j.1365–2923.2012.04234.x.

Boud, D. 1999. "Situating academic development in professional work: using peer learning." *The International Journal for Academic Development* 4 (1): 3–10.

Burgess, A., D. McGregor, and C. Mellis. 2014. "Medical students as peer tutors: a systematic review." *BMC Medical Education* 14 (1): 115. doi:10.1186/1472–6920–14–115.

Burgess, A., C. Roberts, K. I. Black, and C. Mellis. 2013. "Senior medical student perceived ability and experience in giving peer feedback in formative long case examinations." *BMC Medical Education* 13 (1): 79. doi:10.1186/1472–6920–13–79.

Falchikov, N., and D. Boud. 1989. "Student self-assessment in higher education: a meta-analysis." *Review of Educational Research* 59 (4): 395–430.

Henning, J. M., T. G. Weidner, and M. C. Marty. 2008. "Peer assisted learning in clinical education: literature review." *Athletic Training Education Journal* 3 (3): 84–90.

Kneebone, R. L., D. Nestel, C. Vincent, and A. Darzi. 2007. "Complexity, risk and simulation in learning procedural skills." *Medical Education* 41 (8): 808–814. doi:10.1111/j.1365–2923.2007.02799.x.

Ladyshewsky, R. K. 1995. "Enhancing service productivity in acute care inpatient settings using a collaborative clinical education model." *Physical Therapy* 75 (6): 503–510.

Lamb, P. 2015. "Peer-learning between pre-service teachers: embracing lesson study." *International Journal for Lesson and Learning Studies* 4 (4): 343–361. doi:10.1108/IJLLS-03–2015–0012.

Livsey, K., and E. Lavender-Stott. 2015. "Impact of vicarious learning through peer observation during simulation on student behavioural measures." *Focus on Health Professional Education: A Multi-Disciplinary Journal* 16 (4): 64–73.

Nicol, D. 2014. "Guiding principles for peer review: unlocking learners' evaluative skills." In *Advances and Innovations in University Assessment and Feedback*, edited by C. Kreber, C. Anderson, N. Entwistle, and J. McArthur, 197–224. Edinburgh, Scotland: Edinburgh University Press.

O'Regan, S., E. Molloy, L. Watterson, and D. Nestel. 2016. "Observer roles that optimise learning in healthcare simulation education: a systematic review." *Advances in Simulation* 1 (1): 4. doi:10.1186/s41077–015–0004–8.

Santee, J., and L. Garavalia. 2006. "Peer tutoring programs in health professions schools." *American Journal of Pharmaceutical Education* 70 (3): article 70.

Secomb, J. 2008. "A systematic review of peer teaching and learning in clinical education." *Journal of Clinical Nursing* 17 (6): 703–716. doi:10.1111/j.1365–2702.2007.01954.x.

Sevenhuysen, S., M. K. Farlie, J. L. Keating, T. P. Haines, and E. Molloy. 2015. "Physiotherapy students and clinical educators perceive several ways in which incorporating peer-assisted learning could improve clinical placements: a qualitative study." *Journal of Physiotherapy* 61 (2): 87–92. doi:10.1016/j.jphys.2015.02.015.

Sevenhuysen, S., E. H. Skinner, M. K. Farlie, L. Raitman, W. Nickson, J. L. Keating, S. Maloney, E. Molloy, and T. P. Haines. 2014. "Educators and students prefer traditional clinical education to a peer-assisted learning model, despite similar student performance outcomes: a randomised trial." *Journal of Physiotherapy* 60 (4): 209–216. doi:10.1016/j.jphys.2014.09.004.

Sevenhuysen, S., J. Thorpe, E. Molloy, J. Keating, and T. Haines. 2017. "Peer-assisted learning in education of allied health professional students in the clinical setting: a systematic review." *Journal of Allied Health* 46 (1): 26–35.

Speyer, R., W. Pilz, J. Van Der Kruis, and J. W. Brunings. 2011. "Reliability and validity of student peer assessment in medical education: a systematic review." *Medical Teacher* 33 (11): e572-e585. doi:10.3109/0142159X.2011.610835.

Stegmann, K., F. Pilz, M. Siebeck, and F. Fischer. 2012. "Vicarious learning during simulations: is it more effective than hands-on training?" *Medical Education* 46 (10): 1001–1008. doi:10.1111/j.1365–2923.2012.04344.x.

Stigmar, M. 2016. "Peer-to-peer teaching in higher education: a critical literature review." *Mentoring & Tutoring: Partnership in Learning* 24 (2): 124–136. doi:10.1080/13611267.2016.1178963.

Tai, J., B. J. Canny, T. P. Haines, and E. Molloy. 2016. "The role of peer-assisted learning in building evaluative judgement: opportunities in clinical medical education." *Advances in Health Sciences Education* 21 (3): 659–676. doi:10.1007/s10459-015-9659-0.

To, J., and D. Carless. 2015. "Making productive use of exemplars: peer discussion and teacher guidance for positive transfer of strategies." *Journal of Further and Higher Education* 40 (6): 746–764. doi:10.1080/0309877X.2015.1014317.

Topping, K. J., and S. Ehly. 1998. "Introduction to peer-assisted learning." In *Peer-Assisted Learning*, edited by K. Topping and S. Ehly, 1–23. Mahwah, NJ: Lawrence Erlbaum Associates.

Wimshurst, K., and M. Manning. 2012. "Feed-forward assessment, exemplars and peer marking: evidence of efficacy." *Assessment & Evaluation in Higher Education* 38 (4): 451–465. doi:10.1080/02602938.2011.646236.

Wolpaw, T. M., D. R. Wolpaw, and K. K. Papp. 2003. "SNAPPS: a learner-centered model for outpatient education." *Academic Medicine* 78 (9): 893–898.

Yu, T., N. Wilson, and P. Singh. 2011. "Medical students-as-teachers: a systematic review of peer-assisted teaching during medical school." *Advances in Medical Education and Practice* 2: 157–172.

CHAPTER **17**

Building evaluative judgement through the process of feedback

Christina Johnson and Elizabeth Molloy

This chapter focuses on the potential for learners to develop evaluative judgement during feedback conversations in healthcare, offering an illustrative example for any discipline. Feedback in the workplace and the classroom is often enacted as a once-off provision of information to a learner, with minimal engagement of the learner in judgement-making or goal-setting (Molloy 2009, Winstone et al. 2017). We draw on the feedback literature and an empirical case study to argue that feedback can be an important mechanism in cultivating evaluative judgement skills in learners, particularly when it is designed to develop those skills, as well as improve learner performance, across sequential tasks.

Workplace learning is ubiquitous in healthcare, and feedback is commonly held as one of the most important processes in enabling individuals to improve their practice (Archer 2010; Ende 1983; Ericsson 2008). Students learn alongside qualified clinicians amid the hustle and bustle of hospitals and community-based facilities (Delany and Molloy 2009) and, following qualification, many health professionals undertake further training to gain specialist credentials.

Like all professionals in the workplace, health professionals need to develop self-regulatory skills that enable them to learn and perform independently, as supervisors are not constantly available, especially post-qualification. These skills in self-regulation include identifying learning goals, selecting effective learning strategies, monitoring progress and then refining strategies accordingly. Evaluative judgement – understanding what constitutes high-quality work and applying these standards (Tai et al. 2016) – is an essential component of this.

Feedback in theory

Boud and Molloy define feedback as "a process whereby learners obtain information about their work in order to appreciate the similarities and differences between the appropriate standards for any given work, and the qualities of the work, in order to generate improved work" (Boud and Molloy 2013b, 6). This definition aligns with a constructivist view of learning by positioning the learner as an active seeker of information, which they then use to improve their work, and recalls the standpoint that feedback effectiveness can only be determined by its impact on subsequent performance.

The aim of feedback is to help the learner enhance their understanding and skills (Ende 1983). Effective feedback clarifies what the learner is aiming for (the characteristics of a quality performance), how their current performance compares to this standard and what they can do to improve (Hattie and Timperley 2007). Understanding the characteristics of quality work is critical to the development of evaluative judgement (Kruger and Dunning 1999). Standards, protocols, guidelines and rubrics can provide information to help learners clarify what constitutes "good work". However, additional tacit knowledge is required to enable learners to distinguish what good work looks like in a particular context (see Rees et al., Chapter 18). Molloy's (2009) observational study of feedback in the workplace demonstrates that an important role for educators is to "unpack" and "bring to life" standards of work during feedback conversations.

Feedback in practice

Feedback sessions play an important role in the healthcare workplace. Typically, an educator (senior clinician) meets with a learner (student, qualified junior or peer clinician) to review the learner's performance on clinical tasks. This may relate to a specific performance, such as the learner's assessment of an unwell patient, or a longitudinal assessment of the learner's performance. Observational studies have shown that feedback discussions are typically dominated by the educator, and are rarely followed up on (Blatt et al. 2008; Frye et al. 1996; Molloy 2009). This monologic feedback style positions the learner in a passive role and assumes that learners automatically enact desired changes. However, studies of feedback in workplace and classroom settings indicate that learners often do not understand feedback comments, or struggle to apply strategies to improve their work (Boud and Molloy 2013b; Hattie and Timperley 2007). In addition, studies report that educators are reluctant to raise performance problems as they fear the learner may feel insulted or demoralised, at a potential cost to their collegial relationship (Ende et al. 1995; Molloy 2009; Molloy et al. 2013). These characteristics of one-way feedback, once-off feedback, and anxiety from both parties mean that feedback in practice often deviates considerably from the definition of feedback we adhere to in this chapter.

An emerging literature suggests that verbal feedback can assist learners to develop and refine their own judgement (Boud and Molloy 2013a; Molloy 2009; Tai et al. 2016). Self-assessment is frequently inaccurate, with high-performing learners often underestimating their performance and low-performing learners overestimating their performance (Eva and Regehr 2005). The capacity for making accurate judgements can be improved by exposure to peers' performance (for the most competent, who underestimate) or enhancing their performance skills (for the least competent, who overestimate) (Eva and Regehr 2005; Kruger and Dunning 1999). One of the key aspects to improving judgement is the opportunity to evaluate work and to observe how this self-generated judgement compares to the judgements of others (e.g., educator, peer, or consumer). If both learners and educators view feedback as a process with the potential to improve learners' evaluative judgement – a broader goal than improving performance on the next task – we may begin to see different patterns of feedback enactment. The case study below identifies features of feedback that may influence learners' capacity to cultivate evaluative habits.

Building evaluative judgement during feedback: a case study in healthcare

Our research team aimed to find out more about how learners' evaluative judgement could be enhanced as part of verbal feedback processes in the workplace. We had previously developed a Feedback Quality Instrument (FQI) through a literature review and Delphi process; the FQI describes educator behaviours that could engage, motivate and enable a learner to improve their work (Johnson et al. 2016). Many of the FQI items relate to the notion of evaluative judgement and encourage the learner to consider how their performance compares with a quality performance (the standard) and what they can do to improve subsequent performance.

As part of testing and refining the FQI, we collected 36 videos of authentic verbal feedback episodes involving health professionals during routine clinical practice. In order to examine opportunities for learners to practise and develop evaluative judgement, we performed an in-depth analysis on ten of these videos, selected to maximise diversity across health professions, level of experience and gender. Using thematic analysis, we investigated (i) what opportunities learners had to judge their own work, and how they engaged with those opportunities, and (ii) what facilitated or impeded learners' development of evaluative judgement during feedback. Our three major findings are presented below.

Educator's invitations: I want to know what you *think about the quality of your work*

We first looked at how educators created opportunities for learners to evaluate their work. This was a very characteristic opening exchange:

> Educator: Why don't you start off by telling me how you went?
> Learner: I thought it was OK . . . nothing went terribly wrong. [V11]

Most educators initiated the feedback session by asking learners for their overall perspective. Learners almost universally responded by stating that their performance was adequate. Only once did a learner offer some genuine self-analysis by specifying features they had performed successfully to this point.

Following this initial invitation, some educators asked further questions, inviting the learner to evaluate their performance more deeply. This was a common approach:

> Educator: What did you do well? . . . If you had your time again, is there anything you would have done differently? [V9]

Some educators employed other techniques to prompt learners to discuss their performance. One educator described a problem they had observed during the performance and then asked the learner for their perspective on what had happened. Another educator asked the learner to describe how they had introduced themselves to the family of a patient, which prompted the learner to analyse their performance as they replayed their steps. In contrast to those educators who probed further, some educators outlined their own assessment of the learner's performance immediately after the opening exchange. This suggests these educators did not see value in soliciting learners' perspectives or self-assessments.

Overall, educators created few opportunities for learners to make evaluative judgements. Although most educators provided an opening invitation for learner self-analysis, learners' responses were brief, superficial and deflective. They did not offer a genuine analysis of their own performance and their responses echoed the generic nature of the educators' enquiries. Notably, educators did not explicitly ask learners to compare their performance to a standard or target performance. Such a prompt could encourage the learner to undertake a more detailed analysis of their performance, by specifying the aspects that met the standard and those that did not, as well as revealing the learner's understanding of the expected standard.

Learners appeared reluctant to offer self-evaluations. It is important to acknowledge that learners may well be making internalised judgements that they do not express – possibly because they are concerned about articulating flawed judgements or highlighting performance deficits undetected by the educator, or contravening perceived cultural norms where "hearing it from the expert" is a shared expectation of both parties (Bearman et al. 2012; Molloy et al. 2013; Nicol 2013).

Good work looks like this

Our second finding explores how the characteristics of quality work were elucidated during the feedback session. In particular, we consider how educators assisted learners to understand both the explicit and implicit criteria for quality work when applied to a specific context. In our sample, educators focused on describing how the task should be performed. Educators' explanations about "good clinical practice" were characteristically specific and straightforward. They often explained the reasoning that supported their recommendation, adding the "why" to the "what". Regarding an emergency caesarean section operation on a woman in labour, an educator said:

> My advice to you is to always make an adequate incision, that way you won't get stuck not being able to deliver the baby . . . and for labouring caesareans, you can always cut higher than you think. [V12]

To help learners make sense of complex recommendations, educators often used exemplars taken from their own practice. During a discussion about how a junior clinician could engage with a confused elderly patient and stop the family from interrupting without dismissing their important contributions, an educator gave examples of what they might say themselves in that situation:

> I'll often say to the relative, "I understand that you may have things that you know, that your relative doesn't know . . . and I'm very interested. . . . I'm going to talk to [the patient] first and then after that, you'll have the opportunity to tell me things that you think I need to know". [V9]

Although educators' discourse often included descriptions of what "good performance" might look like, it was rare for learners to take the initiative and ask educators for ways in which they could improve their own performance, and even rarer for learners to suggest their own strategies.

Calibration of the learner's judgement through dialogue

Verbal feedback offers a valuable opportunity for educators to assist learners in calibrating their own judgements. This calibration can be achieved by educators confirming or contesting learners' evaluative comments. In this example, the educator enthusiastically validated the learner's opinion:

> Educator: What do you think is an area . . . for development?
> Learner: I think being able to be more confident in my practice.
> Educator: Good! You must have read my notes; previously I said, "Develop confidence in your own ability". [V36]

However, educators seldom challenged learners' views, even though critical appraisal is just as important for calibration as endorsing accurate judgements. Performance analysis from an educator also enables a learner to compare their opinions (whether expressed or withheld) with an expert's opinion. In our case study, educators consistently offered clear and specific comments regarding effective aspects of learner performance:

> Educator: You were very engaging in your talk and your body language was good and you made eye contact with everyone. [V34]

In contrast, educators' corrective comments were characterised by hints, timidity and interspersed with "ums", signifying the difficulties encountered in articulating their thoughts. When pointing out deficits, educators' body language suggested discomfort, such as leaning back from the table, fidgeting and avoiding eye contact.

> Educator: *Um*, in terms of the other part of it, *so the other part* is really, *um*, was around the, *um, the, the* diagnosis, *um*, and again some of the – *some of*

> *the, um*, issues in relation to, *um*, the, *the* way you give feedback to the patient and, *and* the understanding – *perhaps* a more direct feedback about whether there's been adequate medication trials, *um*, as to one of the reasons why the, *the* treatment hasn't worked. [V6]

Our case study suggested that some educators assisted in calibrating learners' evaluative judgements by endorsing or contesting learners' comments, though the latter was rare, and by expressing their own evaluations. Educators frequently commended learners' quality performances or accurate judgements in a straightforward fashion. However, educators tended to avoid corrective comments, and when they did attempt to discuss substandard aspects of performance, their language and nonverbal signals changed markedly to become apprehensive, apologetic and circuitous.

Implications for practice

Evaluative judgement is a valuable skill for all those involved in lifelong learning. If verbal feedback sessions are designed to engage learners, they can potentially act as key occasions for educators to assist learners in developing their judgement capabilities.

In our case study, no learner spontaneously offered a thorough self-assessment and, even when asked, learners matched the depth of their evaluation to that of the educator's enquiry. In addition, educators rarely paid much attention to learners' evaluations. This suggests neither learners nor educators saw the value of self-assessment as a demonstration of learners' evaluation skills and understanding of "good work". As highlighted earlier, learners may be seeking to avoid revealing their internal judgements, in case they are inaccurate or highlight undetected performance errors. Another reason for this pattern may be that learners do not realise that their superficial self-evaluation is insufficient, a notion likely to be reinforced by educators immediately plunging into a monologue. Therefore, it is probable that educators need to be more skilled in coaxing learners to share their authentic opinions. In the case of undergraduate and postgraduate students, assessment can be structured so that evaluative judgements are required from learners, and those attempts and explicit efforts to incorporate new strategies into subsequent tasks are rewarded.

One important factor influencing learner self-disclosure may be the level of trust in the learner-teacher relationship (Bing-You et al. 1997; Carless 2013; Clouder 2009; Molloy et al. 2013; Sargeant et al. 2008; Telio et al. 2016). Lefevre highlights the importance of "the creation of a supportive, safe and trusting environment in which student learning is facilitated and risks can be taken" (Lefevre 2005, 580). Interestingly, in our selected sample of videos, no educators showed any vulnerability in expressing their own challenges or learning deficits at a similar stage of training or in current practice. Reciprocal vulnerability in face-to-face feedback contexts has been hypothesised as an important ingredient in inviting an honest exchange of information (Molloy et al. 2013). Further studies that explore participants' intentions and motivations, both during and after feedback sessions, would be valuable in helping design strategies to embed learners' articulation of genuine self-assessments into routine practice.

So often, standards of work in the classroom and the workplace are implicit (see results by Tai and Sevenhuysen, Chapter 16 and Rees et al., Chapter 18), meaning that learners are more reliant on educators to assist them in gaining an understanding of the desired standard. In our case study, clarifying "what good work looks like" was a major focus for educators when providing feedback. However, educators rarely sought questions from the learner or checked their understanding of concepts, implying educators believed that they could easily transmit complex ideas. This finding aligns with Boud and Molloy's (2013b, 2) description of current feedback practices, which resemble educators delivering "hopefully useful information". Under a constructivist view of learning, a learner makes sense of new information and incorporates it into their mental model by relating new information to their current understanding and resolving any discrepancies (Nicol and Macfarlane-Dick 2006). There are multiple barriers to learners accurately understanding how well they performed a task and how to better approach a task; for instance, the educators' remarks may not be clear, specific or actionable and, even if they are, learners often need to ask questions or obtain further information before achieving an understanding of how to apply new ideas in practice. If educators viewed feedback as "more enabling and less telling", this could change the focus from what educators say to what learners understand (Carless 2006; Johnson et al. 2016; Molloy and Boud 2013).

An earlier observational study of verbal feedback sessions in the hospital workplace, which described how educators socialise learners into the rituals of the professional community, found that feedback appeared to be a one-way transmission of information from educator to learner (Molloy 2009). The consistency of this pattern suggests that monologic feedback is an expected ritual between learners and educators. Calibrating learners' evaluations of their own and others' work is a critical element in the development of evaluative judgement. However, in our case study, learners' evaluations were frequently not sought or discussed in-depth, and so opportunities to calibrate learners' judgements by confirming or contesting them were often missed.

Educators typically find praise or validation of student performance more comfortable than highlighting aspects for improvement. It may be that educators highlight success in order to recognise learners' hard work and progress, thus providing a key motivator for them to continue their endeavours (Kluger and DeNisi 1996; Locke and Latham 2002; Ten Cate et al. 2011). Studies have also suggested that educators are concerned about the potential damage to educator-learner relationships if feedback takes a critical tone (Dudek et al. 2005; Molloy 2009). In our case study, educators adopted a hesitant and apologetic tone when correcting learners' performance, "tiptoeing" around a topic. This reluctance to broach contentious topics reflects feedback described in previous observational studies as "vanishing" (Ende 1983) and "mealy mouthed" (Molloy et al. 2013). We need to consider how these patterns of interaction impact on a learner's development of evaluative judgement: with so much "code" and "padding", how can learners decipher important messages that would help to shape their own judgement?

Based on the literature on learner-centred feedback practices and the empirical case study presented in this chapter, we make the following recommendations to improve evaluative judgement opportunities through verbal feedback:

1. Developing frameworks that describe desirable behaviours for both learners and educators in feedback, to enable learners to express genuine evaluations, develop a shared understanding of the characteristics of quality work, select practical steps to improve subsequent performance, and to establish another opportunity to observe the learner tackling a similar task – that is, to close the feedback loop;
2. Explicitly setting up learner expectations for quality feedback at the outset, by orientating learners to the purpose of feedback (to help the learner improve on tasks *and* to develop skills in evaluative judgement), setting expectations (such as what a genuine learner self-assessment and interactive dialogue might look like) and proposing an outline for the session;
3. Rehearsing practical ways for educators to promote opportunities for genuine learner self-assessment, such as cues to encourage learner participation or pausing to allow sufficient time for learners to respond;
4. Coaching learners and educators on how to discuss aspects of substandard performance and contest opinions through a respectful and honest dialogue, grounded in curiosity; and
5. Further research examining how to create an environment of trust between educators and learners and enable honest appraisal, especially in short-term educational relationships.

Conclusion

Evaluative judgement is a valuable skill for learners in the classroom and the workplace. Our case study findings support an increasing body of work suggesting that educators provide very few opportunities for learners to exercise judgement within feedback processes. Educators often focus their efforts on delivering their own evaluation of learners' performance and clarifying what good work looks like. Orientating educators and learners to the importance of evaluative judgement, and providing practical ways to enable learners to develop this skill, may assist in creating more productive feedback rituals in the classroom, work-based placements, and beyond.

Acknowledgements

We would like to thank the health professionals who volunteered to record their feedback practice. In the name of improvement, these participants rendered themselves vulnerable in allowing their behaviours to be scrutinised and evaluated – precisely the practice we argue for here.

References

Archer, J. C. 2010. "State of the science in health professional education: effective feedback." *Medical Education* 44 (1): 101–108.

Bearman, M., E. Molloy, R. Ajjawi, and J. Keating. 2012. " 'Is there a Plan B?': clinical educators supporting underperforming students in practice settings." *Teaching in Higher Education* 18 (5): 531–544. doi:10.1080/13562517.2012.752732.

Bing-You, R., J. Paterson, and M. Levine. 1997. "Feedback falling on deaf ears: residents' receptivity to feedback tempered by sender credibility." *Medical Teacher* 19 (1): 40–44.

Blatt, B., S. Confessore, G. Kallenberg, and L. Greenberg. 2008. "Verbal interaction analysis: viewing feedback through a different lens." *Teaching and Learning in Medicine* 20 (4): 329–333. doi:10.1080/10401330802384789.

Boud, D., and E. Molloy. 2013a. "Rethinking models of feedback for learning: the challenge of design." *Assessment & Evaluation in Higher Education* 38 (6): 698–712.

Boud, D., and E. Molloy. 2013b. "What is the problem with feedback?" In *Feedback in Higher and Professional Education*, edited by D. Boud and E. Molloy, 1–10. Oxford, UK: Routledge.

Carless, D. 2006. "Differing perceptions in the feedback process." *Studies in Higher Education* 31 (2): 219–233. doi:10.1080/03075070600572132.

Carless, D. 2013. "Trust and its role in facilitating dialogic feedback." In *Feedback in Higher and Professional Education*, edited by D. Boud and E. Molloy, 90–103. Oxford, UK: Routledge.

Clouder, L. 2009. "Being responsible: students' perspectives on trust, risk and work-based learning." *Teaching in Higher Education* 14 (3): 289–301. doi:10.1080/13562510902898858.

Delany, C., and E. Molloy. 2009. "Critical reflection in clinical education: beyond the 'swampy lowlands'." In *Clinical Education in the Health Professions*, edited by C. Delany and E. Molloy, 3–24. Sydney, Australia: Elsevier.

Dudek, L. D., M. B. Marks, and G. Regehr. 2005. "Failure to fail: the perspectives of clinical supervisors." In "RIME: Proceedings of the 44th Annual Research in Medical Education Conference" October 2005 supplement, *Academic Medicine* 80 (10): S84-S87.

Ende, J. 1983. "Feedback in clinical medical education." *Journal of the American Medical Association* 250 (6): 777–781.

Ende. J., A. Pomerantz, and F. Erickson. 1995. "Preceptors' strategies for correcting residents in an ambulatory care medicine setting: a qualitative analysis." *Academic Medicine* 70 (3): 224–229.

Ericsson, K. A. 2008. "Deliberate practice and acquisition of expert performance: a general overview." *Academic Emergency Medicine* 15 (11): 988–994.

Eva, K., and G. Regehr. 2005. "Self-assessment in the health professions: a reformulation and research agenda." *Academic Medicine* 80 (10): S46-S54.

Frye, A., M. Hollingsworth, A. Wymer, and M. Hinds. 1996. "Dimensions of feedback in clinical teaching: a descriptive study." *Academic Medicine* 71 (1): S79–81.

Hattie, J., and H. Timperley. 2007. "The power of feedback." *Review of Educational Research* 77 (1): 81–112.

Johnson. C., J. Keating, D. Boud, M. Dalton, D. Kiegaldie, M. Hay, B. McGrath, W. McKenzie, K. Nair, D. Nestel, C. Palermo, and E. Molloy. 2016. "Identifying educator behaviours for high quality verbal feedback in health professions education: literature review and expert refinement." *BMC Medical Education* 16: 96. doi:10.1186/s12909-016-0613-5.

Kluger, A., and A. DeNisi. 1996. "The effects of feedback interventions on performance: a historical review, a meta-analysis, and a preliminary feedback intervention theory." *Psychological Bulletin* 119 (2): 254–284.

Kruger, J., and D. Dunning. 1999. "Unskilled and unaware of it: how difficulties in recognizing one's own incompetence lead to inflated self-assessments." *Journal of Personality and Social Psychology* 77 (6): 1121–1134.

Lefevre, M. 2005. "Facilitating practice learning and assessment: the influence of relationship." *Social Work Education* 24 (5): 565–583.

Locke, E. and G. Latham. 2002. "Building a practically useful theory of goal setting and task motivation: a 35-year odyssey." *American Psychologist* 57 (9): 705–717.

Molloy, E. 2009. "Time to pause: feedback in clinical education." In *Clinical Education in the Health Professions*, edited by C. Delany and E. Molloy, 128–146. Sydney, Australia: Elsevier.

Molloy, E., F. Borrell-Carrió, and R. Epstein. 2013. "The impact of emotions in feedback." In *Feedback in Higher and Professional Education*, edited by D. Boud and E. Molloy, 50–71. Oxford, UK: Routledge.

Molloy, E., and D. Boud. 2013. "Changing conceptions of feedback." In *Feedback in Higher and Professional Education*, edited by D. Boud and E. Molloy, 11–33. Oxford, UK: Routledge.

Nicol, D. 2013: "Resituating feedback from the reactive to the proactive." In *Feedback in Higher and Professional Education*, edited by D. Boud and E. Molloy, 34–49. Oxford, UK: Routledge.

Nicol, D., and D. Macfarlane-Dick. 2006. "Formative assessment and self-regulated learning: a model and seven principles of good feedback practice." *Studies in Higher Education* 31 (2): 199–218.

Sargeant, J., K. Mann, D. Sinclair, C. Vleuten, and J. Metsemakers. 2008. "Understanding the influence of emotions and reflection upon multi-source feedback acceptance and use." *Advances in Health Science Education* 13 (3): 275–288.

Tai, J., B. Canny, T. Haines, and E. Molloy. 2016. "The role of peer-assisted learning in building evaluative judgement: opportunities in clinical medical education." *Advances in Health Science Education* 21 (3): 659–76. doi:10.1007/s10459–015–9659–0.

Telio, S., G. Regehr, and R. Ajjawi. 2016. "Feedback and the educational alliance: examining credibility judgements and their consequences." *Medical Education* 50 (9): 933–942. doi:10.1111/medu.13063.

Ten Cate, O., R. Kusurkar, and G. Williams. 2011. "How self-determination theory can assist our understanding of the teaching and learning processes in medical education. AMEE Guide No. 59." *Medical Teacher* 33 (12): 961–973. doi:10.3109/0142159X.2011.595435.

Winstone, N., R. Nash, M. Parker, and J. Rowntree. 2017. "Supporting learners' agentic engagement with feedback: a systematic review and a taxonomy of recipience processes." *Educational Psychologist* 52 (1): 17–37. doi:10.1080/00461520.2016.1207538.

CHAPTER **18**

Using workplace-learning narratives to explore evaluative judgement in action

Charlotte E. Rees, Alison Bullock, Karen L. Mattick and Lynn V. Monrouxe

Lifelong professional development is an essential component of professional education, both for the maintenance and development of professionals' knowledge, skills and attitudes and also for safe, competent and ethical professional practice. The development of learners' evaluative judgement is argued to be foundational to this lifelong professional development (Cowan 2010).

Learners need to make evaluative judgements about what they need to learn and how, alongside understanding their progress towards desired performance goals (Cowan 2010). Self- and peer-assessment are thought to facilitate learners' evaluative judgement (Cowan 2010; Tai et al. 2016). Students studying for professions such as medicine report improved understandings of quality through peer observation, feedback and narrating stories about their learning experiences (Tai et al. 2016). Yet to date, the potential for narratives as sense-making activities to explore evaluative judgement in postgraduate professional learners is little understood.

In this chapter, we explore what evaluative judgement means in the context of newly qualified doctors. We describe narratives as sense-making activities (Labov and Waletzky 1967) and use workplace-learning narratives to explore evaluative judgement in action. We present previously unpublished junior doctors' narratives, from a multi-centre UK study focusing on medical graduates' preparedness for practice, to illustrate the types of evaluative judgements that junior doctors make about their performance (and how they make them) in the context of busy workplace environments. We conclude our chapter by summarising what junior doctors' narratives of preparedness for practice reveal and hide in terms of evaluative judgement, ending with key implications for future educational practice and research.

What is evaluative judgement within the context of newly qualified professional practitioners?

In Figure 18.1, we set out the evaluative judgement arena, drawing attention to two dimensions: focus (inward on self; outward on others) and standards (explicit and implicit). We locate evaluative judgement centrally in the figure to reflect its

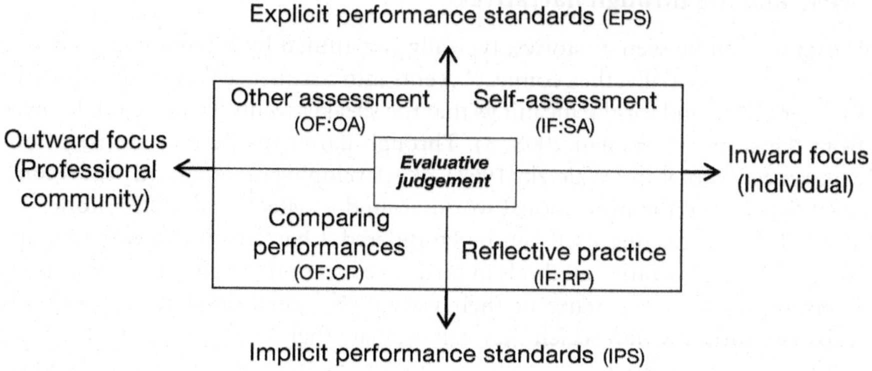

Figure 18.1 Arena of evaluative judgement

position of encompassing attention on the performance of both self and others, against explicit and tacit criteria. As described in Chapter 1, evaluative judgements relate to learners' understandings about what constitutes quality and how they make judgements about the quality of their own and others' work. As is also explained in Chapter 1, there are thought to be four central features of evaluative judgement: (1) learners' understandings of quality; (2) understandings of quality by reference to standards; (3) learners' embodied habits and practices for engaging in evaluative judgement; and (4) learners further extending their understandings of quality through evaluative judgements. In this chapter, we explore evaluative judgement, as demonstrated by postgraduate medical learners, to illustrate the special challenges of evaluative judgement in this context. Here, junior doctors' evaluative judgements can be made against explicit standards such as guidelines, protocols, milestones and workplace-based assessments. However, more often than not, standards are ill-defined and open to interpretation, and judging the quality of performance in the professional workplace may be more commonly informed by the social norms of the professional community. We therefore make preliminary recommendations for developing evaluative judgement in the healthcare workplace.

We think that evaluative judgement in this postgraduate workplace, as in other workplace settings, is made more complex by junior doctors' frequent reliance on tacit understandings of what constitutes quality performance. Both the explicit and the non-explicit nature of what is excellent, acceptable or, indeed, unacceptable performance brings forth variations in interpretation for trainees as they move from one consultant supervisor to another, from ward to ward and from hospital to hospital (Schott et al. 2015). We believe that narratives, particularly those captured by audio-diaries, can be a powerful means of exploring the complexity of trainees' evaluative judgements in action, and could be useful for the development of evaluative judgement in learners in the workplace.

Sense-making through narratives

Narratives can be seen as stories, typically constituted by a beginning, a middle and an end. Essentially, they connect "events into a sequence that is consequential for later action and for the meanings that the speaker wants listeners to take away from the story" (Riessman 2008, 3). Through narratives we make sense of our experiences (Labov and Waletzky 1967), our developing personal and professional identities, and of the professional world around us (Rees et al. 2013; Monrouxe 2016). Indeed, learning itself can be considered a narrative process (Clark and Rossiter 2008). Narrative methods in medical education can give medical learners opportunities to make sense of their own professional development, offering learners a forum within which they can evaluate their own performance (Sadler 2010). One type of narrative approach gaining traction recently in medical education is the longitudinal audio-diary, whereby learners record audio-diaries over weeks, months or years using voice-recording devices, allowing educators to better understand how learners make sense of their learning experiences and developing identities over time (Monrouxe 2009a, 2009b). Narrating events via audio-diaries can help learners to foster their ongoing reflection-on-action: as the narrator attempts to explain (often previously unprocessed) events for an absent other (usually the educator), their story continually oscillates between explanations for others and sense-making for the self (Monrouxe 2009a, 2009b). Thus "the audio-diary method appears to be capturing . . . sense-making-in-the-moment . . . this sense-making process, driven purely by the narrator, [is] hard to capture outside the audio-diary method" (Monrouxe 2009a, 98). As explained by others, repeated storytelling can act as an ongoing form of self-monitoring judgement (Cowan 2010). Therefore, we think that narratives could be used to facilitate the development of evaluative judgement in postgraduate learners.

Workplace evaluative judgement narratives

Postgraduate trainees, who learn their craft in busy workplaces, provide an opportunity to explore how early-career professionals interact with implicit standards of practice to make judgements about their own performances. Preparedness for practice has been referred to as the combination of knowledge, skills and behaviour required at that point or for that role – for example, as new entrants to the workplace, new to a specialty or as new consultants (General Medical Council 2012).

For this chapter, we examine the longitudinal audio-diaries and exit interviews of three postgraduate year two trainees, who were working for the first time as fully registered practitioners (for simplicity, we call them "junior doctors" in this chapter). These three junior doctors were the most prolific diarists across three British countries – England, Scotland and Wales – in our preparedness for practice study (Monrouxe et al. 2014; Lundin et al. 2018). Our England-based diarist was a 25-year-old self-identified British female (we call her 'Cathy' in this chapter), our Scotland-based diarist was a 32-year-old self-identified British female

('Suzanna'), and our Wales-based diarist was a 25-year-old self-identified English male ('Mark').

We found considerable evidence of evaluative judgement in Cathy's, Suzanna's and Mark's audio-diaries as they narrated (and made sense of) their preparedness for practice experiences as junior doctors. Indeed, they narrated evaluative judgements where the performance in question was their knowledge, technical skills (e.g., examination, procedures, clinical reasoning, prioritisation, management) or non-technical skills (e.g., communication, leadership, responsibility). They also exhibited evaluative judgement about their learning, emotions and emotion regulation, personality, identities, ward craft and career choices. For example, Cathy judges her performance negatively when reflecting on her new obstetrics and gynaecology rotation, explaining that she was terrified of making mistakes as she was unsure about how the ward worked:

> I was terrified [**emotion focus**]. New specialty, new wards, new staff, didn't know anyone, didn't know where anything was [**ward craft focus**] . . . I really didn't want to mess things up. (Cathy, first narrative from obstetrics and gynaecology rotation)

Suzanna, on the other hand, judges her performance positively by the end of her four-month longitudinal audio-diary project, explaining that her communication skills are good and that she is rarely discomfited by her communication performance in patient consultations:

> I think I've got quite good communication skills [**non-technical skills focus**]. So there are very few consultations where I think, '*Oh God, that was awful*' [**emotion focus**]. (Suzanna, exit interview for her audio-diaries)

Across our three junior doctors' audio-diaries, we saw evidence of various features of evaluative judgement: (1) comparisons in relation to implicit and explicit predefined standards; (2) comparisons in relation to peers and near-peers (outward focus); (3) comparisons in relation to former selves (inward focus); and (4) seeking and receiving others' feedback on performance. We cover each of these in turn.

Comparisons in relation to standards

All three junior doctors' narratives evidenced their thinking about quality standards and assessing their own performance critically in relation to predefined standards. The standards typically narrated by them were implicit, often gleaned through observing past and present practices of senior role models and reflecting on their seniors' performances in relation to their own, as can be seen in Mark's talk:

> I think it comes down to what you've seen. How much of it you've seen. How often you've seen it and what you've watched your seniors do [**outward**

> **focused, comparing performances**]. All I do really is piece together what's going on with the patient and what my seniors have done in the past to make me think about how I'm going to proceed [**inward focused, reflective practice**]. (Mark, exit interview for his audio-diaries)

However, such implicit standards were not without their problems, as narrated by Cathy; she explains that the implicit standards (i.e., consultants' practices) can differ from one consultant to the next, meaning that the standards constantly change, requiring her to change her practice accordingly:

> So, I work in a team where we have, I think, ten different consultants and they all do things differently [**outward focused, comparing performances**]. So, you have to remember to do things differently depending on which consultant is on-call with you [**inward focused, reflective practice**]. (Cathy, from obstetrics and gynaecology rotation)

However, our three junior doctors also talked about more explicit predefined standards through which they could better understand their performance; for example, externally imposed targets, such as the four-hour waiting time in emergency medicine, and guidelines and protocols were considered. Thus, in the following excerpt, we see how Suzanna's judgement of her performance managing a patient with chest pain on her emergency medicine rotation was positive, based on her self-assessment of her performance against standard protocols for managing chest pain:

> I felt quite well-prepared to deal with the situation [gentleman with chest pain] and acted with the initial management steps to do an ECG [electrocardiograph] reading, give him Aspirin and GTN [glyceryl trinitrate] to see if that had any effect on his chest pain, and then to give him morphine to try and bring the pain down as per a standard practice [**inward focused, self-assessment**]. (Suzanna, first narrative from emergency medicine rotation)

Comparisons in relation to peers

We also saw that our three junior doctors often reflected on their own performance by judging the performance of others (e.g., peers and near-peers) and making comparisons between peers and self. Note that these comparisons can be favourable and/or unfavourable, as illustrated in Mark's first audio-diary from his surgical rotation. Here, Mark reflects on his development as he compares himself favourably to more junior trainees, contrasting this with unfavourable comparisons with more senior trainees the previous year:

> So, to have [more junior trainees] there to delegate towards . . . made me realise quite how far I've come in a year and a little bit that I've been training [**inward focused, reflective practice**] and how much I must have known

> because I was the same as they were only a year ago [**outward focused, comparing performance**]. I remember looking up to the [more senior trainees] and thinking '*I'm never going to be that knowledgeable. I'm never going to understand so many things*' [**outward focused, comparing performance**] . . . You had to look round the other [same year trainees] to realise that they were in very similar situations [**outward focused, comparing performance**] but it was nice to reassure myself that I've got to a situation where I was confident and competent at being a [registered junior doctor] and in the [registered junior doctor] role [**inward focused, reflective practice**]. (Mark, first narrative from surgical rotation)

However, junior doctors do not always work alongside other trainees and are thus sometimes unable to make sense of their own performance by comparing themselves with peers. Indeed, Suzanna identifies this key challenge to evaluative judgement in the context of working on her own in general practice and emergency medicine contexts. She explains that in these contexts, she finds it difficult to benchmark her performance against her peers because they are absent, so she instead attempts to benchmark her performance through exploring her peers' notes:

> I'm not a solo worker, but in A&E [accident and emergency] it's only me who would see a patient and another [registered junior doctor] wouldn't go and see the same patient. Again, when I was in GP [general practice] I was the only one who was in the practice. So, I actually found that quite hard to benchmark [**inward focused, reflective practice**] and be thinking '*well, what would somebody else do?*' [**outward focused, comparing performance**] I'm not sure [**inward focused, reflective practice**] and obviously you could sometimes read through the notes of the previous [registered junior doctors] and see what they did [**outward focused, comparing performance**] but you don't know [**inward focused, reflective practice**]. (Suzanna, exit interview for her audio-diaries)

Comparisons in relation to self

Our junior doctors often considered their own preparedness for practice by reflecting on their former selves (as illustrated in Mark's earlier narrative), typically comparing their current performance favourably with their performance the previous year. We also see this in Cathy's narrative from her obstetrics and gynaecology rotation, where she successfully identifies a sick patient based on her general medical knowledge, learnt over various earlier rotations:

> Something that really went well today was being able to apply my general medical knowledge [**inward focused, reflective practice**] . . . my experience from eight months of general medicine [from previous junior doctor year], working on A&E [accident and emergency] and AMU [acute medical unit]

> really helped in the last 24 hours and helped flag up [the] sick patient [**inward focused, reflective practice**] . . . knowing that I've still got the general knowledge and the general skills that I can apply and adapt to situations for me is really reassuring [**inward focused, reflective practice**]. (Cathy, from obstetrics and gynaecology rotation)

Seeking and receiving feedback on performance

All three junior doctors reflected on and/or assessed their preparedness for practice through seeking and receiving feedback from a multiplicity of feedback providers, including medical seniors, peers and near-peers and other workplace-based clinicians such as nurses, along with patients and their family members. The junior doctors discussed receiving both complimentary and critical feedback on their performance, alongside direct and indirect feedback. We can see an example of indirect and critical feedback received by Mark in one of his rotations. Here, the consultant asks Mark why a radiological investigation had not been ordered on a patient during the night. Mark explains how this feedback triggered critical reflection about his radiological knowledge:

> Occasionally it took me by surprise on a post-take ward round where we'd seen all the patients during the night and the consultant will come in and say '*why not get this investigation?*' It's radiological investigation, which isn't something that had crossed my mind and it made me think perhaps my understanding of what radiology I would use for what . . . perhaps I was a bit weak or unprepared for as a junior doctor [**inward focused, reflective practice**]. (Mark, placement unclear)

Direct feedback from colleagues often included verbal statements about what the trainee had done or not done correctly, whereas indirect feedback included questions posed to trainees (as in Mark's narrative above) or trainees monitoring patient outcomes to establish whether their management of the patient had been correct. We see examples of direct and indirect feedback in Suzanna's narrative from her emergency medicine rotation. She discusses receiving reassurance from her seniors that her management of a patient with respiratory problems was correct, in addition to receiving indirect feedback from the patient's follow-up test results, which showed that the patient's respiratory health had improved after her management:

> The situation was regarding a patient with quite advanced chronic airways disease who came into the A&E [accident and emergency] department with a very high respiratory rate above 40 . . . in a calm manner I did an ABCDE [airways, breathing, circulation, disability, exposure] assessment of the lady . . . I felt that I behaved in a logical manner and . . . the timescale in which I managed the patient was appropriate for her care needed [**inward focused, self-assessment**]. When the seniors came along they reassured me that I had

indeed done the right thing. They added to the treatment plan by adding some steroids, but they suggested repeating the gas in a short while to see what we'd done. I saw on the repeat gas, pH, the blood test that was . . . abnormal to begin with had corrected. So I was pleased with my intervention that I had chosen and used good clinical judgement to make an appropriate plan for this patient [**inward focused, reflective practice**]. (Suzanna, narrative from emergency medicine rotation)

Conclusions

From the workplace-learning narratives of junior doctors presented in this chapter, we can explore evaluative judgement in action. Indeed, the narratives illuminate both trainees' understandings of quality, and how they understand the quality of their own work by making comparisons with implicit and explicit performance standards, whether these comparisons are with respect to their colleagues and former selves (so both outward- and inward-focused, respectively), or through seeking and receiving feedback from others. Indeed, such comparisons seem to help facilitate both their reflective practice and self-assessment of their own performance.

Interestingly, of the four quadrants presented earlier in Figure 18.1, much of trainees' narrated evaluative judgement focused on the "implicit performance standards" end of the quadrants: that is, evaluative judgement in our trainees typically focused on them comparing others' performances in relation to their own [**outward focused, comparing performance**], alongside making sense of their performance through reflective practice [**inward focused, reflective practice**]. Indeed, we see few examples of trainees narrating comparisons of their performance to explicit performance standards [**inward focused, self-assessment**], and we failed to identify examples of trainees narrating others' assessment of their performance using explicit performance standards [**outward focused, other assessment**]. While we see few examples of the "explicit performance standards" end of the quadrants in our three junior doctors' narratives, this is perhaps unsurprising given that they were encouraged to share with us narratives of their preparedness for practice experiences. In other work, where we have encouraged junior doctors to share their narratives of supervised learning events and workplace-based assessment experiences, we might anticipate seeing more evidence of narrated evaluative judgements that involve both other- and self-assessment against explicit performance standards (Rees et al. 2014; Dennis et al. 2018). Therefore, while we see junior doctors naturalistically narrating evaluative judgement in their stories of preparedness for practice, we believe that educators could facilitate the development of evaluative judgement in postgraduate learners through more explicit prompts for evaluative judgement.

We know that people make sense of their experiences, of themselves and of others through narratives. Indeed, an important element of narrative is evaluation, where narrators provide the consequences of events throughout their stories on human desires and needs (Labov 1997). With the multiplicity of examples of evaluative judgement provided in this chapter, we argue that narrative methods have utility for exploring evaluative judgement in professional learning, especially narratives captured in-the-moment through audio-diaries (Monrouxe 2009a). Indeed, as one of our junior doctors Cathy explained: "the reason why I signed up for this study was because it helped me deal with some difficult cases and I found it really useful to go back and reflect on them . . . it makes you look back over your week, what went well and what went badly". Given that audio-diaries are longitudinal, we think they have the potential to encourage learners to develop embodied habits and practices for engaging in evaluative judgement and to further improve their understandings of quality through evaluative judgement, thus facilitating the development of evaluative judgement in learners. However, for this to happen successfully, we think that learners need appropriate scaffolding by educators in terms of advising learners what their stories should focus on. While we drew on the scaffolding of "preparedness for practice" in our junior doctors' narratives, alternative scaffolding for evaluative judgement may be "supervised learning events" and/or "workplace-based assessments" (Rees et al. 2014; Dennis et al. 2018). Whatever educators decide to focus on in their quest to develop evaluative judgements in learners through narrative, we would recommend that they consider all four quadrants in Figure 18.1 and their interplay.

We hope to have shown in this chapter how insights into junior doctors' evaluative judgements can be gained through audio-diary narratives, and how audio-diaries might be used in the future to prompt the development of postgraduate learners' evaluative judgement. We did not ask our junior doctors to share their evaluative judgements with us; we simply asked them to share their stories of preparedness for practice as newly registered doctors. We therefore encourage further work on evaluative judgement in postgraduate professional learning through audio-diary narratives, using alternative educator scaffolding. Finally, we think that research is now needed to explore the potential for longitudinal audio-diaries to provide a window into the development of trainees' evaluative judgements over time. We believe that audio-diary narratives are ripe for evaluative judgement research; the question is whether evaluative judgement researchers are ready for longitudinal qualitative research.

References

Clark, M. C., and M. Rossiter. 2008. "Narrative learning in adulthood." In *Third Update on Adult Learning Theory. New Directions in Adult and Continuing Education, Number 119*, edited by S. B. Merriam, 61–70. San Francisco, CA: Jossey-Bass.

Cowan, J. 2010. "Developing the ability for making sound judgments." *Teaching in Higher Education* 15 (3): 323–334.

Dennis, A. A., M. Foy, L. V. Monrouxe, and C. E. Rees. 2018. "Exploring trainer and trainee emotional talk in narratives about workplace-based feedback processes." *Advances in Health Sciences Education* 23(1): 75–93.

General Medical Council. 2012. "Reviewing the impact of *Tomorrow's Doctors* (2009)." London: General Medical Council. www.gmc-uk.org/5b___Reviewing_the_Impact_of_Tomorrow_s_Doctors_.pdf_50556004.pdf.

Labov, W. 1997. "Some further steps in narrative analysis." *The Journal of Narrative and Life History* 7: 395–415. www.ling.upenn.edu/~wlabov/sfs.html.

Labov, W., and J. Waletzky. 1967. "Narrative analysis: oral versions of personal experience." In *Essays on the Verbal and Visual Arts*, edited by J. Helm, 12–44. Seattle, WA: University of Washington Press.

Lundin, R. M., K. Bashir, A. Bullock, C. E. Kostov, K. L. Mattick, C. E. Rees, and L. V. Monrouxe. 2018. "'I'd been like freaking out the whole night': exploring emotion regulation based on junior doctors' narratives." *Advances in Health Science Education* 23 (1): 7–28.

Monrouxe, L. V. 2009a. "Solicited audio diaries in longitudinal narrative research: a view from inside." *Qualitative Research* 9 (1): 81–103.

Monrouxe, L. V. 2009b. "Negotiating professional identities: dominant and contesting narratives in medical students' longitudinal audio diaries." *Current Narratives* 1 (1): 41–59.

Monrouxe, L. V. 2016. "Theoretical insights into the nature and nurture of professional identities." In *Teaching Medical Professionalism. Supporting the Development of a Professional Identity*, 2nd edn, edited by R. Cruess, S. Cruess, and Y. Steinert, 37–53. Cambridge, UK: Cambridge University Press.

Monrouxe, L. V., A. Bullock, J. Cole, G. Gormley, K. Kaufhold, N. Kelly, K. L. Mattick, C. E. Rees, and G. Scheffler. 2014. "How prepared are UK medical graduates for practice? Final report from a programme of research commissioned by the General Medical Council." UK: GMC. www.gmc-uk.org/about/research/25531.asp.

Rees, C. E., J. A. Cleland, A. Dennis, N. Kelly, K. L. Mattick, and L. V. Monrouxe. 2014. "Supervised learning events in the UK Foundation Programme: a nationwide narrative interview study." *BMJ Open* 4:e005980. doi:10.1136/bmjopen-2014–005980.

Rees, C. E., L. V. Monrouxe, and L. A. McDonald. 2013. "Narrative, emotion, and action: analysing 'most memorable' professionalism dilemmas." *Medical Education* 47 (1): 80–96.

Riessman, C. K. 2008. *Narrative Methods for the Human Sciences.* Thousand Oaks, CA: SAGE.

Sadler, D. R. 2010. "Beyond feedback: developing student capability in complex appraisal." *Assessment & Evaluation in Higher Education* 35 (5): 535–550.

Schott, M., R. Kedia, S. B. Promes, T. Swoboda, K. O'Rourke, W. Green, R. Liu, S. B. Stansfield, and S. A. Santen. 2015. "Direct observation assessment of milestones: problems with reliability." *Western Journal of Emergency Medicine* 16 (6): 871–876.

Tai, J., B. J. Canny, T. P. Haines, and E. K. Molloy. 2016. "The role of peer-assisted learning in building evaluative judgment: opportunities in clinical medical education." *Advances in Health Sciences Education* 21 (3): 659–676.

CHAPTER 19

Creating an agenda for developing students' evaluative judgement

David Boud, Phillip Dawson, Joanna Tai and Rola Ajjawi

By placing evaluative judgement on the agenda for curriculum reform in higher education, this book points to an underdeveloped, but potentially highly fruitful, direction for adding value to current courses. The "capability to make decisions about the quality of work of self and others" (Ajjawi et al., Chapter 1) is already implicit as an outcome to be developed in university courses, but many of the preceding chapters have argued that it should be actively pursued, rather than taken for granted that it will occur.

We are not suggesting that university courses currently neglect to cultivate students' capacity to develop their evaluative judgement. A cursory glance at any course will uncover multiple examples of activities that foster aspects of judgement which can be mapped to the practices described in this book. What is not occurring, however, is a concerted effort to develop the skills of students across the curriculum and to link evaluative judgement to the substantive learning outcomes for a given discipline or profession. If university courses are promoting this, then it is not well articulated and we do not sufficiently appreciate how they go about doing it. Furthermore, it is not clear how they might be assisted in this process. It is also not clear how we might judge students' progression along the paths to developing their evaluative judgement capability, other than observing improved work. This is rather indirect and may not help us diagnose problems in judgement rather than execution.

Many different theoretical perspectives have been introduced in this volume. These include social constructivism, cognitive psychology, practice theory, sociomateriality, ontological/epistemic fluency, and identity. These perspectives all have useful contributions to make to this area. They provide tools by which others can interrogate the various ideas which have been proposed and which we take forward here. However, it is not the role of this chapter to attempt to bring these together or suggest where any one theoretical perspective might be fruitful in the quest for further understanding of evaluative judgement and how it might be fostered.

What we seek to do in this final chapter is to point to practical directions that may be taken by those who wish to form an agenda for applying these ideas in course development. This treatment is exploratory, seeking to open up further discussion of how evaluative judgement might be considered and structured into courses.

The development of evaluative judgement involves more than introducing a set of activities to the curriculum. It involves a repositioning of the formation of students within a discipline or profession, and a reinterpretation of the notion of students' development over time. It prompts a new focus on questions such as the development of generic attributes, the structuring of a curriculum, and what constitutes progression from one level of sophistication to another. It also focuses on the role of assessment in learning and how it can contribute, not just to the judgement of students by other parties, but to the judgement by students of themselves and their peers, and where educators and other people can fit into this.

Components of evaluative judgement: a learner focus

While there is more work that needs to be done to fully conceptualise the notion of evaluative judgement and how it might be fostered, we know enough to suggest a pragmatic way forward that can assist in planning courses, especially for the area that Robert Nelson (Chapter 5) has identified as hard evaluative judgement. If we logically examine the notion of evaluative judgement and break it down into its constituent elements, we can identify things done well at present and aspects which may not be done well or at all. This analysis will vary from course to course and from unit to unit in any given course. Also, there will be variation between courses and across disciplines in terms of the objects and practices of evaluative judgement. Different kinds of task are involved, drawing on different knowledge domains and different kinds of knowledge within them. In our considerations, we need to keep in mind that, as Ajjawi and Bearman point out in their chapter (Chapter 4), standards reside in the practices of academic and professional communities and are not always explicit, or explicable. In addition, each discipline and profession has its own signature pedagogies which characterise the ways in which it is learnt and these in turn will influence the development of evaluative judgement; see, for example, Dall'Alba (Chapter 2) and Bearman (Chapter 15). While it is not possible to examine these variations here, we can nevertheless begin to focus on what might be some key components of the notion. For each of the components identified, we discuss first how they might be framed and secondly consider design implications which show how the developing judgement can readily sit alongside other aspects of study and assessment.

Discerning quality

Once it is agreed that a given type of work needs to be produced, students need to appreciate what constitutes good work of that kind. As Sadler points out, it is necessary to "induct students into sufficient explicit and tacit knowledge of the kind that would enable them to recognise or judge quality when they see it and also explain their judgements" (Sadler 2010, 542). Without being able to recognise good work, they are unlikely to be able to produce it for themselves. A key part of this capability is discerning quality. While some features of high-quality work end up being codified in standards and criteria, such condensed statements might not be a good starting point for students. After all, if students could fully decrypt the language of standards and criteria they would probably already be operating at a level superior to that of the course they are studying.

After reaching a basic familiarity with the kind of work that is to be produced, and having developed some of the discourse and knowledge needed to discuss it, a useful starting point can be to expose students to samples of work of various qualities so that they can begin to appreciate what distinguishes one from another – perhaps through the use of exemplar pedagogies like those discussed by Carless et al. (Chapter 11). This is a process of discernment through induction. Learners are given practice in noticing what differentiates one piece of work from another. "Work" is used here to describe any product or performance that learners aspire to be able to enact for themselves.

Discerning quality is a central feature of variation theory, developed by Ference Marton. He argues that learning is a process of making increasingly sophisticated discernments. The expert can distinguish many more features of a phenomenon or problem than a novice. In this view, learning is the building of a repertoire of variations in the phenomenon of interest. This body of work provides many studies and illustrations of how quality can be discerned (Bowden and Marton 1998).

Developing the capacity of students to discern quality is not new. It has been advocated by authors on study skills for at least 40 years. A simple example of this approach was established by Graham Gibbs in the 1970s (1981). First-year undergraduate students are given examples of essays written in response to an assignment similar in kind to the one for which they are preparing. Through discussion in small groups, students distinguish which essay was better than the others. They are then asked to identify exactly how one is better or worse than the others. These differences are noted and a list of distinguishing features assembled by the group. Thus, a set of distinguishing features is generated and students are introduced to the notion of criteria. Students take these features and use them to prepare their own essays. The power of the process is that students do not need to be given direct instruction on quality features, and so long as the exercise is undertaken in diverse groups with sufficient discussion, students realise that they have the capacity to begin to discern quality for themselves. Later variations on such approaches are taken up in the chapters by Henderson et al. (Chapter 12), Thompson and Lawson (Chapter 14), Tai and Sevenhuysen (Chapter 16) and Carless et al. (Chapter 11), who enter into some specific discussions on how we can get this to occur in various contexts and configurations.

Discernment of quality is not something that begins or ends at first year, as Nelson recognises (Chapter 5). It is a persistent feature of learning and practising anything, as illustrated in the chapters by Carless et al. (Chapter 11), Henderson et al. (Chapter 12) and Rees et al. (Chapter 18). Thus, opportunities to prompt discernment of quality can be included at transition points in programmes, when students move from producing one kind of work to another that is qualitatively different. For example, students moving from small-scale reports or essays might need to revisit their discernment of quality when faced with producing a research report or Honours project. Indeed, there is some suggestion that moving from one form of assessment to another that requires a quite different approach might require additional efforts in discernment, as students tend to regress a little when producing work in a new form (Boud et al. 2015).

While making judgements of the work of others and benefiting from feedback processes is likely to develop connoisseurship, it does not necessarily lead to learners being able to generate good work themselves. So then, what do we need to assist learners in the transition from appreciating the work of others to generating good work of their own? A learner could develop high levels of evaluative judgement, and be assessed as such, but not be able to create good work. The transition from discernment to manifestation is an important one.

Judgement processes

How is a judgement made with respect to any learning outcome or type of work? This is one of the most underdeveloped areas in our understandings of evaluative judgement. When educators pass judgement on students' work they traditionally use implicit yardsticks to judge quality, and they are not very good at tapping their own communities of practise to reaching a common view (Price 2005). More simply, they compare students against each other to gain a spread of marks. While the latter process has the virtue of being much easier to undertake, it is now no longer acceptable. In an era of explicit learning outcomes, students must be judged against a defined standard using appropriate criteria (Boud 2017). Officially, comparisons between students are residue of an earlier policy era; however, these comparisons are difficult to escape from as they have shaped much current assessment practice, and there is evidence they may contribute to the calibration of our judgement.

Judgement against a standard, rather than with respect to other students, is now required. It is the norm in most work settings. In technical areas, the notion of a standard is quite straightforward. Indeed, industry quality standards for products and processes are ubiquitous and are, for example, published internationally by the International Organization for Standardization (ISO). Companies are held accountable for consistently meeting ISO norms. In most aspects of university work it is not possible, or even desirable, to be quite so formal or rigid. However, some notion of a standard is needed, both for certification of students and to assist them in meeting these requirements. While this may come from a written specification, standards are more typically embedded in examples of work: in texts, in course materials and in captured performances. These provide a yardstick for judgement.

Identifying and utilising standards is a central feature of learning. While standards may be provided to students in many courses, and in vocational courses they are enshrined in professional standards statements, they invariably need to be contextualised and explicated for any given task, and they need to be performed, as Ajjawi and Bearman point out (Chapter 4). Working with and appreciating standards is a pre-requisite for developing judgement based on them. Modelling of this use is needed from teachers, who can represent the kinds of processes that they are helping to prompt in students.

Modelling and embodiment, or even representations of standards, are insufficient in themselves. Rubrics present an example where standards are contextualised by teachers but may remain opaque to students. While rubrics (a marking grid representing the various learning outcomes for an assignment and criteria and levels of performance for each) are manifestly a representation of the standards required for a given assignment, they are often not in a form that can be readily appreciated or, when feedback is provided in terms of the categories of the rubric, understood. An example of how this might be addressed is given in the chapter by Ajjawi and Bearman (Chapter 4), which describes how students can go through a process of co-constructing a rubric for an assignment and thus appreciate, through direct experience, how standards and criteria are created and instantiated in the form of a rubric.

Judgements may be made through comparison with the work of others, as given in the example on p. 000, or with oneself, as when a learner seeks to improve their own work from previous assignments or through working on drafts. Students need to discern the key features of their own work, and that of others, and then judge what else is needed to improve their work.

Fostering judgement processes requires opportunities within courses for students to engage in practising judging and to receive feedback information on the judgements they make. This is needed whether or not rubrics are involved, and can be undertaken on a regular basis with each new class of students. Importantly, students must not just appreciate the standards that they will apply; they must also get opportunities to compare their judgements with those who have greater expertise. An example from our own teaching experience is to ask students to appraise their work against a set of features of good work that they have generated in class. These are used to compile an assignment attachment sheet, on which each student writes qualitative statements indicating how their accompanying assignment addresses the criteria that have been agreed. When their marked work is returned, they receive comments solely on how well they have judged their own performance. This focuses on discrepancies between their own judgement and that of the assessor. Thus, feedback here is primarily focused on improving students' judgement of work of this kind, and secondarily on improvement of the work itself. This process can be enhanced when, prior to submission, students share their draft with a peer, receive comments and modify their own work accordingly. Of course, this can only be done effectively in a standards-based context in which students are not penalised when the work of their peers improves. Further examples of how feedback may be optimised to develop students' evaluative judgements can be found in the chapters by Henderson et al. (Chapter 12) and Johnson and Molloy (Chapter 17).

Managing biases

All judgements are subject to beliefs, assumptions and biases of different kinds, as Joughin and Dawson point out (Chapters 6 and 10, respectively). It is the nature of human judgement that a fully objective assessment cannot be made. The best we can do is to recognise our own biases and seek to manage them. This is just as much a problem when teachers or assessors judge students' work as it is when students do it for themselves or each other. A whole repertoire of approaches has been developed to manage biases in marking, which can be adapted to the present context (e.g., the Better Judgement website).

The most important step for this aspect of developing evaluative judgement is to accept that the judgements that anyone makes will be biased, and to recognise where the sources of bias may reside. As well as the biases and their sources discussed by Joughin (Chapter 6), the most common bias in self-judgement is the desire to do well and interpret one's own work in the best possible light. For example, when confronted with a marking scheme with model answers, many students are tempted to give themselves the benefit of the doubt. For this reason, it is vital for students to access multiple sources of information and be open to a multiplicity of judgements by others that they are encouraged to reflect on. These sources include different teachers, different peers and anyone to whom their work is visible or who could be invited to view it. We recognise our biases through seeing our work through the eyes of others. Temptations for bias are even stronger when there are incentives for distortion, for instance through the allocation of grades or rewards for the quality of the work, rather than the quality of the judgement. Strategies for promoting metacognitive checking of evaluative judgement processes are presented by Lodge and colleagues (Chapter 7).

Assessing quality trustworthiness of sources and others

Any given learner usually has access to considerable material and human resources that could potentially assist them in making effective judgements of their work. However, some of these sources could lead to worse judgements, or potentially even harm the development of their evaluative judgement capability. How then can they know what to rely on and what to be sceptical of? As far as material resources are concerned, in the era of the Internet this is part of the basic requirement of distinguishing what counts as a trustworthy information source (or not) for any given purpose. For example, when online source evaluation is not explicitly taught, students tend towards heuristics that can be somewhat unhelpful, such as looking to confirm pre-existing beliefs or going on the reputation of the source rather than the quality of the information (Metzger and Flanagin 2013). The development of skills for judging the quality of sources of information need to be considered alongside other aspects of learning skills development around the use of sources and evidence for any aspect of academic work. Interventions intending to develop students' information literacy or domain-specific critical thinking skills could fruitfully consider these capabilities through an evaluative judgement lens.

When it comes to direct information from other people, further considerations apply. A feature which may be overlooked in making judgements is an affective one. When undertaking a feedback process with another person, how does one judge what reliance to place on their comments? Can they be trusted in what they provide? This is already an active but overlooked consideration when students receive information from staff (Telio et al. 2016). Some comments are believed and others are not. The basic question to be asked is: Does this person have my best interests at heart and do I think that what they say has credence? Only when the answer is in the positive can the information provided be regarded as secure. With no knowledge of the other person, they can only be judged in terms of their position (a teacher, a peer) and on the content and manner of the information they offer. Information which appears to be disrespectful can be ignored, and the rest treated cautiously. The question to consider is: Is what the other person communicates significant enough and trustworthy enough to take the effort to act on it?

The converse of judging the trustworthiness of others is being trusted oneself; that is, ensuring that information provided can be relied upon and be seen to be trustworthy by the other person (Carless 2013). Trust is a reciprocal process: trust begets trust, and when offering comments to others it should be expected that the trustworthiness of the provider is taken into consideration by the recipient. Maximising one's own trustworthiness to others involves being interested in their learning, eliciting what they want, appreciating the appropriate criteria to use and communicating that to them, pitching the level of comments suitably for what you know of them, and contextualising information suitably; in short, knowing what you are doing and communicating it authentically.

A challenge comes when there is different information coming from different sources. Clearly, the value of what others say relative to the work considered is of first importance; balancing different inputs then involves making judgements about the source and the perspectives they hold, and their relationship to the recipient and the work.

Seeking opportunities for practice

Evaluative judgement is a complex process which needs as much practice as does generating the work that is being judged. It is an embodied process that needs to be enacted, not just studied or thought about, as Dall'Alba emphasises (Chapter 2). She draws attention to the importance of developing evaluative judgement over time, as students become the professionals they aspire to be. Development needs to be undertaken across the different domains and subject matters of a programme. It is not a generic process which, once learnt, can be applied universally, but rather, as Bearman highlights, is instead embedded within disciplinary and professional practices (Chapter 15). This implies that multiple opportunities are required for the practice of judgement across a course or programme, many of which require accompanying feedback processes using multiple sources of feedback information, as discussed by Thompson and Lawson (Chapter 14) and Ellis (Chapter 13). The obvious occasions for practice are when tasks are undertaken as part of the normal curriculum. However, when new ideas are being introduced or new processes of development are used, there may be a need for explicit instruction, practice and feedback in how to judge appropriately. As Goodyear and Markauskaite discuss (Chapter 3), it is also important for students to gain exposure to situations in which intrinsic feedback from the environment can "bite them back", allowing students to thus learn from the world in which they operate rather than from any deliberate pedagogic intervention.

A well-designed curriculum would map these occasions and opportunities for practice over units and years, and provide mechanisms to allow students to track their development. This requires digital enablement to store artefacts, record information about judgements and feedback, allow easy navigation across occasions, and provide clear summaries of progress in developing judgement as well as meeting programme learning outcomes. There are various devices to aid different aspects of this (for instance, see Thompson and Lawson, Chapter 14), such as e-portfolios, specialist platforms (e.g., *REVIEW*™) and dashboards; however, they need to be well integrated into the usual learning management systems to be effective. Forums for reflection are also needed, to assist learners in utilising the information available through such enabling devices to take responsibility for managing the development of their own evaluative judgement across a programme. Such approaches require a programmatic view of curriculum design and assessment, rather than the fragmented one common in a unit-centred approach to courses. As tempting as it may be, developing one course unit focused on evaluative judgement is unlikely to have much effect; evaluative judgement must be integrated into day-to-day activities across units.

Enabling conditions of courses

While we have emphasised the need for activities to be included in the curriculum to promote the development of evaluative judgement, such activities cannot be enacted independently of the many other aspects of teaching and learning that pursue other desirable goals. From the learning-centred perspective we have been discussing in this chapter, the most important condition is emphasised by Boud and Falchikov (2007) in their notion of promoting informed judgement: the self-identification by students as active learners. This refers to the need for all students to navigate the transition between seeing themselves as *consumers* of courses – the responsibility for which lies with others – to *learners*, as they realise that they are the principal agents for their own learning and that only at their own initiative can they benefit from the opportunities available to them. Different students make this transition at different points, some long before they enter university. It is only through an effective transition pedagogy, which starts in first year and ensures that all students have shifted in this way (Kift 2015), that effective development of evaluative judgement can proceed. Transition is nonlinear, and continues throughout and beyond the university; evaluative judgement should be revisited when major transitions occur, such as when learning key threshold concepts, or when entering placements in the workplace.

Several contributors have identified ways in which consideration of self-regulated learning can provide useful ways of thinking about practising evaluative judgement and the enabling conditions of courses, along with specific suggestions about how it can be introduced. Introducing evaluative judgement practice is one important way in which self-regulation can be promoted and developed, as discussed by Bennett et al. (Chapter 9), Panadero and Broadbent (Chapter 8) and Lodge et al. (Chapter 7).

The effective use of the elements of evaluative judgement development outlined here are contingent on having good quality feedback processes throughout a programme (Boud and Molloy 2013). These involve the careful selection of tasks, sequencing of activities so that capacity for evaluative judgement can build systematically, and feedback comments arranged from multiple sources (teacher, peers, etc.) and timed such that they can be utilised for the next task. Feedback for the development of judgement needs to be considered programmatically, not just in relation to each unit; capacities need to build over time and across different subject matter.

Conclusion

In conclusion, there is a clear agenda to be pursued to enable the general goal of developing learners' evaluative judgement within higher education. Individual teachers will readily find ways of doing so, drawing on examples given in this book. The more substantial challenge is to develop learners' evaluative judgement systematically across the curriculum across many diverse disciplinary areas. At first sight, it may appear that this is an additional burden for an already overloaded programme. However, closer consideration suggests that this agenda is simply one of ensuring that graduating students are able to do what the curriculum claims. A focus on evaluative judgement is a focus on the core feature of education itself: there is no point in graduating students who do not know what they can and cannot do. They need to be able to judge good work when they see it – whether it is their own work or that of others. Anything less is a failure on the part of the institution to graduate capable students who can continue their learning.

References

Boud, D. 2017. "Standards-based assessment for an era of increasing transparency." In *Scaling Up Assessment for Learning in Higher Education*, edited by D. Carless, S. Bridges, C. Chan, and R. Glofcheski, 19–31. Dordrecht, The Netherlands: Springer.

Boud, D., and N. Falchikov. 2007. "Developing assessment for informing judgement." In *Rethinking Assessment for Higher Education: Learning for the Longer Term*, edited by D. Boud and N. Falchikov, 181–197. London: Routledge.

Boud, D., R. Lawson, and D. Thompson. 2015. "The calibration of student judgement through self-assessment: disruptive effects of assessment patterns." *Higher Education Research and Development* 34 (1): 45–59. doi:10.1080/07294360.2014.934328.

Boud, D., and E. Molloy. 2013. "Decision-making for feedback." In *Feedback in Higher and Professional Education*, edited by D. Boud and E. Molloy, 202–218. London: Routledge.

Bowden, J., and F. Marton. 1998. *The University of Learning: Beyond Quality and Competence in Higher Education.* London: Kogan Page.

Carless, D. 2013. "Trust and its role in facilitating dialogic feedback." In *Feedback in Higher and Professional Education*, edited by D. Boud and E. Molloy, 90–103. London: Routledge.

Flinders University. "Better Judgement." Better Judgement website. www.flinders.edu.au/medicine/sites/better-judgement/.

Gibbs, G. 1981. *Teaching Students to Learn: A Student-Centred Approach.* Milton Keynes, UK: The Open University Press.

Kift, S. 2015. "A decade of transition pedagogy: a quantum leap in conceptualising the first year experience." *HERDSA Review of Higher Education* 2: 51–86.

Metzger, M. J., and A. J. Flanagin. 2013. "Credibility and trust of information in online environments: the use of cognitive heuristics." *Journal of Pragmatics* 59: 210–220. doi:10.1016/j.pragma.2013.07.012.

Price, M. 2005. "Assessment standards: the role of communities of practice and the scholarship of assessment." *Assessment & Evaluation in Higher Education* 30 (3): 215–230.

Sadler, D.R. 2010. "Beyond feedback: developing student capability in complex appraisal." *Assessment & Evaluation in Higher Education* 35 (5): 535–550.

Telio, S., G. Regehr, and R. Ajjawi. 2016. "Feedback and the educational alliance: examining credibility judgements and their consequences." *Medical Education* 50 (9): 933–942. doi:10.1111/medu.13063.4649

Index